PRAISE FOR "YOU HAVE TO SAY THE WORDS"

"You Have to Say the Words goes beyond other books to take a real-life honest look into the situations managers face every day in the trenches. Kathy Ryan's advice has universal application that can guide even the most experienced leaders, reinforcing critical lessons and inspiring them to help develop managers who struggle with these skills. Most importantly, this book is a road map for less experienced leaders, showing them a way to build confidence and reassuring them that their discomfort in addressing performance issues is a natural part of the growing process. It should be required reading for aspiring managers and seasoned executives alike."

John Romanowicz, General Manager, House of Blues Entertainment

"As an outplacement consultant, I often work with clients who arrive in my office bewildered as to the reasons for the termination of their employment and angry about the mixed messages they received from their managers leading up to it. In this very practical book, Kathy Ryan draws on her extensive experience as an HR Professional and a Business Coach to make the case for much needed straightforward and honest communication from managers to employees regarding performance expectations and workplace behavior. She also provides a wealth of tools and examples that will help both new and experienced managers improve their ability to "say the words" that lead to clear and productive communication with employees."

Roger E. Pickard, VP / Managing Consultant, Lee Hecht Harrison

"Finally, a book comes along that actually says the words! Kathy Ryan helps you to break through the mental blocks that keep you from doing just that. The content is very relatable and the stories represent the types of issues that managers struggle with on a daily basis. I highly recommend investing in this book as a must read for anyone in management and human resources. It will become your go-to reference tool."

Kimberly Hunt Khouzam, VP, Human Resources,
Retail and Entertainment Industry

"Kathy Ryan has put into words what every manager must know in order to effectively manage and mentor their employees. With clear and concise examples, Kathy eloquently provides the "real world" dialog necessary to handle the difficult conversations that are typically avoided in the work place. "You Have to Say the Words" was not merely a pleasure to read but is also a treasure chest of tools I now have at my fingertips to apply to my managerial responsibilities."

Anthony Paolini, Vice President, Instructors Network, Inc.

YOU HAVE TO
SAY THE WORDS

An Integrity-Based Approach for Tackling Tough Conversations and Maximizing Performance

By Kathy Ryan

Published by:
Achievement Press, LLC
P.O. Box 770844, Orlando, Florida, 32877

Although the author and publisher have made every effort to ensure the accuracy and completeness of information contained in this book, we assume no responsibility for errors, inaccuracies, omissions, or any inconsistency herein. Any slights of people or organizations are unintentional. The advice and strategies contained herein may not be suitable for your situation. You should consult with your organization's Human Resources department and/or an attorney for specific application as appropriate.

Printed and bound in the United States of America.

First Printing 2011

10 9 8 7 6 5 4 3 2 1

ISBN 978-0-9837565-0-7

ATTENTION CORPORATIONS, UNIVERSITIES, COLLEGES, AND PROFESSIONAL ORGANIZATIONS: Quantity discounts are available on bulk purchases of this book for educational or gift purposes, use in corporate training programs, or as premiums and sales promotions. Special books or book excerpts can also be created to fit specific needs. For information, please contact Achievement Press LLC, P.O. Box 220844, Orlando, FL 32877; website *www.achievementpress.com.*

ACHIEVEMENT PRESS

Developing Leaders from the Inside Out
www.achievementpress.com

Author's Note

I believe providing people with honest and timely feedback is the single greatest growth opportunity area for most managers in business today. Many managers avoid confronting performance or behavior issues until circumstances force them to act, and then their lack of comfort or skill communicating difficult messages sabotages their effectiveness. Your willingness to read this material in an effort to improve your skills already sets you apart from your peers, and I applaud your initiative. You are already demonstrating some of the qualities of an exceptional leader.

Throughout this book, I offer examples and stories that draw heavily from my experience as a human resources manager, leadership trainer, and coach. They are used to illustrate key learning points and to assure you that you are not alone in struggling with tough conversations. I hope you enjoy these stories. They are written to entertain as well as educate.

Some stories and conversations are described to the best of my memory as they occurred, while others are a composite of people and situations I encountered throughout my career. To ensure complete confidentiality and to protect the privacy of my coworkers and clients, I have changed the names, personal descriptions, and any other identifying characteristics. I respect these individuals greatly and share their stories with you not to exploit them but as a powerful learning tool. I am profoundly grateful to each of them for the lessons they taught me as I became a better leader, and person, as a result of working with them.

Thank you all.
Kathy

Warning: Disclaimer

This book is designed to provide you with information on how to prepare for, conduct, and document performance conversations. It is offered with the understanding that the publisher and author are not engaged in rendering legal advice, mental health counseling, or other professional services. If legal or other expert assistance is required, the services of a competent professional should be sought.

It is not the purpose of this book to replace or override your company's existing human resources and progressive discipline policies, but to complement, amplify, and supplement their effectiveness. You are urged to read all the available material provided by your employer, to learn as much as possible about coaching and counseling from other texts, and to tailor the information to your individual needs.

Every effort has been made to make this book as complete and accurate as possible. However, this book should be used only as a general guide and not as the ultimate source of performance counseling and progressive discipline information. The templates are provided as reference only and should be tailored to your specific circumstances. Furthermore, this book contains information on coaching, counseling, and documentation that is current only up to the printing date.

The purpose of this book is to educate and entertain. The author and publisher shall have neither responsibility nor liability to any person or entity with respect to any damage or loss caused, or alleged to have been caused, directly or indirectly, by the information contained in this book. If you do not wish to be bound by the above, you may return the book to the publisher for a full refund.

Table of Contents

Introduction

Over my twenty plus years in human resources, I developed a strong commitment to having honest and direct conversations in the workplace. Too many times I witnessed the devastating consequences of a manager's failure to speak the truth to employees about their performance or behavior. Even with all the management and leadership training available, managers today still consistently avoid providing candid feedback to their people and frequently stop short of saying the words that need to be said. Whether driven by a lack of confidence, a fear of conflict, or a desire to be liked by their people, many managers hesitate to tell team members exactly what they need to hear in order to improve their performance.

But within this pervasive environment of candy-coated messages and misleading silence, lies a tremendous opportunity for you as a leader. By finding the courage and developing the skills needed to deliver honest and direct feedback to your people, you can easily distinguish yourself from your peers and positively impact productivity, performance and the overall morale of your team. And it comes down to six little words that will make all the difference for you.

YOU HAVE TO SAY THE WORDS

During my career coaching leaders, the phrase "You have to say the words" became the best piece of advice I could give everyone to help them immediately elevate their effectiveness and take their performance to a higher level.

This belief in saying what needs to be said, even if it is uncomfortable to do so, became the cornerstone of my leadership philosophy and communication style. The advice offered in this book has been distilled from my coaching sessions with hundreds of managers as I helped them improve their communication skills and become more effective leaders.

Throughout my career, I've been a part of delivering thousands of difficult messages to employees, many times resulting in the termination of their employment. It often gave me a starring role in one of the worst days of their lives, and I appreciated the responsibility that came with that role.

To help me dig deep to find the strength and courage to say what needed to be said in those conversations, I always tried to maintain my perspective and remember these three things:

1. **Being honest is a value I hold and I believe it is the right thing to do.** As a leader, it is my responsibility to be honest even if the message is going to be unpleasant to hear.
2. **No matter how uncomfortable I was feeling about delivering a particular message, the recipients were probably going to feel worse.** In recognition of this I tried to keep my focus on them and off my discomfort.
3. **Providing honest feedback to team members demonstrates your respect for them as individuals and employees.** While they might not like what you have to say to them after all is said and done, most people will appreciate that you had the courage to say it.

I used to joke with people that human resources wasn't just a job; it was a way of life. I think what I was trying to say is that I believe it is impossible for me to have one set of values for my job and another set for my personal life. Who I am as a person has to be in alignment with how I behave in my job. I now understand that this is true for all leaders, not just for human resources managers. It is not possible for you to preach the value of behaving ethically to your team during the day, then skip out on your bar tab during happy hour after work. Your values as a leader can't be called into question or people will not trust you.

As for me, I have a fundamental belief that people deserve to be treated with dignity and respect. It is not just important to me because it was my job throughout my career to ensure it; but it is a personal value I maintain. Because of this core value, I was willing to push through whatever discomfort I was feeling in the moment to say what needed to be said, even if it hurt people's feelings to hear it. If it was important feedback that they needed to make critical changes in their performance, then I had an obligation to share it with them.

By using your own moral compass as a guide and by building your confidence and inner strength, you can conquer any fear, anxiety, or discomfort you may be experiencing when you provide others with candid feedback regarding their performance. Knowledge and practice are the keys to overcoming reluctance and that is why I brought all my best tools and advice together in one place to help you, when the time comes, to say what needs to be said.

I believe honest feedback is the silver bullet when it comes to improving overall performance in organizations today. Too many companies sabotage their ultimate success by spending too much time and resources on systems that track performance rather than dealing effectively with behavior and performance issues directly when they occur. This acceptance of substandard performance at all levels within the organization is like pulling back on the reigns of a racehorse; you won't fall off the horse that way, but you are unlikely to win the race either.

In this book you will learn what goes into preparing for and successfully conducting tough conversations in the workplace. It is important that you continue to develop your skills so you are well-equipped to respond to any situation that arises, as you can never completely predict the twists and turns one of these challenging discussions will take.

I have assembled within these pages a collection of best practices, great advice, and a few cautionary tales. You may even be able to see yourself or one of your coworkers in some of the stories I share. My hope is that you can learn from the experiences of others to build your influence and develop your own reputation as an honest and well-respected leader.

If you are new to management and haven't spent much time developing your leadership skills thus far, there is no need to fret. Here you have the opportunity to learn from the best practices and mistakes of others. Because you are in the early stages of your career, I encourage you to decide now what kind of leader you want to become. The information provided in the first two sections of this book will help you to understand the qualities needed for exceptional leadership.

If you are a seasoned manager or leader, you will find the information contained in these first sections a confirmation of lessons you've learned and a wonderful refresher on how to fine-tune those areas where you may have strayed a little along the way. Time spent on your personal development is never wasted. You should strive to become a life-long learner. As they say, the best time to plant a tree is twenty-five years ago; the second best time is today!

In Section 2, I identify the basic and advanced skills you will need to develop in order to increase your effectiveness when communicating performance feedback. Subsequent sections provide you with tools to help you prepare for, execute, and document your conversations. There is even advice on how to talk about those sensitive topics that many of us find particularly challenging.

This book is meant to be functional. You can read through starting from the beginning or jump right to the section that pertains to an area where you have an immediate need. However, there is so much valuable information available here that if you do skip around, I encourage you to go back at some point and read it from the beginning. Better yet, read the information, practice the skills, and then teach someone else what you've learned. Teaching others is really the best way I know of to help you fully absorb and incorporate new material.

If you currently struggle with finding the strength and confidence to deliver honest feedback, to ultimately "say the words," then the advice and tools offered in this book will most likely make you feel uncomfortable and may even press some buttons for you. That is to be expected. If it was easy, everyone would be doing it consistently. I ask that you work through your discomfort and try to apply your new skills as soon as possible. With practice, it will become easier to say the words that need to be said, but it will take time to build your confidence. Commit to investing in your development and press on through any awkwardness you may be feeling, secure in the knowledge that by providing your people with honest feedback you are giving them the greatest gift you can as their leader.

SECTION ONE:

YOUR LEADERSHIP STYLE

1 Chapter

A Commitment to Honesty

*The trouble with most of us is that we would rather
be ruined by praise than saved by criticism.*

Norman Vincent Peale

Before we go any further, let me share my definition of honesty with you since this is such a critical value for our discussion of tough conversations. Some people define honesty as being truthful, or not lying. While speaking the truth accurately as you know it is a big part of what it means to be honest, my definition goes far beyond that. It also includes having the courage to speak up when it would be easier to remain silent. When situations arise in the workplace where you might find it easier to say or do nothing, make the decision to maintain your integrity, operate with honesty, and speak up.

For instance, let's say your coworker makes an open request for feedback following a presentation she just did. You know she made some mistakes, but you choose not to say anything and allow her to believe it was fine. This is not being honest. Have the courage to do what is right, even if it is uncomfortable or difficult for you. Every day you are presented with situations that will challenge your character. Step up and provide feedback when others remain silent and you will become a trusted and respected leader.

Being honest with people about their performance isn't always as simple or as easy as it may sound, but you already know that or you probably wouldn't be reading this book. In any human interaction there are numbers of ways a message can get lost, muddled, or misunderstood, and conversations with employees are certainly no exception. The employee is often nervous, worried about losing his job, or even defiant, and his heightened emotions can easily filter out critical parts of your message.

To make matters worse, many people don't realize in the heat of the moment that their defenses have been triggered. Instinctively their mind tries to protect them from any information that they perceive as harmful so their defense system kicks in. These defenses do a fine job shielding them from pain, but they also get in the way of their comprehension. Often people are not even fully aware that their defenses prevented them from hearing information accurately, so they blame any resulting misunderstandings on the other person engaged in the conversation.

In order to cut through their defenses and the resulting mental fog, it is critical that you are clear, candid, and direct in your feedback. If you are in a leadership position it is only a matter of time before you will have to communicate a difficult message, such as telling an employee that he has bad breath, is underperforming, or he may lose his job if he is late again. Because many managers are uncomfortable with confrontation or being the bearer of bad news, they will do whatever they can to put off these tough conversations for as long as possible.

It Isn't Real Until You Say It

Since your ultimate goal in any conversation is to have your message completely and accurately understood, it is absolutely essential that you are crystal clear when communicating with others, especially when providing them with performance feedback or information related to their employment. Any perceived grey area or vagueness in your language leaves enough wiggle room for the employee's well-established defense system to deflect, reinterpret, or argue your message. Any efforts on your part to soften the blow or skirt the real issue will give the employee just the opening he needs. In fact, that is exactly what happened to a fellow manager and friend of mine when he was speaking to his employee, Dave.

Dave's Story

I was sitting with one of my department managers, Paul, and we were waiting for his employee to join us, a young man named Dave. Dave was about to lose his job, although he didn't know it yet. This was not the first time Paul and I had spoken to Dave about his performance. Paul informed Dave on a number of occasions over the past several months that he was not performing at an acceptable level. There were several areas where Dave's performance continued to drag behind the rest of the team. Dave had been given ample opportunity to improve his performance, but his efforts continued to fall short. As his manager, Paul had decided that he was done investing in Dave, and it was time to end his employment. Paul believed he had been clear with Dave during his previous conversations that termination was a real possibility, and today was the day.

I was the human resources manager at the time, and I was joining the meeting primarily as a witness to the termination. As an HR manager, my philosophy had always been that the line manager should be the one to drive counseling sessions and termination meetings. It is the manager's responsibility to actually say the words that terminate employment. I believed then, as I do today, that if HR managers terminate employment they have effectively taken themselves out of the internal grievance process as an objective resource. This forces disgruntled employees to seek remedies outside of the organization and increases the company's legal exposure.

Of course, over the years in response to specific situations I have made exceptions to this philosophy in practice. There were conversations where circumstances dictated that I jump in and actually terminate the employment of the individual because the manager froze or got hopelessly lost in the conversation, but as a general rule I usually tried to remain a supporting player.

So in keeping with my philosophy on this day, Paul was all set to do the talking. I had worked with Paul for a number of years and knew we both shared the belief that whenever possible, actual termination meetings should be very short, approximately five minutes or less. Any longer and you can run the risk of not maintaining the employee's dignity or saying more than you should in an effort to make him, or you, feel better. Both of these situations can end up hurting your reputation and placing you in a tenuous legal position. So once Dave joined us in the conference room, Paul got right down to it.

"Dave, you and I have spoken on several occasions about the need for you to improve your performance. You still are not meeting my expectations as I have outlined them to you. In our last meeting, I gave you a final warning and I explained that if you did not show immediate and significant improvement, I would have to make a tough decision. That time has come."

Paul sat back in his chair allowing a little relief to show across his face now that it was all said and done. Dave tilted his head to one side, furrowed his brow and said, "I understand and I have really been trying to do the things that you asked me to do, and I feel that I have been doing a lot better. I really thought that everything was okay now."

I could see Paul wasn't quite sure where to go with this. In his mind, Dave no longer worked for him and this was beginning to sound like he wanted to get back into a discussion about his performance. He said to Dave, "I appreciate that you have been trying, but it really hasn't been enough. You are a nice guy Dave, it's not personal, but I think we should move on."

Dave leaned forward in his chair. He really wanted Paul to know he was sincere. "I agree. I want to put all this negative stuff behind us as well. I like being here and I really like working for you Paul." Paul sat there silent and stunned.

Dave, feeling he was on a roll, went on to highlight all the good things he got from working for Paul and the company. As Dave spoke, I could see the frustration start to rise on Paul's face like a thermometer on a hot afternoon in July.

Finally, when he'd had enough, Paul sat straight up in his chair and planted his feet squarely on the floor. Putting a hand on each of his knees, he leaned forward toward Dave and said, "I just don't see you as part of my team." The frustration was now evident in his voice.

Dave was unshaken. He reached out his hands in front of him in a pleading gesture. "Oh, but I want to be on your team!" he exclaimed. "I just know I can do better."

At this Paul abruptly stood up, shot me a look of utter amazement and frustration, and walked out of the room. This was actually a first for me. I had never had a manager walk out of a termination conversation before, and quite frankly, in that moment, I wasn't really quite sure Paul was coming back.

Dave looked up at me with big, bassett hound brown eyes. He was not agitated; on the contrary he looked almost peaceful. I knew that as far as Paul was concerned, Dave's employment had been terminated. But Dave wasn't catching on, and I could see how confused it left him.

A minute or two passed, although at the time it felt like an eternity. Finally Paul reentered the room. He had a good head of steam under him now and he walked straight over to where Dave was still sitting and looked down at him. Clearly, Paul had gathered his thoughts while he was outside the room.

"Dave," he said, "This is it, I'm done. You're fired. You no longer work here. I'm sorry, but you need to leave now." With that, Paul shook Dave's hand and left the room.

Dave blinked a few times as the meaning of the words started to sink in. I sat with him in silence, allowing him to collect his thoughts and emotions. When he was ready, I explained the details of his final paycheck and the disposition of his benefits. I then walked with him down the hall to the front door of the building, said goodbye, and wished him well. Once I was sure that Dave was fine and that he had left the building, I returned to Paul's office.

"What happened?" he asked as soon as I walked in. "Why did Dave just sit there? Why wouldn't he leave? How many times do I have to fire the guy?" I could see that he was totally amazed by Dave's lack of understanding and reaction.

"He didn't understand his employment was being terminated," I said, "because you never said the words, not until the very end."

Until Paul actually said the words "You're fired," Dave did not get the message. He was too caught up in trying to plead his case, and the vagueness of Paul's words allowed Dave to feel he still had some maneuvering room.

Paul and I began to sort through the conversation. We realized that while Paul thought he was being direct and very clear with Dave, his message had gotten lost.

"I was trying to spare Dave's feelings by not coming right out with it," he said shaking his head back and forth. "I was hoping I wouldn't have to be so blunt, but in the end he forced me to blurt it out because he just wasn't getting it."

Sure enough, Dave didn't get it because he didn't want to hear that he was losing his job. In softening his message and using euphemisms for "you're fired," Paul had given Dave and his emotional defense system the wiggle room it needed to hang onto any glimmer of hope it could find. And hang on he did!

"You have to say the words," I told Paul. "You didn't actually terminate his employment until you were crystal clear and specific at the end. It may have felt harsh, but it wasn't until then that you were really direct and clear. It was then that it became real for Dave."

Maybe someone else would have been able to read between the lines and would have understood Paul's meaning right away, but not Dave. Dave wanted to cling to every last bit of hope he could find in his manager's words. He liked his job and wanted to keep it.

"I don't think you have to be harsh or uncaring in how you communicate the termination," I said. "Your message can still be filled with compassion and tact, but the lesson here is you have to be very clear and specific with your language, no matter how uncomfortable it makes you feel."

The Courage to Be Honest

That situation helped me to crystallize the basic foundation of my leadership philosophy. From that point on, "You have to say the words" became my mantra and a standard for how leaders need to communicate during difficult conversations. It signifies my desire to be totally honest with employees and to state messages in a clear and concise manner so that they have the best chance of being understood. Before almost every important conversation I had after that meeting with Dave, you could hear me say, "Ok, so who's going to say the words?"

I encourage you to adopt this philosophy of "saying the words" for yourself, and to commit to the belief that honest feedback is the best way to reinforce or alter an individual's behavior and performance. For some people, the consequences of their bad behavior or poor performance does not become real to them until you actually state in clear and concise language, that what they are doing is unacceptable and their behavior could potentially become job threatening.

When you think about it, it is unfair to ask employees to "read between the lines" to find your hidden message when their job or welfare is at risk. Your responsibility as a leader is to bring all of your experience and skills to bear on the situation and to demonstrate the courage to say clearly what needs to be said. It is the only way to effect positive change and improvement within your team and organization. You hold the key; the question is, do you have the courage to use it?

Types of Tough Conversations

So what makes a conversation tough? Well, not to give you too squishy of an answer, the definition of a tough conversation really varies by individual situation. What seems like a tough conversation to you might be very easy for someone else, so it is a subjective experience. For our purposes, I am going to embrace a very broad interpretation of "tough."

If **you** feel a conversation you are about to have is going to be **difficult or uncomfortable** for **you or the employee** in any way, then it qualifies as a tough conversation. For most of us, situations that would fall under this definition can be sorted into one of these four categories:

- Behavior issues
- Performance issues

- Sensitive topics
- Terminations

Let's briefly look at each one of these categories and identify the types of issues that you would typically address within each.

Behavior Issues

Although behavior issues can certainly impact performance, they are distinct from performance issues in that they are usually related to a specific incident or behavior rather than the overall performance of the employee. They are the employee's unwanted actions that need to cease or the desired actions that need to begin immediately. Most of the time an employee is expected to demonstrate this change in behavior quickly, as the shift doesn't require additional training or entail a significant learning curve.

Examples of commonly addressed behavior issues include

- Attendance or lateness problems.
- Inappropriate outbursts or inability to manage emotions.
- Improper communication issues such as use of profanity or rudeness.
- Insubordination.
- Cash handling errors.
- Failure to follow a company policy or procedure.

Obviously there are other situations that fall into this category, but this list gives you a good idea of the problems encountered most frequently. As a general rule of thumb, if you find yourself telling an employee, "Don't ever do that again," you are probably dealing with a behavior issue rather than an overall performance issue.

Behavior issues are typically best dealt with using a progressive discipline process which includes a series of warnings that increase in seriousness for each offense. Each step of the progressive discipline process includes feedback to the employee as to why his behavior (or lack of it) is unacceptable and some form of documentation that confirms the feedback and outlines the potential consequences if the issue has to be addressed again. Each step along the process increases in formality and urgency until eventually the employee's employment is terminated as a result of the behavior.

The goal of addressing behavior issues in this manner is to provide employees with critical feedback on a timely basis regarding any behaviors negatively impacting their performance so they can make immediate adjustments. It sets a finite limit on unwanted behavior and the feedback ensures the employees are fully aware of the issues and the potential consequences of their continued unacceptable behavior. It also chronicles the company's efforts to assist employees by providing them with feedback and documents the decision to terminate the employment of those unwilling or unable to change.

Performance Issues

Issues falling into this category are typically related to an employee's failure or inability to meet performance standards and job expectations. These problems cannot be corrected simply by the warning "Don't do this again." Performance issues are more pervasive and tend to need a longer period of time to correct. Additional training and support may also be required to assist the employee in improving his performance to an acceptable level.

Examples of commonly addressed performance issues include

- Failure to meet stated sales or performance goals, usually measured over a 3–12 month period of time.
- Inability to effectively execute a number of job responsibilities.
- A lack of knowledge or skills that negatively impacts performance.
- Difficulty establishing or maintaining positive relationships.
- Poor habits (e.g., organizational, decision making, interpersonal) that become obstacles to achieving performance goals.
- Poor discernment and decision-making skills.

Performance issues are addressed using a slightly different form of the progressive discipline process. While each step in the progressive discipline process increases in urgency and severity of consequences if the problem persists, employees struggling with performance issues are usually given a longer period of time (generally 30–90 days) to correct their issues before escalating to the next step. The extended time, often called a probation period, is typically necessary to give employees enough time to demonstrate the needed change or to acquire the additional knowledge or skills.

Documentation for performance issues frequently includes an action plan listing suggested activities for employees to accomplish during the probation period which can assist them in demonstrating their improvement. The goal is to provide employees with a "road map" that provides specific feedback as to where they are falling short of expectations and suggest actions they can take to elevate their performance. The responsibility remains with the employees to complete the activities and demonstrate the needed improvement.

Here again, the progressive discipline process serves to document the company's attempts to assist employees in improving their performance and to formally outline the consequences if the improvement isn't forthcoming. This documentation becomes especially important if legal action is initiated.

Sensitive Topics

Not surprisingly, some of the topics that fall into this category can make the strongest leader go weak in the knees. Sensitive topics are the last thing in the world most people want to talk about, but when these very personal issues crop up in the workplace and negatively impact performance or career advancement, they must be addressed head on.

Examples of sensitive topics that many managers find uncomfortable addressing include:

- Personal hygiene, body odor, bad breath.
- Appropriateness of dress, professional image.
- Office romance, sexual behavior.
- Medical, mental health issues.
- Personal or family related problems.
- Alcohol, drug abuse.
- Harassment.
- Bereavement.

Leaders need to know how to effectively handle delicate issues such as these in the workplace with compassion and sensitivity. If you manage enough people, you will eventually have to address a sensitive subject that may be negatively impacting performance, perception, or team morale.

In subsequent chapters, I will offer you some specific suggestions to use when initiating these types of sensitive conversations as well as communication tools (such as I-statements) that will help you to provide employees with candid and specific feedback.

Terminations

Because this is one of the most important and intimidating situations a leader needs to successfully manage, there is a whole chapter later in the book dedicated to the process of conducting terminations (see Chapter 15). For some managers, the thought of ending a team member's employment is a responsibility they do not want, so they avoid the conversation like the plague. When finally forced to terminate employment, discomfort and fear can block their ability to effectively communicate critical information during the meeting, leading them to mismanage the termination process.

No one enjoys ending someone's employment, and if they do, they have no business being in a leadership position. I have found that termination conversations are best handled much like one would handle removing a band aid: quickly and efficiently. If you worry too much about how much it is going to hurt and allow your sympathy for the individual to get in the way, you actually become less effective with the delivery of the message and that could end up making it a more painful experience for everyone involved.

When delivering a termination message, people don't want to hear about how hard this is for you or how bad you feel about terminating their employment. They should be the focus of this tough conversation, not you or your feelings. Expressions of remorse or guilt may make you feel better in the moment, but you should avoid stating that you are "sorry to have to do this" as you may end up further agitating them. Your apology may also give them the perception that there is wiggle room in your decision because you feel bad, which can prompt them to argue or try to negotiate the termination and prolong the conversation.

Tough conversations come in all shapes and sizes and, because of this, it is harder to feel confident and comfortable that you know what you are doing in every situation. You will need to rely on your intuition and experience to help navigate the process, to understand the limits of your compassion, and to determine the appropriate time to initiate or escalate the progressive discipline process. Addressing issues directly will show your humanity as a leader and demonstrate your respect for the individuals who work for you.

KEY LEARNING POINTS FROM THIS CHAPTER

- Your goal with any conversation is to have your message completely and accurately understood while demonstrating compassion and respect for the individual you are counseling.

- Any attempts to "soften the blow" of your message with vague language will dilute your message, lead to misunderstandings, and for some individuals "protect" them only from facing the reality of their situation.

- When it comes to delivering critical feedback, you must have the courage to be direct. You have to say the words you are most uncomfortable saying.

- A tough conversation is any conversation that you feel is going to be difficult or uncomfortable in any way, for you or the employee.

- Tough conversations typically fall into one of four categories: behavior issues, performance issues, sensitive topics, or terminations.

- Behavior issues are usually related to a specific incident or behavior.

- Performance issues are typically related to an employee's failure or inability to meet job-related standards or expectations.

- While uncomfortable to talk about, sensitive topics must be addressed when they negatively impact an individual's performance or relationships.

- Keep the focus on the employee during a termination discussion, rather than your feelings, and do not belabor the message.

2 Chapter

Build a Strong Foundation

Try not to become a man of success.
Rather become a man of value.

Albert Einstein

A reputation for honesty is not built during just one conversation. It is created over time through each and every interaction you have with people, formal and informal, where you demonstrate who you are as a leader and the value you place on honesty. Your ability to address issues directly and to say what needs to be said in order to support the growth and development of your people builds your credibility as a leader. To avoid these conversations is to send a clear message that you are not interested in their well-being or their future, and that you put your own comfort above their welfare.

Your character and your values are the foundation of your leadership style and, like the foundation of a house, the more solid it is, the higher you can build on top of it. If you have a solid character and honor values such as honesty and integrity, you will develop trust and credibility with people. These qualities are at the core of your ability to provide effective feedback. If people don't trust you, they won't listen to what you have to say—even if it is information they desperately need to hear.

Building Influence

As a leader you need to be able to build influence with others. True leadership does not come as a result of a promotion, your position, or your title, no matter how impressive it sounds. The only person you really impress with your title is yourself—and maybe your mother. Influence cannot be mandated; like respect, it must be earned. Influence is built on credibility, respect, and trust. A certain title or position may buy you time to build your influence because people are taught to respect individuals in positions of authority, but it won't carry you forever.

Your ability to build the needed influence to lead people is directly related to the strength of your character and the qualities you demonstrate as a leader. You make decisions every day that either enhance or destroy your character. If your character is flawed, you will not be able to hide it from others. People follow individuals they know, like, and trust, and if they do not trust you or your intentions, they will not support you. It's as simple as that. Leaders who fail to learn this lesson are unable to effectively build trust and influence with their people. To help illustrate this point, let me tell you about Robert.

Robert's Story

Robert had recently been promoted from within his department to the department manager position, and he was absolutely thrilled. This was his first real management position, and he thought to himself he finally had made it. He spent his initial few weeks as a manager sitting in his office organizing files and attending meetings as the new head of the department. It felt good to him to be on top, and he was settling into a comfortable routine.

Like many new managers, Robert realized quickly that he was uncomfortable addressing performance issues directly with his team. He had been promoted from within the department, and his former peers now reported to him; he felt awkward giving his friends feedback when they made a mistake. Instead of fully embracing his new leadership role and addressing performance issues directly with real-time coaching and counseling, he focused instead on enforcing the department and company rules. This felt a lot safer to him, and he thought it would be a good way for him to establish his authority right out of the gate. "Rules were rules," he said, and his staff wouldn't be able to argue with his judgments if they broke a rule.

Robert's discomfort with having candid conversations with his former peers led him instead to create a list that he kept in his desk drawer. He figured keeping track of problems was a good idea for a leader as eventually he would have to write a performance review for each of them and his list would come in handy. Each time one of his team members did something wrong, he noted it on his list. By the end of six months, almost everyone in Robert's department was on the list for something they did.

Meanwhile, Robert was enjoying the freedom and the perks that came with his ascension to the management ranks. He began taking long lunches with his colleagues and often slipped unnoticed out of work to head home early. When the department entered its busy season at the end of the year and his team was forced to work overtime and weekends, Robert still kept to his 40-hour-a-week work schedule. He thought to himself how lucky he was that he didn't have to stay late or work weekends anymore.

As you might imagine, Robert's work ethic and leadership philosophy did not sit well with his team. While they had been willing to cut him some slack while he settled into his new role, their patience was running out. They often grumbled that it wasn't fair that they had to work late and give up their weekends and Robert didn't. After all, he was their team leader. They tried to hint at their frustration, but Robert dismissed their comments as playful banter and did not take them seriously.

Over the months, as Robert's team struggled with his lack of commitment to the department, his relationships began to suffer. Eventually, his team stopped communicating with him at all. Morale dropped and mistakes began to occur. Even though Robert was aware of the slipping performance issues, he never addressed the mistakes directly with his people, choosing instead to note the errors on the "secret" list that he kept in his desk. When one of the team's mistakes resulted in the company losing significant revenue, the problems then rose to the attention of the general manager, to whom Robert reported. The GM called Robert to his office to discuss the productivity and quality issues.

Robert knew that his boss was very concerned. Productivity was down and mistakes were being made. Robert wanted to show his boss that he was aware of the problems, so he brought the list he had been keeping to the meeting. When Robert sat down, the GM asked him to explain what was going on in his department. Robert reviewed the infractions members of his team had committed during the last several months and suggested that there were a few people in particular whom he believed had not been pulling their weight.

The GM asked Robert, "Have you addressed any of these issues directly with your team members?" Robert responded, "Oh, I'm sure they know exactly what they are doing wrong. How could they not? The customer complaint forms go directly back to the person who made the mistake!" This wasn't a lie; Robert truly believed that his people "instinctively" knew they had been dropping the ball lately.

Based on Robert's comments about poor performance and with the specific information he had on the list, the GM instructed Robert to select the two members of his team who currently had the most issues and place them on performance probation in an effort to improve their performance and eliminate the productivity and quality issues within the department.

Well, you probably can guess what happened next. Robert's staff was caught completely unprepared. When Robert met with the first of his people, James, to place him on performance probation, James was totally caught off guard by what he was hearing. He had never had a performance problem before; in fact, he thought he was one of the strongest members of the team. After hearing the feedback, James became very angry and raised his voice to Robert: "This is the first I am hearing of any performance issues, and in fact, I don't believe I have any issues," James said heatedly. "I am going to need to see proof of what you are saying as I think you are absolutely wrong!"

The confrontation unnerved Robert, and he was having a hard time coming up with specific examples off the top of his head to support his feedback to James. Then he had a thought: To help him refresh his memory, Robert reached into his file drawer and pulled out his list.

Reading from his "secret" list, Robert proceeded to cite the exact dates and times in the last six months when James had broken a departmental rule or made a mistake. James was furious that Robert had not given him this feedback immediately when the issues occurred. He felt ambushed and utterly betrayed by his boss and friend. "There is obviously no use in continuing the conversation as it is clear to me that you aren't going to change your mind and that you are setting me up for failure," James shouted. James refused to sign his performance probation memo and stormed out of the office.

By the time Robert called the second employee, Laura, in for her discussion, she already knew all about the conversation with James and Robert's now-infamous "secret" list. Laura went right on the offensive as soon as she sat down in Robert's office.

"I demand to know what you have written about me on your list!" she stated folding her arms across her chest. Robert tried to dance around the issue and minimize the impact of the list, but Laura was having none of it. She was so insistent that Robert was forced to take out the list again and review the notations he'd made about her, just as he had done with James.

As he read each item, Laura debated the accuracy of each and every comment, and then out of utter frustration, she began to sob. The sight of Laura crying really upset Robert as he didn't know what to do when a woman started to cry, especially someone he considered to be a friend. He tried to comfort her by again minimizing the issue and taking back some of what he had said. "It's not really all that bad," Robert said. "I can explain away more than half of these mistakes because you were working so much overtime, you must have been exhausted."

After more than an hour of Kleenex and consoling, Robert decided to let Laura off the hook with just a warning, no performance probation. Later he said, "It just didn't seem like the right thing to do with her crying and all."

He thought he had handled the two conversations about as well as could have been expected, but Robert's troubles were only just beginning. With lightning speed, the news of the secret list spread throughout his department. Team members didn't feel safe, even the ones Robert considered to be excellent performers. No one felt they could trust Robert anymore after this.

When James found out that his coworker, Laura, had not been put on performance probation as he was, he went to human resources to complain. Fueled by frustration and the momentum of recent events, several of Robert's staff decided to band together and request a group meeting with the GM so they could air their concerns about the list as well as Robert's leadership style.

During that meeting, they informed the GM that they didn't trust Robert and because he was withholding feedback, they all worried about the security of their jobs. They also took that opportunity to share their frustrations about Robert's management style: his unfair treatment, his short work days, the long lunches, and their perception that he felt he was "above" helping out. All of this quickly added up to a department and a manager in crisis.

The general manager called Robert in for another meeting to further discuss the situation and to provide him with the feedback he'd received from his team. As the HR manager, I sat in on the meeting. The GM asked how the meetings with James and Laura had gone. "Not very well," Robert admitted. "I really don't know what happened. I knew they wouldn't be happy, but their reaction really surprised me."

The GM shared with Robert the feedback that he had received during his meeting with Robert's team. Afterward he asked him, "What do you think went wrong here, Robert?"

Robert thought about it. While he recognized that he should have given people more feedback, he wasn't sure what he had done that was so wrong that it made everyone turn on him like that. "I thought everything was going so well," he said sadly. "I thought they were my friends."

Over the next couple of days, the GM and I met with Robert to help him identify where he had made his mistakes and to coach him through the changes he would need to make immediately with this team. Robert needed to significantly shift his leadership paradigm as he had made several fundamental mistakes regarding his relationships with team members. He believed that respect came automatically with the manager title and position, but he had just learned the hard way that he could not demand respect: he had to earn it.

Robert also had thought that since he was promoted from within and his people all knew him that he didn't have to build relationships and establish his credibility. We reminded him that people don't care how much you know until you show them how much you care about them. He had done nothing to establish his credibility in this new position or to show that he cared about the welfare of his people. Eventually, his team grew tired of giving him the benefit of the doubt and withdrew their support.

Finally, Robert understood how his failure to deliver honest and timely feedback had undermined the relationship he had had with his entire team. His list was the equivalent of virtually pulling the performance rug out from under each of his team members, and with the discovery of that list, team members lost any trust he had built. Robert was going to have to start over again with his team and mend what was broken before he could begin to exert any influence going forward.

While he might seem like a lost cause to you, Robert's story eventually did have a happy ending. It took more than a year for him to correct his issues and establish his credibility, and the road was not without its share of bumps. He worked hard to rebuild the trust he'd lost with his team and learned to provide real-time feedback. With our help and support, Robert improved his communication skills and improved his attitude toward his job and his interactions with the team.

Unfortunately, there was a casualty in Robert's department. As a result of the turmoil and stress, one of the team's best performers resigned. She accepted a job at another company because she was afraid Robert wouldn't be able to make the needed changes, and the entire situation had left her feeling insecure about her continued employment.

To Robert's credit, even though he made some major mistakes in the beginning, he remained open to feedback and was able to transform the difficult situation into a tremendous learning experience. He changed his behavior and his attitude and tried to apply the lessons he learned in that first year of management throughout the rest of his career.

Robert's story is certainly not unusual. By far the most common mistake managers make is withholding honest and specific feedback from their direct reports because they find the process of delivering feedback awkward, uncomfortable, and intimidating. Like Robert, they make the decision that it is easier to ignore issues or to save feedback for a time when they really need the "ammunition," rather than addressing problems as they occur.

You don't have to make the same mistakes Robert did. Make it a priority to become an expert at communicating feedback. Take pride in your ability to do it well. Build confidence by developing your communication skills; you will become more comfortable confronting issues and you will significantly increase your influence with others.

Developing the Qualities of a Leader

Becoming an exceptional leader is as much about being honest with yourself as it is about being honest with others. If your decisions and actions are not in alignment with your values and what you believe to be important, people will perceive that disconnect, and they will have trouble trusting you. In order to demonstrate respect for others you must hold as a value the importance of treating people with respect or it just won't work.

To ensure that you are starting out with the best foundation possible on which to build your leadership legacy, I've identified several qualities and values that are directly linked to your ability to provide open and honest communication to your team. By developing these qualities, you will not only enhance your leadership ability, but you will see a trickle-down effect that will positively impact all aspects of your life. You can't help but become a better person when you pursue becoming a better leader: It is all connected.

Become a Person of Character

Your character is at the heart of who you are as a leader. It demonstrates to the outside world your moral and ethical compass. Unlike other qualities you possess, character is not something you are born with. No matter your background or family circumstances, you can make a conscious decision to choose the type of person you want to become at any time.

A commitment to honesty is a big part of developing good character. When you value and practice honesty by providing individuals with accurate and timely feedback on their work performance, you build a foundation of trust, which gives you something to draw from when you need to address a performance situation down the road. If you don't truly value honesty, you will bail at the first hint of discomfort and do anything to avoid having the tough conversation.

The last thing most managers want to do is terminate employment. Unfortunately, it does happen and when it does, you never want to be in the position of terminating employment when the individual isn't fully aware that their job was in jeopardy because you weren't totally honest with them. I could not have continued to do this type of work for over twenty years without making a commitment that I would do all that I could to help people understand the reality of their situations before it was too late.

Accept that it is your responsibility to treat people with dignity and respect and your actions will build your credibility as a leader and promote trust between you and your team. When you walk your talk, people trust that you mean what you say, and they will see you as a person of integrity. If your words and actions are not in alignment, you will be perceived as untrustworthy and as having a hidden agenda. People won't know which to believe—your walk or your talk.

Be Trustworthy

Your role as a leader is to find out where your people currently are and to get them to follow you to where you want them to be. People will not follow a leader they do not trust. One of the saddest situations I've observed is when someone loses her job for a behavior or performance issue she could have corrected if she had just been told about it before it got to a point of no return.

Building trust with your staff is a challenging task. The process cannot be rushed, and it can't be granted just on the basis of your position or experience. It takes a long time to develop trust with your team members and, unfortunately, it can all be lost in an instant as we saw with Robert. Trust is absolutely that fragile and should not be taken for granted. Here are some common ways leaders break trust with their people:

- Not following through on a commitment or promise
- Gossiping
- Failing to accept responsibility for their mistakes
- Taking credit for their people's work
- Lying
- Avoiding responsibility
- Holding on to or actively hiding information that should be shared

Avoid these and other trust-breaking behaviors. Being honest with your people about where they stand in terms of their performance is vital to building and maintaining their trust. If your people trust your intentions and they believe you to be a person of good character, you can give them almost any feedback and the relationship will survive.

Communicate Your Expectations

While people are motivated to effectively perform their job duties for a variety of reasons such as money and career advancement, successful leaders also understand that many people are equally as driven by the desire to please their boss. The trouble is some leaders are not very clear about the behaviors that make them happy or do not communicate to their team when their priorities have changed. This can lead individuals to feel like they are running in circles trying to please their boss.

By clearly defining and communicating performance standards and expectations, you are giving people a road map for success and showing them exactly what they need to do to make you happy. Your consistent feedback lets them know when they are on target and when they have fallen short of your expectations. Some people, once they know their goals, are naturally driven to succeed and will self-correct when they get offtrack. These individuals may seem like they do not need a lot of feedback from you, but what happens if you don't give them feedback and their assumptions are wrong?

I've always coached my managers that an absence of any feedback is the same thing as giving positive feedback. For most people, unless told otherwise, they assume that their performance is acceptable and that their manager is happy with them. Unfortunately this is not always the case, and when there is a disconnect between perception and reality, it can lead to devastating consequences.

In order to achieve outstanding results, you must provide your team with plenty of feedback, both positive and constructive, as it relates to your standards and expectations. Lack of honest and timely feedback leads to all kinds of problems for everyone involved, including the following:

- Team members can't improve their performance because they are unaware that there is an issue.
- Managers can't get the results they need because they are allowing unsatisfactory performance to continue.
- The HR manager gets cranky when a department manager finally decides to remove the under-performer because she was never fully informed of her issues and given a chance to improve.
- And finally, the company may face an increased chance of legal exposure as a result of the lack of documentation and is hampered in its efforts to defend a lawsuit.

Your role as a team leader is to achieve results through the efforts of other people and you will be judged on that ability. Effectively articulating your standards and expectations while addressing performance issues as they arise allows you to be fair to your employees, achieve results, maintain morale, and protect the interests of the company.

Leading is an active process, not a passive one. You should praise and reward positive performance consistently. You need to actively monitor poor performance and develop your people every day or you will not achieve results. If you choose to ignore issues rather than address them too many times, eventually someone will wonder about *your* results and *your* effectiveness as a leader. And if that should ever happen, I'm confident that you would want your manager to give you honest feedback in a timely manner so you can correct the problem: so pay it forward.

Become a Servant Leader

I have worked with a number of individuals such as Robert from our earlier story, who were so focused on what a management position could do for them they lost sight of the true nature of leadership. Your primary function as a leader is to serve the best interests of your people. Focusing on "what's in it for me" makes you an arrogant leader and gives people the impression that you will sacrifice them for your own agenda. It will also erode any trust you have developed with them.

Some managers think they can hide their personal agenda and spin situations so that they appear to be taking action on behalf of others. If you are one of these leaders and you think you are being clever, I'm here to tell you you're not. Chances are very good that your team is far more perceptive than you give them credit for. They see through your smoke screens, know when you are promoting yourself at their expense, when you don't hold yourself to the same standards you enforce with them, and when you use your title as a "get out of jail free" card for bad behavior. Most people can smell a self-serving attitude a mile away, and they will want none of it.

Adopt the attitude of a servant leader. Be more concerned with helping others to succeed than you are in promoting yourself. Come to work every day to look for ways you can help your team by

- Eliminating obstacles to their productivity and success.
- Finding additional resources to make their jobs easier.
- Showing them appreciation.
- Rewarding and recognizing their achievements.
- Investing in their growth and development.

Servant leaders believe the path to their success lies in serving the needs of the people they lead first. They are not interested in directly raising their own profile within the organization but in ways they can increase the growth, cooperation, and success of their team. Become a servant leader. Practice humility. Remember what leadership expert and author Ken Blanchard says, "People with humility don't think less of themselves; they just think of themselves less."

Invest in Yourself and Others

The most successful people know that they are a "work in progress" and have therefore never finished growing and developing their skills. Develop an attitude of continuous learning, and then share your knowledge and skills with others. Talk to your people about their goals, career and personal, and then look for ways to help them achieve those goals by investing in their development. In some instances, you might consider reimbursing them for attending a program or seminar that increases their technical skills, or you may simply spend time mentoring them. Investing in their growth doesn't have to mean a large financial expense.

Invest in your own development as well, even if the company you work for doesn't reimburse you for all of your expenses. Use your car as your own personal classroom, and listen to audiotapes and books on CD that focus on business skills and on general personal development. Expand your mind and your knowledge as you commute to work or run errands around town. Your local library should have a large selection for you to check out.

Once you learn a new skill or hear a fresh idea, share it with the people you work with. If you find a book you especially like, add it to your library at work and encourage your team members to read it as well. Start your own book club to encourage learning in a fun environment. They say the best way to learn something new is to teach it to someone else, so make sharing your knowledge a regular part of your routine.

Think about the people you are investing in and developing as the next generation of leaders. Have you given any thought to the legacy you are creating as a leader? Many people don't consider their legacy until the latter part of their career, but legacy is something that you should think of at any stage of your life. The reputation you build today will cast a long shadow and will follow you for quite some time, so you should decide now what you want your leadership legacy to be.

Make the decision today to make developing and investing in others a part of your legacy. Understand that your actions speak louder than your words. You will motivate more people to grow if you model an attitude of continuous learning yourself. Dedicate yourself to personal growth and you will inspire others to do the same. Lift people up and encourage more out of them than they ever thought possible. Serve your people and hold as your intention to help them grow and be their best. What an incredible legacy that would be!

KEY LEARNING POINTS FROM THIS CHAPTER

- Your ability to influence people is directly related to the strength of your character and your ability to build trust. You demonstrate your integrity by being honest and authentic with others.

- You will achieve only a limited amount of respect as a result of your title or position, the rest must be earned.

- You establish credibility and loyalty when you place the needs of the individuals you lead above your own. Be more concerned with helping others succeed than you are in promoting yourself.

- You destroy trust and undermine your credibility when you withhold performance feedback from your people.

- In order to be a better leader on the outside you need to become a better leader on the inside.

- People do not follow a leader they do not trust. Avoid trust-breaking behaviors such as gossiping and withholding feedback.

- Clearly articulate your expectations and standards for performance so that employees understand what is expected of them and they have a road map for success.

- Consider the leadership legacy you are creating with today's actions. Invest in your own personal growth and dedicate yourself to the development of others.

3 Chapter

Get Out of Your Own Way

*Almost all our faults are more pardonable than the
methods we think up to hide them.*

Francois de La Rochefoucauld

If you have ever been in the position of coaching and counseling another individual, you know there are times during a conversation when you can be your own worst enemy. Some people can push your buttons like no others, causing you to lose control of your emotions and the conversation. As much as we might try to avoid it, regrettably, sometimes we end up dragging our personal emotional baggage into our conversations.

Let's face it, we are all human. In addition to our strengths, knowledge, skills, and experience, we also bring our own sets of fears, insecurities, biases, and negative personality traits into each and every interaction. We are a whole package, for better or worse. When a button gets pushed and you react or when a negative bias or stereotype you hold interferes with your objectivity, it can mean disaster for you as a leader.

Your Dark Side

Maintaining your composure in emotionally charged situations is hard work, and sometimes it can take your focus off the discussion at hand. You may find that you are expending as much energy trying to keep your "stuff" down as you are trying to manage your employee's emotions.

The "stuff" I refer to are those things that lurk just underneath your surface that, when triggered, can immediately impact your demeanor, your ability to remain objective, and your sense of control. I call this stuff your "dark side," and it's a term I freely use today because I grew up during the first Star Wars era and, quite possibly, because I am still shocked by the fact that Darth Vader is actually Luke's father. But then again, who isn't?

These powerful emotions tend to stay in the shadows until they are in-advertently triggered during a conversation, and then their intensity might surprise you. It is in these shadowy areas of our personality that we are most vulnerable as individuals and especially as leaders. At times, we can react and make decisions based on these deep emotions and beliefs and be totally unaware that they are negatively affecting our judgment. You might have heard this situation referred to before as a blind spot.

The emotions associated with these shadow areas are typically intense and the buttons or triggers that set them off are hard-wired. In other words, you've had some of these fears, issues and beliefs since you were a child, so they are not going to be so easy to eliminate. It may feel as if they are almost part of your DNA. But you can still work to minimize their negative impact once triggered.

For example, here's a very real scenario I've seen play out a number of times over the years:

A manager has some significant insecurity around her competency levels and one of the strong fears she holds is that one day people will find out that she doesn't really know what she is doing. In essence, she's been faking it. As a result, this manager is very unlikely to admit a mistake, especially in front of an employee. Any suggestion that she's made an error triggers a strong defensive and emotional reaction in her and she may not even be aware this buried insecurity has been tapped into.

During a counseling session one of her employees goes on the offensive and tells her, "You're wrong, it's entirely your fault," and "You don't know what you are doing." The accusation sets off an exaggerated and disproportionate emotional response in the manager because of her hidden fear and insecurity. She yells back at the employee, defending herself and throwing blame elsewhere as it is tapping directly into a very real insecurity about not being good enough. She may not even be totally conscious that the employee triggered something on her "dark side," but the real clue that it is there is the intensity of emotion ignited by the employee's statements.

Her exaggerated emotional response and her inability to take responsibility for her mistakes have the potential to sabotage the conversation. If the manager remains unaware of this insecurity and responds defensively and emotionally each time it is triggered, her responses will eventually erode trust within her team, irreparably damage relationships, and undermine her credibility.

Once an area of your dark side is engaged during a counseling session with an employee, it is almost always a conversation stopper. The flood of emotions you feel will likely divert your focus away from the employee to you, while you try to manage your defenses and maintain control of your own emotional reaction. The negative impact could significantly change the tone and the direction of the discussion, making it difficult for you to get back on track without stepping away from the conversation.

Self-awareness is critical to managing your dark side because once you identify where you are vulnerable, you can begin to develop strategies to effectively neutralize your emotions. You may never be able to totally eliminate some of your hot buttons, but with self-awareness you can learn to recognize where they are, minimize any defensive reactions, and manage the emotional fallout.

The heat of the moment during a counseling session is not the appropriate time to try and work through any issues you have had hiding in the shadows, so while we have the time now, let's take a walk "on the dark side" and see if you might recognize some places where you are currently vulnerable.

Fears

Are you afraid of dealing with someone who is aggressive, yelling, crying, or physically intimidating? Are you afraid to own the feedback you give because you are worried the recipient won't like you or will be angry with you, or you will have to defend your position at some point? Maybe you worry about retaliation if you terminate someone's employment.

Most of us have a type of personality or a kind of situation with which we are uncomfortable or even fearful of handling. Whether your fears are valid or not, when triggered they can grab hold of you and kick in your innate fight-or-flight response system. Once that happens, it becomes very difficult to maintain your objective demeanor and maintain control of the conversation.

A personal example can help to illustrate this. Because of my upbringing, when I started my career I was very uncomfortable dealing with people who shouted or yelled at me. I grew up in a very restrained family environment, and I remember only rare occasions when my parents raised their voices to my sister or me. In fact, we knew we were in real trouble when things got too quiet. So when I entered the workforce, dealing with someone who was raising his or her voice or yelling as a way of expressing emotion was something that I really did not know how to handle, and it created tremendous fear in me.

Because I had no experience handling people who were angry and confrontational, when those situations occurred, it stopped me dead in my tracks. If employees became angry and raised their voices as I was counseling them, I became totally unnerved. I had a very real physical reaction to this fear: my heart pounded, my face got hot, my hands shook, and my mind raced so quickly that I couldn't speak. I was literally the human version of a deer caught in headlights. I quickly realized that I would have to conquer this fear if I was ever going to be an effective leader.

To help manage my anxiety, I read books on how to deal with difficult people. These books offered me concrete strategies for handling someone who was angry or emotional. I also role-played potential emotionally charged situations with a fellow manager before I went into the actual conversation in order to practice the techniques I'd learned for diffusing emotions.

My greatest improvement came when I learned to make a distinction between people who were angry *at me*, and those who were just angry *at a situation* and venting that anger to me. I found that once I made that important distinction, I could easily deal with expressed anger when it wasn't personal or directed at me. This helped me to deal effectively with 99 percent of the situations where I encountered anger in the workplace.

Is there a type of person or a situation that you are afraid of handling? If so, you may want to do some research or get coaching support to give you the tools to better deal with your emotions. With fears, sometimes the anticipation of the encounter is worse than the reality of it. Fear is an emotion we create in our minds that then gets transferred to our bodies, so validation of the information you hold around a fear is very helpful in eliminating it.

Also, keep in mind this definition of fear. Fear is

False   **E**vidence   **A**ppearing   **R**eal.

Sometimes additional information is all you need to shine a light on your fears, adjust your perceptions, and maintain control of your emotional responses. That is, unless we are talking about snakes—then I am very comfortable holding onto that fear.

Insecurities

Even the most seasoned leader can feel insecure going into a tough conversation. You wonder if you have your facts straight. Will you say the right things and will you be able to control the conversation? You get those little butterflies in your stomach as you anticipate how the conversation will play out. These thoughts are natural for most managers and this type of minor insecurity usually starts to dissipate once the conversation begins and you settle into the flow.

But there is a much deeper and more destructive type of insecurity that is of a greater concern for leaders. It is the insecurity that prevents leaders from trusting others, building positive relationships, and communicating honestly. This insecurity permeates their interactions with everyone and undermines their team's ability to build trust and function effectively as a group.

Insecure leaders are often uncomfortable providing people with negative feedback. If they are forced to do so, they are unlikely to completely own it, preferring to pass it off as someone else's feedback or concerns. It is scary for them to take responsibility for negative feedback, making themselves a target for the employee's dissatisfaction.

Here are some other behaviors you might observe when dealing with insecure leaders. They

- Try to hold down or sabotage exceptional performers on their team because they are afraid of being "out-performed."
- Will not hire exceptional performers because they do not want the competition.
- Are more concerned with being liked than with being an effective leader.

- Isolate their team from other departments; they are afraid of their "dirty laundry" getting out.
- Sabotage relationships between team members so that people are only comfortable talking with, and going through, them.
- See everyone and everything through their filter of insecurity so they have trouble developing trust; people are either "for or against" them.
- Have difficulty accepting responsibility and quickly fall into victim mode when cornered.

Insecurity isn't always manifest by the leader passively hiding in the shadows, trying to remain unseen. Sometimes insecurity turns into an aggressive and dominant leadership style that is always on the offensive, rolling over people and situations with such force that it drains the energy from a room. These leaders do not give people the chance to question their decisions, so there is no debate or free exchange of opinions and ideas on their team. It is the ultimate "my way or the highway" attitude.

While confidence and a healthy ego is important for any leader, deep insecurity can also manifest outwardly as an over-inflated ego; a false bravado that almost dares people to challenge it. More than a few times I've had managers come to me demanding that we terminate the employment of one of their people because the employee "talked back to me, and I'm the boss." I am always concerned when leaders rely more on their position or title to grant them authority than their ability to build influence. Insecure leaders demand respect as a privilege of their title rather than appreciating that respect has to be earned.

I have found it very difficult to help the deeply insecure leader. During my years of coaching leaders who struggle with significant insecurity, I have often heard them say that any day they expect their manager to figure out that they don't know what they are doing and to fire them. It must be awful to come to work every day feeling that way and unfortunately, their problems won't be solved with a good pep talk or the latest self-help book.

If you feel that your insecurities might be getting in the way of your effectiveness as a leader, then you might consider seeking the assistance of a qualified counselor. Often the issues that lie at the base of these problems are deeply rooted in a person's personal life as well and are therefore most effectively handled by a professional.

Biases

I am using the term *bias* here to describe any belief, tendency, or preference you may have toward a particular perspective that interferes with your ability to be objective and impartial. It is not uncommon when you hear the word *bias* to immediately think about the very serious forms of ethnic, racial, and gender bias. These forms of bias are insidious, and there is obviously no room in a healthy workplace for any of them.

But in addition to these biases, I'd like you to think about some potentially less obvious ones that may be part of your belief system. They could be hiding just under the surface and they can be as destructive to your credibility and the productivity of your team as overt prejudice. Your biases are part of who you are, and you bring them into each and every decision you make. You may already be aware of how some beliefs might interfere with your objectivity, but others may be so deeply ingrained that you are not conscious of them.

To illustrate this, here are a few statements I've heard over the years that indicated to me at the time that the person making the statement might have a potential bias that could interfere with his or her ability to be objective.

- "I will never again hire a woman manager in her child-bearing years because she will end up getting pregnant and going out for six months."
- "He's from the South so I am concerned he won't be able to keep up with how fast we move here."
- "I would have hired him, but he takes public transportation to work so I don't feel he's reliable."
- "I don't like to hire young mothers as their kids will make them late all the time."
- "I will get rid of anyone who has an affair. If a wife can't trust her husband because he cheats, why should I?"
- "I feel he deserves more money; he has a family to support and she is single."
- "He's not a candidate for this job. Realistically at his age, he's just looking to coast to retirement."
- "This guy is really a drain on the department and I should let him go, but I feel bad, he just had a baby and he needs the job."

I believe that none of the managers making these statements meant to be unfair or to discriminate. Whether these beliefs were conscious or unconscious, the result was that it affected their judgment, their results were compromised, and people were adversely affected in the process. The more ingrained a bias or belief, the more likely we are to passionately defend it if challenged and the less likely we are to question it.

Be honest with yourself. Do you believe any of the following?

- Single mothers are unreliable.
- Men with families need their job protected more than single women.
- Older workers are less productive than younger ones.
- Minority employees will immediately claim discrimination if you try to give them negative feedback.
- A woman would never lie about an incident of sexual harassment.
- Anyone placed on a performance plan will eventually lose their job.
- A certain group or class of people can't be trusted.

Take an honest look at your strongly held beliefs and become aware of how they might impact your decisions. Be cautious that they don't inadvertently influence your decision making process when hiring, determining compensation, applying discipline, and terminating employment. Increasing your awareness of the areas in which you may have a bias now will help you to head off trouble down the road.

Personality Traits

In addition to those emotions and beliefs that skulk about on our dark side, each of us is made up of personality traits that can either support or impede our ability to flex our style enough to meet the needs of every tough conversation. While in many ways your personality is long developed by the time you reach the workplace, you can learn to identify how the behaviors and perceptions associated with these traits can become a distraction during a counseling discussion. Like the other shadow areas, you may be unaware of the negative perceptions that others have of you and their impact on your relationships.

In the following pages, I've identified several of the most common personality traits displayed by leaders that negatively impact the quality of communications and can quickly become obstacles to building effective relationships.

Emotionally Distant

People want to feel connected to their leader on both a professional and personal level. Managers who keep their distance by showing minimal emotion and withholding personal information never really connect fully with their team. Allowing your compassion, humanity, and respect to show to your employees is a very positive thing. No one wants the person disciplining them or terminating their employment to act like a cold-hearted fish. It's okay to show that you have empathy for them and their situation.

A poker face is a good asset to have when dealing with some staff issues, but in normal daily interactions it makes you hard to read, and leaves your staff unsettled and unsure of what you are thinking and feeling. Let your personality shine through. Employees love to work in an environment in which they can have some good-natured fun with their coworkers and boss. Restraint is a good quality in a leader; but too much restraint and you will be perceived as unapproachable.

Some leaders believe in total separation between their work and personal life. I believe you should let your people into your life, even if it's just a little. Share some details of your time outside of work. Talk about your family so they have a sense of who you are as a person. Ask them about their lives and fully listen to them when they speak. If a team member tells you his son has been sick, make sure you circle back and ask how he is doing. You'd be surprised how important it is to people that you listened to them and demonstrated your caring by following up.

Heart on the Sleeve

The opposite trait of being emotionally distant is to wear your heart on your sleeve. As much as these managers might try, they can't help but to let their emotions hang out there for all to see. They feel what the employee is feeling so sympathetically that it interferes with their ability to control the conversation and deliver their message. Any emotion they are feeling can be read on their face and is immediately communicated through their body language.

For these managers, emotions also get in the way of their decision-making process. Managers who feel too much sympathy for their employees might tolerate unacceptable behavior and performance for too long, delay discipline because they feel bad, or stop short of delivering an honest and effective message, all in an effort to spare their employees' feelings. Their inability to set their emotions aside makes them ineffective leaders and leaves them vulnerable to easy manipulation by more savvy employees.

For these managers, it takes practice and self-discipline, but they can learn to be less transparent with their emotions without turning into ice kings and queens. Over the years I have realized a couple of things about my emotions:

- By demonstrating an overabundance of emotion I am enabling people to stay in victim mode longer, preventing them from accepting responsibility, taking corrective action, and moving forward.
- An inability to control my emotions is likely to be perceived as a weakness by my employees and my boss, and both may lose respect for me.
- Savvy employees will use my emotions against me in an attempt to defend themselves or avoid discipline.

You want to demonstrate your compassion for an individual, but you don't want to let your guard down and show every emotion unfiltered as it comes up for you. When you allow yourself to feel and demonstrate the full weight of your emotions during a counseling session, you run the risk of saying something inappropriate. This can damage your efforts to have a productive discussion and ultimately the strength of your company's legal position.

If you believe you are having trouble managing an emotion such as anger or sadness during a conversation, excuse yourself and take a 10-minute break so you can compose yourself. It is better to take a break than to continue the conversation with your emotions out of control.

Impatient

I've worked with many leaders who were impatient by nature. It was not uncommon for them to appear as if they were disengaging when the story got too long or detailed for them. Most were usually just so focused on getting to the point where they could begin to fix the problem that they tried to rush the process. What they didn't realize is that in their haste to get to the point where they could begin to problem solve, they often left people feeling unappreciated and unheard.

I've learned over the years that some people just need you to listen to their story; that's it. They are perfectly capable of solving their own problems; they just need a good sounding board to work through their thought process. Don't be too quick to jump in and offer solutions. In fact, you will have greater success in your performance coaching if you allow people to come up with their own solutions. They will tend to feel a greater sense of ownership and investment in implementing any solutions they were a part of designing.

Some leaders "take back" tasks that they've delegated because things aren't getting done as quickly as they want, or give so much instruction to how a task ought to be completed that there is no room for the employees to learn and grow by accomplishing it on their own. People need to make mistakes in order to advance their skill levels and gain knowledge through their experience. That's how we get battle scars as leaders, and each of those scars represents a wealth of learning, so don't be too quick to micromanage the process.

If this describes you as a leader, remember one of your goals is to accomplish results *through* others and to teach them to be self-sufficient. Try to continue to work through the person to whom you have delegated rather than jumping in to save her if you think she is taking too long. And don't try too hard to protect your people from experiencing their own failures. There is a valuable lesson in failure if you let go of the process enough to find it. If you continue to micromanage your people for the sake of expediency and quality, they will never become self-sufficient and be able to grow beyond their current positions.

You want team members you trust and can delegate to with complete confidence, but sometimes in order to get to that point people need to learn from their own mistakes. And that means that you just might need to let them fall. This is especially important if you are trying to determine if an individual has a performance issue that needs to be addressed. If you are too quick to take back tasks or give too much detailed instruction, a struggling employee will never actually make a mistake or fail, making substandard performance harder to document and creating an obstacle to growth. It also leaves you doing a lot of extra work.

Don't be afraid to delegate to your team members. Make sure you are clear in the beginning about your level of urgency, any critical time frames and your expectations for the task. If one member drops the ball, don't immediately cut her out of the process. This might be an excellent developmental opportunity for your employee here if you take the time to coach her through it.

Arrogance

While confidence in a leader helps to put people at ease and makes them feel comfortable that someone is actually in charge, overconfidence in the form of arrogance is incredibly destructive in a leader. Humility is the safety valve that stops confidence from building to the point that it explodes into arrogance.

Leaders who are arrogant damage the cohesiveness of their team by placing themselves and their needs above everyone else. It can be "their way or the highway" and they rarely admit mistakes or accept ownership of problems. They have a narcissistic view of the world, and they are often perceived as driving their own personal agenda to the detriment of others. They are poster children for the WIIFM ("What's In It For Me?") club and are mainly focused on cashing in on the perks that their position affords them.

In counseling conversations, arrogant leaders tend to appear closed to other interpretations of a situation and are reluctant to admit any part they may have played in creating a problem. This reluctance to accept responsibility for their actions makes having a two-way discussion with them nearly impossible. I have found that they do not like to explain their thought processes or to defend their decisions, and in a situation where there is conflict with an employee, they believe the employee is always at fault. Providing these leaders with feedback can be a bit like hugging a porcupine; they are not very receptive and in the end, you are the one who feels hurt.

Arrogant leaders have never learned that it's not the position that makes the leader, but the leader who makes the position. I've seen it time and time again, once arrogant individuals make it to the management level they believe the rules somehow don't apply to them anymore and they start to take liberties: long lunches, flexible work schedules, and expecting their direct reports to make sacrifices they are not willing to make themselves.

Make sure you take a healthy dose of humility regularly to keep your ego in check. Become a servant leader; define your role as one of serving the needs of your people rather than finding ways for them to serve you. Enter every conversation with an open mind and be receptive to feedback. Adopt the One Percent Rule when it comes to feedback; ask yourself, if only 1 percent of what this person is telling me is true, what can I do to solve the problem and create positive change?

If you don't adopt an attitude of servant leadership, you may find people and circumstances conspiring to provide you with more than enough opportunities to "forcibly" practice humility. I have found a direct relationship between a manager's level of arrogance and his team's commitment to taking him down a peg or two.

These are a few of the qualities and attributes that can undermine your leadership and your ability to conduct effective conversations with employees. Do any of these resonate with you? If so, you might want to do some more inner work to help you mitigate their negative impact. Remember, self-awareness, followed by a well-designed and executed plan to address your weaknesses is the answer. Well, that and, in some cases, a really good therapist twice a week.

Getting caught with a portion of your dark side emerging during any conversation with an employee is like falling into quicksand, the harder you struggle to get out, the faster and farther down you sink. Your best bet is to avoid this hazard altogether.

Avoiding the Conversation

Heaven knows, in the short term, it is a lot easier to ignore a problem than to hit it head on. Maybe this is why so many managers avoid giving their people critical feedback. Whatever the reason, any short-term benefits you receive from sweeping a performance issue under the proverbial rug are outweighed by the long-term damage it can do to your team and your credibility as a leader. As they say, you can run but you can't hide. Eventually, you will need to face the situation in order to resolve it.

We've all been there. You avoid saying something to one of your team members about an issue and you think the issue has gone away on its own, then one day—bam! It's now a huge problem and everyone is wondering how it got this bad and they are looking to you for answers. In fact, this is one lesson I had to learn the hard way myself.

My Story

My learning curve as a young manager was pretty steep. At 22 years old I was in my first real job right out of college and I had almost 30 people reporting to me, most of them with significantly more work experience than

I had. I had no clue what I was doing most of the time when it came to people management. Fresh out of a multiweek management training program I tried to apply the lessons I had been taught. In the training we had covered the mechanics of coaching, counseling, motivation, and discipline, but talking about it in a classroom setting was one thing, dealing with actual employees was a completely different experience.

My efforts to apply my newly gained knowledge with my team were met at best with indifference and at worst, with insubordination as they outright refused to follow some of my directives. "I don't let my daughter tell me what to do," one woman said to me, "so why should I listen to you?" I had to hand it to her, it was a good question, one that really hadn't been addressed in my recent training.

When I joined the management ranks in the mid-1980s, people didn't talk much about being a good leader; the emphasis was on management and systems, directing others to get the job done. So to my way of thinking, it seemed if I could just get my team to listen to me, I would be a successful manager. It was a simple philosophy: if my staff liked me enough they would do what I asked, productivity would go up and morale would be high. This would surely impress my boss. I had succeeded in reducing modern management theory to the equivalent of wanting to be invited to sit at the "cool kid's table" in high school.

So I quickly became the manager who tried to be cool and was everyone's friend. I said yes to every request, and I avoided giving my team honest feedback because I was afraid of hurting their feelings and alienating them. Plus, the thought of confronting them about a performance issue just plain scared the heck out of me! Any illusion I had of power and influence given my title was quickly crushed by anyone who even remotely pushed back at me.

As it turned out, my methods ended up being successful with most of my staff because they were all good people who just wanted to come to work, do their jobs, and enjoy themselves. But for those employees who were underperforming or who exhibited behavioral problems, their performance remained unchecked, as I was unwilling to rock the boat by addressing issues or pushing them to improve. It was enough for me that on the surface we looked happy, got most of the work done, and all pleasantly coexisted.

My wakeup call came one afternoon when I was about six months into my job. Our office had the typical corporate setup with several rows of cubicles stretching from one end of the building to the other. Our department had approximately 100 team members and my unit of 30 sat right in the middle of them.

I was standing in my unit, leaning on a cubicle wall, talking to a member of my team. Out of the corner of my eye I could see Sharon, another member of my team, striding purposefully down the aisle right for me, papers clutched in her hand. She was clearly agitated. I knew she was prone to emotional outbursts and that she had "gone off on" others before, but I had failed to address this issue directly with her. In my youth and inexperience, I was hoping the problem would just disappear and I wouldn't have to confront Sharon. That was my first mistake.

To be honest, I don't really remember what Sharon said to me that day or what I had done to make her so angry. What I do remember is the humiliation and horror I felt as this woman loudly and *very* publicly berated me in full view of my team as well as the rest of the department. Her words were biting and her voice seemed to carry as if she were wearing a concealed microphone. All over the office heads began to pop up and down over the cubicle walls, faces assessing the danger like I was standing in the middle of a field of prairie dogs with a hungry coyote approaching.

As she stood there ranting at me, my mind raced. Somewhere in the back of my brain a little voice told me that I should stop her immediately and take her off the floor to talk, but I couldn't move. I was absolutely stunned and paralyzed with fear. Although the tirade only lasted a minute or so, it seemed like an eternity to me. During the entire encounter, I had not uttered a single word. When she had finished what she wanted to say, my embarrassment and humiliation complete, she turned on her heals and marched away triumphantly. I looked around the office for some sign of support as onlookers sheepishly disappeared from sight behind their cubical walls.

I did the only thing I could think to do: I slipped into my office, which was really just a cubicle with higher walls than any of the other cubicles on the floor, and laid my head on my desk. I felt like crying, but resisted. Even though no one could see me I was acutely aware that the cubicles were far from offering the level of privacy I needed for a complete emotional breakdown.

One of the other managers in the department who had witnessed the encounter came into my cubicle and sat with me. She was a compassionate woman, but today she was about to deliver some well-deserved tough love.

"Kathy," she said, "you can *never* allow this to happen again." I was with her so far. I could easily go the rest of my career avoiding this particular brand of humiliation. "What happened was entirely your fault," she said. That one stung as I was enjoying my role as a victim.

She continued, "This is not the first time Sharon has gone off like this on someone and up until this point, you chose to look the other way. You should have disciplined her the last time she did this." She was right, but as they say, hindsight is 20/20.

"At the very least, you should have taken control of the situation, stopped Sharon immediately, and brought her into the conference room for privacy."

"I was afraid to confront Sharon," I admitted. I was feeling very defeated at this point. "You need to toughen up," she said. "You are going to have to have a lot of uncomfortable conversations in your career, but you have to have them, it's your job." She slapped her hand on the desk for effect, "So suck it up!" She left me alone in my cubicle and as I reflected on what had just happened, the adrenaline subsided and the weight of her words began to sink in.

I had made a big mistake by not addressing Sharon's issues directly with her when she acted out before. I allowed my anxiety over a confrontation with her to intimidate me and I totally avoided the tough conversation. I also let my team down. By not addressing the negative behavior of one of its members, I allowed a problem to fester and impact the working environment of my star players, those people who made us all look good with their performances. I should have had more respect for them and addressed Sharon's behavior issue when I had first heard of it. Instead, I allowed the team to continue to suffer her tirades. In the end, I let my fears guide my decisions and I chose to do nothing.

As a result, the problem escalated and I got a taste of my own medicine. Maybe if I had tried to correct the behavior when it first occurred, I could have saved myself the humiliation and public embarrassment of Sharon's outburst. But I didn't, and that day I learned the hard way the cost of ignoring behavior issues.

Make the decision now to never allow yourself to be intimidated into avoiding a tough conversation. In order to be an exceptional leader, you are going to have to become as skilled as you can in talking to people about issues that are very personal, sometimes embarrassing, and often job threatening. You don't earn respect as a leader by ignoring issues; you earn it by valuing your people enough to address problems directly with them before it's too late. And as I found out early in my career, their respect is far more valuable to you, and effective for you as a leader, than their friendship.

Minimize the potential damage inflicted on your relationships by recognizing what fears, insecurities, biases, and personality traits you possess that get in the way of your current effectiveness, and then develop a plan to manage these areas and eliminate their negative impact. By successfully identifying and neutralizing any negative baggage you automatically carry with you into a conversation, you will not only better manage your own inner demons, but you will also become a more consistent and reliable leader for your team.

KEY LEARNING POINTS FROM THIS CHAPTER

- In addition to our strengths, we all bring our own unique set of "baggage" into every interaction: our fears, insecurities, biases, and personality traits. Some are known to us, others linger just outside of our consciousness hiding in our "dark side."

- Limiting beliefs and emotions lurking in our "dark side" leave us vulnerable, especially during tough conversations. Self-awareness is the key to neutralizing their negative effects.

- Get coaching and support to help you more effectively deal with types of people or situations in which you are currently uncomfortable or fearful.

- If you believe you may have some significant insecurity to manage, seek the support of a professional counselor.

- A bias is any belief, tendency, or preference toward a particular perspective that interferes with your ability to be objective and impartial. Honestly assess any biases that may impact your effectiveness.

- Identify personality traits that might get in the way of your demonstrating compassion, humility, or patience during a difficult conversation.

- Ignoring performance and behavior issues is never the best response. Don't let your fear or discomfort with having a tough conversation prevent you from addressing a problem. It rarely will resolve on its own.

- Practice and experience will help you to refine your skills and build your confidence. Ultimately, most people will respect you for being honest with them.

SECTION TWO:

DEVELOP THE TOOLS

4 Chapter

Filling Your Toolbox: The Basic Skills

Men must be honest with themselves before they can be honest with others. A man who is not honest with himself presents a hopeless case.

William J. H. Boetcher

Your Virtual Toolbox

I am a visual learner, so I've found it helpful to liken the leadership skill development process to a carpenter adding new tools to his toolbox. A good carpenter needs a variety of tools to effectively perform his job. If he only has a hammer and a saw, he is limited as to the kinds of projects he can handle. Each tool he uses has a very specific purpose and situations when they work best. The carpenter keeps his tools in a handy toolbox, so that when he is on the job he can quickly reach in and pull out the best tool for the job before him.

The process of becoming a more effective leader is like being a good carpenter. Each time you learn and master a new leadership or management skill, you are adding another tool to your handy toolbox. The more tools in your toolbox, the better equipped you are to handle a wide variety of problems and situations because you already have the right tool for the job in your virtual leadership toolbox.

For example, as a new manager you typically learn the basic skills involved with coaching. If someone is late for work, you can handle that conversation comfortably because you have that tool or skill at your disposal. But what happens if one employee gets into an argument with another employee because he used a racial slur? Now you are dealing with a more complex issue and that conversation will require a higher level of skill (a better tool) to address the problem.

In order to prepare yourself to handle almost any problem situation or tough conversation, you need to continually add more specialized tools to your toolbox. You do this by further refining and developing your communication skills and by increasing your knowledge and experience. Some skills and knowledge can be acquired quickly and easily by attending a one-day seminar and by reading books on the subject. Others will require a more prolonged effort and plenty of practice. Many higher level leadership skills are learned on the job with your manager and mentors coaching you through the process as you practice your skills. This is where you learn from experience and your mistakes.

Take a moment to think about your current skill set. Be honest with yourself: how full is your virtual leadership toolbox?

Psychology professor Abraham Maslow said, "If the only tool you have is a hammer, you will see every problem as a nail." Amen to that, Abraham! I have known many managers who didn't make their personal development a priority, which limited their effectiveness; they knew only one way to react to a problem and they reacted the same way to every problem whether it was appropriate or not. Some knew how to have a direct and forceful conversation (the hammer), and they were very good at it because they used that skill over and over again. But not every situation needs a hammer, and when they encountered a conversation that required a softer touch, they came across as harsh, insensitive, and overly heavy-handed.

Exceptional leaders know that people and their problems do not come in a "one-size-fits-all" package and they value the ability to flex their style so they can respond appropriately to each employee. Your ability to flex your communication style to meet the needs of any conversation will distinguish you as a leader and set you apart from your peers.

As you can see, preparing yourself to conduct a difficult conversation actually begins long before you sit down with the employee. It starts with developing some basic skills and tools of the trade that will prepare you to handle those conversations effectively.

The Basic Skills

Several basic qualities and skills are essential for you to develop so you can effectively manage your way through most coaching and counseling conversations. These are the essential tools you should carry with you in your virtual leadership toolbox. By developing these skills, you will be able to effectively handle most general conversations you need to have with your employees, coworkers, and even people in your personal life.

Direct Feedback

There are a number of reasons people are not clear or direct when communicating with others. We've already spoken about the anxiety many people experience just at the thought of providing honest performance feedback. If this describes you, you will need to come face to face with this fear and find a way to work through your discomfort if you are ever going to master the art of the tough conversation. You need to be able to deliver direct and honest feedback with tact, while demonstrating respect and compassion for the individual.

Fearful managers are purposely vague and evasive with their message in the hope that the employee will be able to read between the lines and relieve them of the responsibility of having to say what is uncomfortable. I know just how difficult it is to look someone in the eyes and tell him that he made a mistake and may lose his job. Suddenly you have a strong urge to make the situation less awkward and uncomfortable, so you talk around the issue, hoping he will catch on and intuitively get what you are really trying to say without you actually having to say it.

Some managers are comfortable with being direct but are more anxious about the potential of triggering an emotional reaction from the people they are counseling. They worry that employees won't be able to handle it emotionally if they are too direct and "hit them between the eyes" with feedback and they worry about being able to manage the emotional reaction. In my experience, people have a tremendous capacity to receive unpleasant information as long as it is offered in an effective and compassionate way. If this is your concern, building your confidence and skills will help to minimize your anxiety.

Nonetheless there are those few who, no matter what you do or how well you phrase your feedback, will naturally have a visible emotional reaction.

Sometimes this is more about them releasing pent-up anxiety in the moment than it is about real pain. You should never allow your fear of a specific response to get in the way of addressing an issue. Later I will give you some tools that you can use to help defuse strong emotions and prevent them from derailing your conversation.

I can also tell you with absolute certainty that the more honest you are with your feedback, the better chance you have of helping people to grow and correct any problems. I have seen managers literally have the same conversation three and four times with the same employee because they stop just short of being completely honest each time. Because the affected employee doesn't have all the information he needs, he misunderstands the urgency to make changes or the potential consequences if he doesn't until one day he crosses a line and loses his job. This is frustrating and unfair for everyone involved and leaves you open to criticism and possible legal action.

Bottom line, if you are being less than straightforward when conducting coaching and counseling sessions because you are uncomfortable giving honest and direct feedback or are afraid of the reaction you will get if you do, I offer you the same wisdom that was given to me over twenty years ago when I admitted to a similar feeling: "Suck it up!"

As a leader, it is your responsibility to use honest feedback as a tool to develop your people and improve their performance. To choose not to do so is just another way of saying you are choosing to not do your job. The idea that you are trying to spare people's feelings, while understandable, is flawed. It is actually more compassionate to tell them exactly where they are falling short and to give them the opportunity to correct the problem before they permanently damage relationships or lose their jobs. Letting people know where they stand in terms of performance is one of the best ways you can demonstrate your respect for them.

If you believe that part of the reason you are less than clear and direct is because you have difficultly articulating what you want to say at that critical moment, you are certainly not alone. Here are some suggestions to help you to find the right words:

- Write notes for yourself ahead of time using key words or phrases. There is nothing wrong with glancing at a notepad in front of you while you are having your counseling conversation. Use your notes to get started in your discussion and to keep you on track. In addition to ensuring that you cover all the points on your agenda, glancing at your notes affords you a wonderful, natural opportunity to pause to gather your thoughts and emotions. As long as you don't read directly from your notes or allow them to become an artificial barrier between you and the person to whom you are speaking, having prepared written notes does not negatively impact your credibility or professionalism.

- Consider joining Toastmasters International, attending a Dale Carnegie professional development course, or other public speaking course. These programs give you the opportunity to speak in front of groups on a regular basis, and they provide you with immediate feedback on your speaking and platform skills. Regular practice will help you manage any discomfort and build confidence. It will also teach you how to organize your thoughts when speaking extemporaneously, allowing you to better articulate your message.

Whatever method you choose to improve your communication skills, it is critical that you become as skilled as you can in this area. You will be able to get right to the point in a tactful and compassionate way, which helps to reduce some of the anxiety people feel during difficult conversations. Employees won't spend their energy trying to read between the lines of what you are saying in order to figure out your message, so that energy can then be put toward better understanding the issue and looking for ways to resolve the problem.

Active Listening Skills

Active listening is the process of hearing *more* than just the words that are being said. It is a way to demonstrate that you understand what the person is saying, and in some cases not saying, and recognize and acknowledge any emotions they may be feeling. By using active listening skills you show your employees that you are totally focused on them and that you are fully engaged in the listening process.

When you use active listening skills you

- Begin to establish rapport with the employee.
- Demonstrate that you are paying attention.
- Check your understanding of what is being said.

- Help to diffuse their emotions.
- Establish your desire to have a two-way dialogue.

Active listening is a skill that you will find valuable in any conversation. It is easy to use and once you get the hang of it, you will no longer have to concentrate on each step as it will just flow naturally. In fact, you may already demonstrate most of these steps. This is a great skill to master and once you do, you will find that it helps to improve all of your relationships.

The four steps of the active listening process are the following:

1. **Acknowledge** what you are seeing and hearing.
2. **Summarize** and paraphrase what has been said.
3. **Empathize** with how they are feeling.
4. **Probe further** using questions to gain a better understanding.

To help illustrate each step of the process, let's say Carol, one of your employees, has just come to tell you about an issue she has with her co-worker Danny, who is ignoring her requests for help.

Carol: *"I need your help. I have this big project due and the data input is taking me a lot longer than I expected. I asked Danny a couple of times if he could help me out, but he isn't responding. I really don't know how much more I can take."*

Here's how you would demonstrate each step of the active listening process with Carol.

1. Acknowledge

Acknowledge what you are seeing and hearing. Respond in a way that shows you hear and understand what has been said. You want to show you have heard not only the words, but any emotions the speaker is feeling as well. To Carol, you might say something like:

You: *"So each time you asked Danny to help, he ignored you. That sounds like it was a very frustrating situation for you."*

A statement like this demonstrates that you understand the problem (Danny ignores her) and also acknowledges the emotions she is feeling. In this case, Carol is frustrated with Danny.

Carol: *"It is! He knows how important this project is. I asked him first thing when I got in this morning if he would have time to help. He said he would see. Then, as he was leaving for lunch I asked him again, as I wasn't even sure if I would be able to take lunch today. He said he would help when he had time. Finally, just a few minutes ago I saw him coming back from the coffee place down the block with a latte. I asked him if he had time now, and he said he was still busy with his work. It looks like he has time to go get coffee but he can't help me!"*

2. Summarize

Periodically paraphrase the content of what the employee has said to you thus far. You want to summarize the key points in your own words. It is an opportunity for you to make sure you are hearing the facts accurately. The longer the story, the more frequently you will need to do this. Again you might say something like this to Carol:

You: *"Okay, on three separate occasions today you asked Danny for his assistance on your project and even though he agreed, to your knowledge he has not helped, is that correct?"*

You distill what Carol has said down to the core issue, repeat it back to her, and then check to make sure you understand it correctly. If you don't have it right, she has the opportunity to correct your understanding before you get too far down the wrong road.

Carol: *"I thought we were all part of the same team here. If I don't get this project done we all look bad. I can't believe he would just blow me off like that. Doesn't he care about anyone other than himself?"*

3. Empathize

Here is your opportunity to show that you understand how the employee is feeling about the situation. Using your own words, reflect back to the employee the feelings you are hearing and the reasons behind them, without adding any judgment or opinion. You might say to Carol:

You: *"I can certainly understand how feeling ignored by Danny could anger and disappoint you and cause you to question his commitment to you and the team."*

If the speaker has used words to describe feelings, reflect them back in your statement; otherwise, describe the unspoken feelings you are observing. The words the speaker uses and the body language shown will give you clues. The speaker may not have actually said she was angry, but you can often pick that up from her tone and body language as she retells the story to you.

Carol: *"It just seems so strange. He's normally such a team player."*

4. Probe further

Now it is time to probe deeper and to ask follow-up questions so that you can fill in any blanks or gain a better understanding of the context of the situation. You could ask Carol:

You: *"Can you tell me a little more about your relationship in the past with Danny? Has he ever acted this way toward you before?"*

People frequently leave out important details when they are telling their story, especially if they get emotional and animated. Make sure you completely understand the issue and use questions to get at any details they may have missed.

Adapt Your Feedback Style

Another skill critical to helping you guide and improve performance is for you to be able to match your communication style to the employee's so he is best able to receive and understand your feedback. Over the years, I have had to flex my style in a lot of directions in order to help people lower their defenses to receive the feedback I was offering.

With some people I needed to be very direct and get right to the point, more of a "right between the eyes" approach. With others, I had to ease into the conversation with some small talk to help them relax before I got to the main point. Getting to know your people and the way they best accept and receive feedback is an essential skill for you to have in your toolbox.

So how *do you* find out how your people like to receive feedback? Well, one way is to observe how they react in general conversations. Notice their body language to see when they seem to get defensive and listen for how they like to give other people feedback. While this will give you some good information, it is not the most reliable way. I have often encountered people who like to give feedback in a very different way than they like to receive it.

The best way I know to find out how others like to receive feedback is to just ask them directly. I have found that asking them during a general conversation, well before a problem situation arises, is the most effective way to get this information. If you have never done this, I strongly encourage you to have this conversation with everyone who directly reports to you in the near future.

If you are new to a team or if a new member has just joined your team, it is a great question to ask during your individual "get-to-know-you" conversations. You can work it into the discussion in a way that is nonthreatening. Here you have the opportunity to set expectations by finding out how they like to give and receive feedback while also sharing your preferences with them.

But if you are already well into your assignment I suggest meeting one on one with your team members to obtain this information or working it into other general performance related conversations. I might ask the question like this: *"I would like to learn a little more about you and your style when giving and receiving feedback. First of all, how do you typically prefer to give people feedback?"*

Ask them first how they like to give other people feedback. This helps you to establish that you are a leader who is open to receiving feedback from your team and it is good for you to know their comfort level with telling the boss when there is a problem. People who immediately answer with something like, "Oh don't you worry, I'm not shy," are usually pretty comfortable giving their manager feedback. These are people you will want to keep close as they will help you to keep your finger on the pulse of the team.

On the other hand, individuals who hem and haw and can't really answer the question are people you will need to reach out to specifically on a periodic basis. They probably don't give feedback to others often enough to know their preferences, so you will need to ask them directly for feedback if you want it. They are probably not comfortable with the feedback process and are unlikely to seek you out to share information, especially if they feel it is something you won't want to hear. It is a good idea to let both types of individuals know your expectations of when they should communicate with you and the types of issues you'd like them to bring to your attention.

Once you've gathered enough information about how your team members like to give feedback, ask the second question: *"Great. Now, I know everyone is different and I want to make sure that I provide you with feedback in a way that is most effective for you. Specifically describe for me how you like to receive feedback."*

Some people will need to sit a moment and think, as they have never been asked this question before. But if you give them enough time and space they will come up with an answer. Encourage them to be as specific as possible. Don't accept "I don't know" as an answer. Prompt them if they seem stuck.

Here are some examples of prompts to use:

- Do you like to receive feedback directly without small talk, or do you prefer to socialize a bit before we get down to the important part of the meeting?
- Do you prefer that all conversations of this sort take place in my office or are you okay if we have the conversation privately in another location?
- Do you want to get right to fixing the problem after you receive constructive feedback or do you like some time to absorb the information before you are ready to start problem solving?
- Do you worry about showing emotion in front of your manager and if so, how can I best support you if this happens?

You can see why I suggest having this conversation at a time when defenses are low and your employees are not worried about what you are going to say to them. The timing is optimal when there isn't a specific issue you need to address immediately.

But what if you haven't gotten this information from a team member and now you have to have a tough conversation with him? I would still do a short and sweet version of this process right up front before you begin your meeting. I might say something like this:

> *"You and I have never specifically talked about how you prefer to give and receive feedback, and I am sorry I did not do this sooner in our relationship. With that being said, I have some feedback to share with you and I would*

like to know how best to do that so that you can receive it with an open mind. Then we can discuss the feedback and our next steps. So how would you like me to proceed with the conversation?"

You will be able to tell from their immediate reaction to this question how you should proceed. If the employee offers some version of "bring it on," you are probably okay to be direct and get right to the point. If he hesitates and struggles to answer, that's your cue to take the conversation back a few steps and proceed in a gentler manner, providing more explanation and background leading up to the critical information.

If you've been working with your team for some time and have had occasion to have multiple performance conversations with them, you may believe you already have a good sense of how they like to receive feedback and can tailor your style to meet their needs. Even though you feel you may know them, you should take a few moments to validate your impressions with a direct conversation.

Manage and Diffuse Energy

Tough conversations, by definition, are riddled with anxiety. Anxiety can manifest as excess energy stored up in your body. It is uncomfortable to hold onto this energy and your body's natural response is to look for a way to release it. In conversations, the most common way to release pent-up energy caused by anxiety is to start talking and to keep on talking. Think about the last time a friend called to share some exciting news with you—I bet it was 10 minutes before you could get a word in edgewise! Talking helps people to relax. Plus, while they are speaking, you are receiving valuable information you may find useful later in the conversation.

We will cover the three phases of a counseling conversation in more detail later, but for now, let's agree that getting your employees to release some of their anxiety and nervous energy will help them to relax and allow them to be more open to hearing what you have to say. The process is fairly easy in theory; the challenge is in finding the right moment to turn the conversation over to them and then for you to sit back and be silent.

Generally, when speaking with those who like to get their feedback quickly and directly you should let them know what the topic of the discussion is right up front, and then as quickly as you can give them the floor to let them speak. Because they like direct communication and don't need the small talk, they will appreciate getting right to the point of the conversation.

In contrast, when you are speaking with those who prefer to ease into the conversation and work up to addressing the issue at hand, engage them first by asking some general questions related to the topic of the discussion. This allows them the opportunity to release some of their anxiety while responding and to gather their emotions before you get to the heart of the matter.

Either way, your goal is to get employees engaged and talking quickly in the conversation because, as they talk, they will expend some of their energy, helping to make them more receptive to hearing your feedback and keeping their defenses down.

This sounds simple, but there is a catch (you knew there had to be). In order for them to talk, you need to STOP talking. You have to be quiet and listen to what they are saying. This can be very challenging because often you are also anxious, and talking also helps *you* to release *your* pent-up energy. So it is also natural for you to want to start talking and keep talking until you've delivered your entire message. Don't let this happen. No matter how jumpy you may feel, you have to resist speaking excessively at the beginning of any conversation.

I have seen managers go into a meeting feeling anxious about what they have to say to their employee and as a result, they start talking and don't stop until they are completely done delivering their message. There is no room for the employee to respond or add his input. By the time the manager stops speaking, the employee has totally shut down and is only responding with one-word answers.

Once you get to this point, your verbal "dumping" is unlikely to encourage the employee to reopen the discussion to correct any misinformation or to provide you with additional details. The conversation ends up being totally one-sided. He may be left with the impression that it's pointless to try to offer further explanation as it is clear to him that you are not interested in his side of the story or you would have let him talk. This does nothing to promote understanding between you and your employee or to foster an honest and productive relationship with other team members.

In most cases, the conversation you will want to have with your employee is a two-way dialogue, so the quicker you can get the employee talking, the better. Once he is talking, your job is to move into receiving mode and to listen. Use your best active listening skills to help you get the most out of what is being said.

You also need to be okay with silence in a conversation. This is actually a tremendous coaching tool if you can get past any preconceived feelings that silence is a bad thing. If you ask a question and he doesn't answer immediately, sit in silence and allow the space for him to collect his thoughts, to get hold of his emotions, or even to concoct a really good story.

Silence naturally slows down the pace of your conversation so use it to help maintain a comfortable flow in your dialogue. Silence can also make people a little anxious, but that's okay, because in order to release that energy they will eventually begin to talk, which is what you want. Be cautioned though, if you don't get comfortable with silence it may increase your discomfort as well, so don't allow your anxiety to fill the silence. If you do, it will keep your conversation one-sided.

Consistency

There are many compelling reasons for leaders to be consistent with their messages, but at the top of the list is predictability. People want their leaders to be predictable. Inconsistency unnerves your team and makes them feel like they are walking on eggshells.

Employees want to know that if they do something right, it will be right each and every time they do it; and if they do something wrong, it will always be wrong. They want to be able to trust that everyone is treated equally and that discipline is consistent regardless of the leader's personal relationships or mood on any given day. Even though they may never tell you directly, your people want to know exactly where they stand in your eyes at all times.

The trouble usually begins when otherwise well-meaning managers start to apply policies and disciplinary processes inconsistently. When they do, they send mixed messages. For example, if you consistently address lateness issues and have a formal process for disciplining lateness, then people know what to expect when they are late. Their behavior will actually self-correct because they know exactly what will happen if they are late again and most will want to avoid the consequences.

When you apply policies or discipline inconsistently, you quickly lose control of your team's behavior and your people will start to resent you when you eventually try to enforce structure and discipline. To illustrate this point, think about how you would feel in the following situation:

Your department status reports need to be completed and turned in by Monday at 10 a.m., but that doesn't seem to be a hard deadline and no one has ever said anything to you in the past when you've been late. In fact, you know other managers are frequently late with their reports as well. But this week, when you submit your report a day late (as you have often done), you receive a written warning for missing deadlines from your manager. You are understandably confused and you even feel that the discipline has been a little too harsh given the fact that timeliness has not been enforced before. To make matters worse, later that day you find out that the other managers (your peers) who were late with their reports did not receive a written warning as you did. There doesn't seem to be an obvious explanation as to why you were disciplined and others were not.

Would the inconsistency in treatment from your manager anger you and leave you wondering what your leader is thinking? You bet it would! The reality is the more consistent you are with the way you communicate your messages, your discipline, and the way you interact with people (your mood and attitude), the better your team will be at understanding your standards and expectations and they will behave accordingly. They will know where the boundaries are and will make sure their behavior does not stray outside of them. Inconsistency breeds chaos and contempt for the leader. No one wants to tiptoe around every day, wondering what mood you are in or what will happen next.

The easiest terminations are the ones where the employee comes to the meeting fully understanding and expecting the termination because he was warned it would happen, and he trusts that you as a leader will always follow through on what you say you will do. It is never a good feeling when a manager reprimands an employee and the employee defends himself by naming half a dozen other people on the team who did the exact same thing but were never disciplined for it.

Being consistent also has a financial impact on the company that goes well beyond the cost of training and managing an individual team member. Your organization's ability to adequately defend employment lawsuits can be significantly impaired if its managers are not consistent with how they handle disciplinary situations, especially those that involve termination of employment.

It's very dangerous and expensive when there is a disconnect between what you say you will do and what you actually do, when it comes to discipline. Most companies have an employee handbook or a collection of written policies that they share with employees during the orientation process. When defending legal actions, your written policies may be one thing, but the practices of your managers are another. For instance, if your company policy says that you terminate employment on the seventh absence but a manager has a practice of allowing double that amount of absences before she terminates employment, the manager's practice will carry more weight when defending the termination than the published written company policy. In fact, what managers actually do on a consistent basis becomes the unofficial policy of the company, regardless of what the handbook says.

Taking this example a step further, after establishing a precedent of allowing up to 14 absences before ending employment, that manager now suddenly enforces termination on the seventh absence for one employee. Following the stated policy will seem arbitrary, like it came out of left field, which will put him very quickly into the middle of legal quicksand.

Even if you are not sued, there can still be financial repercussions to inconsistency. It is not uncommon for companies to lose unemployment hearings because a manager did not behave or discipline in a consistent manner. In one particular case, a company terminated the employment of one of its employees for lateness. Prior to the termination, the employee was given a final warning that stated the next time she was late, her employment would be terminated, which she signed. Three weeks later, the employee was late for work and her employment was terminated.

On the surface it sounds like everything was handled correctly, but during the unemployment hearing additional information was discovered. It was noted that in the three weeks between the final warning and the termination, the employee had been late two other times but was not fired as indicated by the final warning. The manager explained he felt sorry for her.

The unemployment hearing judge ruled that because the manager had been inconsistent in his discipline the employee could not have had a legitimate expectation that she would be fired on that "final time," since the manager's discipline seemed to be a moving target. The judge granted the former employee full unemployment benefits which cost the company thousands of dollars. Those benefits would not have been paid if the manager had followed through with the next step of the discipline process as stated in the company policy and in the final warning, which would have terminated her employment the very next time she was late.

Leaders are paid to be consistent, but also to be fair. Sometimes those objectives can seem to be at odds with one another. Discerning the right course of action is a decision-making skill that certainly can involve some "grey areas," so let's take a moment to make a distinction between consistent and equitable treatment.

Some managers believe they need to treat everyone *exactly the same* in order to be consistent. No exceptions to the rules or policies. For them it is easier, no matter the circumstance, to dispense discipline exactly the same for everyone. By holding tight to the written policy, they think they are on solid ground and above reproach with their discipline.

Unfortunately, this thought process lacks the flexibility our workplaces demand. Situations are rarely exactly the same, problems are seldom black and white, and the individuality of people adds an inescapable element of uncertainty to every situation. Like it or not, managers have to use their discretion.

The goal of every manager should be fair and equitable treatment, not identical treatment. This definition may open the door to more subjectivity than most managers are comfortable with, but it is the right way to treat your employees. Leaders are more effective when they seek to be consistent, but also when they apply some level of discretion to handling employee situations.

I think most leaders would agree that it doesn't make sense to treat your best performers *exactly* as you would your worst performers in the early stages of the disciplinary process. The reality is that a good performance track record does buy an employee some leeway in determining how a first offense is treated. But this flexibility should not turn into a free pass for any and all bad behavior.

The farther into the disciplinary process the employee gets, the less manager discretion should be a factor. By the time you get to the part of the process where written and final warnings need to be issued, even the best performers can exhaust any goodwill they have earned. I have seen several outstanding performers lose their jobs because of something as controllable as lateness, and even though it broke the manager's heart to do it, ending their employment was the fair thing to do for the rest of the team. Exceptional leaders understand that there are times when acting in the best interest of the team may mean that they have to make a decision that is detrimental to an individual.

The bottom line when deciding how to reward and discipline your employees is to be consistent and, if you make an exception, you need to be comfortable explaining your thought process if challenged. Once you make an exception to your stated policies you need to be prepared to defend that decision and to make the same exception if it comes up again.

There was a time when managers could get away with hiding the reasons behind their decisions, adopting a "because I said so" attitude, but not anymore. Employees value and demand transparency from their leaders and the organizations for which they work. If you are making sound decisions based on fair and equitable reasoning, you will have nothing to fear from this new level of transparency.

Learning to master these five basic skills—providing direct feedback, using active listening skills, adapting your style, managing and diffusing energy, and behaving consistently—will give you the necessary foundation to communicate effectively with your team and promote healthy and productive relationships. These skills are also the initial building blocks that lie on top of your leadership foundation. Mastering these skills establishes you as a leader who is able to relate and communicate with a variety of personality types and one who cares about investing in the development of your people. Effectively incorporating these basic skills into your coaching and counseling process demonstrates respect for your people as individuals and your commitment to their success, and are desirable in any leader.

KEY LEARNING POINTS FROM THIS CHAPTER

- Exceptional leaders continuously add skills to their "virtual tool-box" so that they are able to flex their style to meet the needs of any situation.

- The basic skills leaders need to demonstrate in any coaching or counseling conversation are direct feedback, active listening, adapting feedback style, managing and diffusing energy and consistency.

- Write down key words and phrases on a notepad to use as a reference to help you remember specific points you want to share during the feedback session.

- The four stages of the active listening process are:

  - **Acknowledge** what you are seeing and hearing.

  - **Summarize** and paraphrase what has been said.

  - **Empathize** with how they are feeling.

  - **Probe further** using questions to gain a better understanding.

- Make a point to find out from your employees how they like to receive feedback, and then adapt your style to increase the chances that the feedback will be received and understood accurately.

- Get people talking early in the conversation to help them release any pent-up energy and lower their defenses.

- Your people want you to be predictable as a leader. Apply policies and discipline fairly and consistently and don't be afraid to explain the reasoning behind decisions.

5 Chapter

Take It to the Next Level

Good instincts usually tell you what to do long
before your head has figured it out.

Michael Burke

Advanced Skills

In addition to the basic skills we covered in the last chapter, there are several advanced skills you can acquire to assist you with the more sensitive and complex conversations. While you can research the mechanics of each of these skills, most of them are best learned through practice and experience, trial and error. Once you master the basics, you can begin to incorporate these higher level skills which will add more depth and layering to your coaching and communication style.

Trust Your Intuition

Research on personality types indicates that we all have the ability to tap into our intuition and inner guidance, although it does seem that some people are more comfortable using this skill than others. I rely heavily on my intuition while coaching individuals and in particular, during difficult conversations. My intuition, or insight, has been honed by years of performance coaching and my observations of human behavior. For me, my intuition shows up as a little voice that whispers thoughts quietly into my consciousness. I have heard others refer to their intuition as a "gut feeling," "sixth sense," or "hunch." Whatever you call yours, it can be a very useful tool to help you get to a deeper level of understanding in your conversations.

You might use your intuition in conversations with employees to sense when there is

- Something more to the story that they are not telling you.
- A disconnect between what they are saying and what they are really feeling.
- A chance they are not being truthful.
- A deeper issue or problem hidden beneath the one you are currently addressing.
- A pattern developing.
- Information that doesn't "make sense."

Use your intuition to help guide you when determining the direction of a conversation or when making decisions regarding discipline. When I started my career in management I accepted what people said and did at face value. But experience taught me to trust when my little voice said something was not right or there was more to the story. You never want to act solely on your intuition and totally disregard the facts of a situation, but you can effectively use it to guide you to further validate and investigate.

Think Strategically

I had a mentor once who gave me some great advice. She said, "Kathy, as a leader you want to play chess, not checkers." She was telling me that I needed to be more strategic; to think several steps ahead rather than just responding to what was happening right in front of me. I called it "fire fighting." I would get so busy with all the immediate problems in front of me as if each was "on fire," that I found it difficult to take the time to think about how to prevent the problems from happening in the first place. It was a real challenge to find the time to strategically think several months ahead in order to prevent problems rather than just reacting to them. This situation is not unique to HR managers. All managers can find themselves so preoccupied on a daily basis with immediate issues that they forget to make the time to think long term and be strategic.

But when it comes to counseling an employee, it always pays to think several steps ahead of where you actually are in the conversation. This takes some finesse as you need to still focus on what is being said in the present while simultaneously mapping out where you want the discussion to ultimately go. In order to think a few steps ahead in the conversation, I find it helpful to spend some time before the meeting determining what I want to actually accomplish with the employee. I pick a goal or desired outcome for the discussion, and once I have that finish line in sight, it is easier for me to mentally "see" what steps I still need to take to get there.

To illustrate this using a very simple example, let's say my employee was late to work today. My goal by the end of the conversation is to make sure he knows it can't happen again and to set up the next step of the disciplinary process if it does. Here are the steps of the conversation as I have mapped them out in my head:

- Find out why my employee was late today.
- Help him understand how his lateness negatively impacts the team and business.
- Remind him of the company policy regarding lateness.
- Convey to him my expectation that it won't happen again.
- Explain to him what will happen the next time he is late.

Even though it is a rather simple issue to address, you can see how thinking through the steps will help you to stay on track and enable you to reach your goal. If the employee starts to talk about another employee who is taking too many breaks, you can easily steer him back on point to finish your conversation, and then revisit the break issue later if necessary.

When dealing with more complex issues, all the steps for a discussion might not be that easy to see at first, instead, they will unfold for you "real time" as you speak with the employee. Give thought as to where a comment is likely to take your conversation before you make it. If the employee introduces a new topic, ask yourself "am I prepared to go down that road in this conversation or will it likely lead to a conversational dead end?" The more experience you have coaching and counseling employees, the easier it will be for you to think through these scenarios on the fly.

Thinking strategically also means considering the future implications of a decision you make today. In order to be consistent, you will need to be mindful of any precedents you set when making exceptions to established policies or practices. Before you make an exception, always think ahead to make sure it is something you can live with each and every time the exception comes up again. If not, don't make it.

Develop a Poker Face

The ability to have a good poker face is a valuable skill for a leader. There are so many times when you need to have a neutral expression on your face in order to avoid embarrassing your employee, communicating your emotions, or seeming judgmental. Employees who are already hesitant to share sensitive or very personal information will be looking at your face for a clue about what you are thinking and to see if there is any judgment there. If they don't like what they see, they are likely to shut down.

For instance, employees may need to share extremely personal information with you in order to help explain an absence and they will be looking at your face for any signs of disapproval or judgment. Seeing negative feelings played out on your face might stop them from confiding further in you. This is especially important when investigating a claim of sexual harassment. It is often difficult for a woman to explain to a man how she felt sexually harassed because she worries about him taking her claim seriously. Because she is already feeling vulnerable, any look which hints at a negative judgment or dismissal will stop her in her tracks.

There will be times when employees get carried away telling their story to you and they share way too much personal information. Maybe they share the specifics of a medical condition, their sex life, past transgressions, or questionable activities outside of work. Whatever your personal feelings about a certain subject, it is helpful to be able to hide those feelings when you want to and remain neutral in your facial expressions. That way your reaction does not derail the forward momentum of the conversation. As my mom used to say, "Sometimes you just need to let it go in one ear and out the other."

Think on Your Feet

Whatever your plan is going into a conversation, chances are good you will be thrown a curve ball at some point so you need to be flexible enough to respond in the moment. Your intent might be to counsel an employee about her poor performance and lack of focus, but halfway through the conversation she tells you that she just found out that her husband has a serious illness and she is distraught. You need to be able to immediately put on the brakes and take the conversation in a new direction.

I have seen managers so rigid in their focus that they could not respond to a change in direction when new information was presented. In one case, I watched in disbelief as the manager literally slid a written warning for bad behavior in front of an employee at the end of a meeting when it was clear from the additional facts presented that the she was not even involved in the situation. The manager was so focused on the preplanned path of giving a warning that he could not respond appropriately in the moment to the new information.

Being able to think on your feet does take a certain amount of confidence. If you are plagued with doubts as a manager and second-guess your decisions, you will have difficulty with this skill. You need to be comfortable stopping a meeting midstream, and even undoing everything that was already agreed to, if the situation warrants it. Don't get too attached to a certain path or outcome. Your ability to ebb and flow with the tide of the conversation will make you a better manager and will take your leadership to the next level.

Adding these advanced skills to the set of basic ones we covered in the last chapter will increase your flexibility and options when coaching and counseling employees, and it will equip you to handle almost any conversation. Granted, you can never be fully prepared when dealing with people, but that's what I enjoy most about being a leader. People are full of surprises so there is always an opportunity to grow and increase your knowledge. After two decades in human resources you would have thought I'd seen it all, but there are still times I find myself shaking my head in disbelief saying, "Didn't see that one coming." The good news is once you've seen a situation, you will know how to best deal with it the next time it comes up, and that is how you develop and hone your leadership skills.

KEY LEARNING POINTS FROM THIS CHAPTER

- Your intuition can be one of your greatest assets during any conversation. Experience and practice will help you to tap into this "sixth sense." Trust where it leads you, but look to validate your intuition with facts whenever possible.

- Never enter a conversation without a clear idea of what you want to accomplish in the discussion and an understanding of the future implications of any decisions you make.

- The ability to mask your emotions is not just helpful when playing poker. There are times when you will need to communicate a completely neutral message with your body language, especially your facial expressions, in order to avoid shutting down a conversation.

- Don't be afraid to respond "in the moment" to information presented during a conversation, even if it means changing direction or overturning a prior decision. Never sacrifice what is right for what was planned.

SECTION THREE:

FOLLOW THE PROCESS

6 Chapter

The Development Process

Men are developed the same way gold is mined. Several tons
of dirt must be moved to get an ounce of gold.
But you don't go into the mine looking for dirt;
you go in looking for the gold.

Dale Carnegie

In most situations, tough conversations are not isolated events. They are, in fact, an important part of the larger growth and development process that all managers should be engaged in with their people. The quality and frequency of your communications with employees will significantly impact their overall performance level and ultimate success.

It is your responsibility to be an active part of their development and growth. While the individual activities that make up the development process are usually easy to execute, it is here in these common, everyday activities, that we as leaders inadvertently drop the ball. Your engagement in the development process starts the day you meet your new employees and your commitment to following through will set them up for success.

While the specifics may vary by organization, there are typically five major activities involved in any effective development process:

- Set clear expectations.
- Provide timely and consistent feedback.
- Provide both coaching and counseling.
- Document performance.
- Follow through.

You need to ensure that you are engaging in all five of these activities in order to develop your employees' skills, improve their individual performances, and grow them into a high-functioning team.

Set Clear Expectations

This may come as a shock to you, but your people aren't psychic. No really, they can't read your mind. You might wish they would sometimes, but they can't. So why then, do we make the mistake of treating them like they can?

If you don't actually articulate to your employees your expectations, they won't really know for sure what you want. They might be able to guess, and many are very good at guessing, but there remains a good chance that they will be off the mark at some point, at least a little. Sometimes as a leader you can get caught up in your own world and forget to state clearly what you want.

I was blessed to work with several really exceptional assistants over the years. They made me look like a rock star every day, which couldn't have been an easy feat! In fact, they were so good at doing their job and anticipating my needs that I was occasionally lulled into thinking that I didn't have to express my thoughts anymore; we basically operated on auto pilot. I assumed that they would know what I was thinking and they would just do it. Inevitably, something would be missed jolting me back into reality, and I would realize that I was not communicating all my expectations as I should. This was not their fault: it was entirely on me. I was expecting them to read my mind.

As a leader it is your responsibility to clearly articulate your expectations. You need to start by virtually drawing employees a mental picture of specifically what it looks like to be an outstanding performer on your team. You can do this by providing a written job description for them during orientation and engaging in a good goal-setting process. This way they are set up for success from the start, and they know exactly what you expect them to do and at what level they should perform.

You also communicate your expectations verbally on a daily basis in the normal course of operations. When you are talking with your team members about their performance and your expectations, imagine that you are answering this question for them: "What behaviors or activities would I be engaged in right now if I were an outstanding performer on this team?"

Your answers to this question, such as, "An outstanding performer would respond to all client emails within 24 hours," or "Someone who exceeds my expectations would always demonstrate a positive attitude and would never gossip about their coworkers" will provide them with an understanding of your expectations. It's important to be as specific as possible when sharing performance standards and expectations verbally in order to give your employees a very clear understanding of what they need to do to be successful in their jobs.

Expectations should not be something you talk about once or just when employees are hired. Things change over time; even priorities get rearranged. You need to share your expectations frequently and in a variety of different ways. Whether you are casting your vision for the new year, orienting a new manager to your team, or just delegating tasks, you need to be crystal clear about what you want in terms of performance and behavior.

People also learn and retain information in a variety of different ways. So to cover all the bases, use a variety of methods to state expectations: verbally, in a group setting, one on one, in writing, and by using visual aids such as posters or progress charts. The greater the challenge or expectation, the more methods you should use to communicate it and keep the goal in front of them at all times. This ensures that your message is received and understood by everyone, whatever their learning style.

When it comes to performance expectations, you can't articulate them enough. I used to start this process of drawing a mental picture of my expectations as early as the interview process. When interviewing candidates for a manager position, I would set aside some time to talk about our team's culture and the values we collectively held as leaders. I wanted to make it clear right from the beginning to all candidates what our expectations were of leaders on our team. I didn't go into great detail at that point, but I did share enough about our culture, the way we communicated, how we liked to give feedback, and some of our more important expectations that the candidate could easily decide if we were a good fit.

As an example, in one company I worked for, our leadership team liked to give a lot of feedback, both positive and constructive. We put a high priority on offering feedback in real time, meaning literally as we were observing the behavior we would offer feedback. I would explain to candidates interviewing for leadership positions that if they worked for us, they could potentially be getting feedback from not only their boss, but their peers and even direct reports almost daily. To be successful with us, they would have to be open to receiving that level of feedback, without getting defensive, and be willing to engage in conversations around the feedback.

I knew from experience that for some people who were not used to this type of environment, who may have received feedback from their manager only once a year at review time (if that), they could find it difficult to transition to our culture. Our environment could easily lead them to feel like they were getting frequently beat up, and I wanted people to understand our culture and expectations *before* they were hired to improve retention.

In addition, once new leaders came onboard, I would spend a couple of hours with them going through our policies and practices. I covered the formal policies that were written in our handbooks and management guides as well as the "unofficial" policies that people are often left to discover on their own. These are the policies and practices that every company or work team has in force, but are not typically written down anywhere. For instance, maybe it is frowned upon for professional level employees to leave work prior to 5 p.m., even though the handbook states employees can start their workday at 7 a.m. and end at 3 p.m. That way a new manager knows the expectation is that she will work until at least 5 p.m. each day.

Provide Timely and Consistent Feedback

Once you've set the expectations with your team, it is critical that you let them know when they are on track and when their performance is slipping. Feedback that is given immediately or within a relatively short period of time after a behavior or activity is the most effective kind of feedback you can provide because the behavior is still fresh in the employee's mind. She can remember everything she did or said to meet your expectations so she has a good chance of being able to repeat the behavior again. She can also remember exactly what she did or said that led her to fall short of expectations. Again, since the experience is still fresh in her mind she can easily see her mistakes and correct her behavior. This type of immediate feedback is called real-time feedback.

Real-time feedback is an excellent way to reinforce positive behavior and also to correct substandard performance. By providing real-time feedback, you let people know immediately whether their performance is in line with your expectations or if it needs adjustment. It provides them with additional information to help them to fill in any gaps in that mental picture of what an outstanding performer looks like and leads to a quick recovery when they stumble or fall.

Too often managers make the mistake of waiting before providing their people with performance feedback. Because of the rapid pace of most work environments, the longer you wait to give feedback, either positive or constructive, the less chance you have of your feedback being meaningful to the employee and resulting in positive behavioral changes. Think about how you would feel in the following situation.

> *You stay late one night in order to complete a project you know is important to your boss. Just before 11:00 p.m. you place the finished project on her desk and head home. Even though you were there working late, the next morning you are in early so you can catch up on the rest of the work that you didn't get to because of the project. Mid-morning, your manager comes over to your desk and in front of several of your coworkers enthusiastically thanks you for your hard work and your dedication to the team.*

I'm sure you can see how meaningful that would be to you and how it might positively impact any decision in the future to go the extra mile for your boss.

> *Now take the same scenario, only the next day, you don't hear anything from your manager. In fact, your extra effort isn't recognized at all and you are not even sure she cares that you stayed late and came in early. How inclined would you be to extend yourself in a similar situation again? You probably wouldn't be very motivated at all. And even if your "above and beyond" effort made it into your next performance review eight months later, would it be as meaningful as if you had been praised and acknowledged the next day? Probably not.*

The same philosophy holds true when you are giving constructive feedback in an effort to correct behavior or improve performance. Here is an example similar to the one above.

> *You have an important project due and the deadline is tomorrow morning. You know your boss absolutely needs that information, but instead of focusing on the priority, you spend the afternoon cleaning out your file cabinet. You go home at your normal time and opt not to inform your boss that you will not have the project completed by the appointed time.*

The next morning your boss calls you into her office to ask about the status of the project and you inform her that you do not have it done: you just ran out of time. After asking you to close the door and sit down, she proceeds to counsel you on the importance of meeting your deadlines. You discuss together where you went wrong in your decision-making process and you understand how important it is not to do this again. You leave the office feeling bad that you let her down but determined not to let it happen again. Because she gave you timely feedback, you can immediately correct your behavior and ensure that it does not have a lasting negative effect on your overall performance.

In contrast, using our same example situation again, you come in the next morning and you do not hear anything from your manager regarding the project or the missed deadline. It takes you a couple of days, but you eventually get the information pulled together and you put it on her desk. In fact, she is sitting there when you drop it off. She doesn't say anything to you regarding the missed deadline then, and you don't hear another word about the project or the deadline after that so you assume it wasn't a big deal. You start to think that when she gives you a deadline, it has some flexibility in it so you are unconcerned when you miss another couple of deadlines and do not receive any feedback.

Eight months later in your annual performance review, you receive the feedback that you are consistently late with assignments and your overall performance score and increase amount have been lowered as a result of this issue. Now you are beside yourself! You are wondering why she didn't tell you that this was an important issue before and that it was affecting your performance. Rightfully so, you are very angry. Trust between you and your manager has been significantly damaged. If she had only told you that it was a problem after the first time, you could have corrected the issue long ago.

I understand that while reading these examples you may consider this to be such a simple concept that there is no reason to belabor the point. But the truth is that these scenarios play out in workplaces exactly this way each and every day. Managers get distracted and need to be continually reminded about the positive effects of praising using real-time feedback. And for many managers, their discomfort with providing constructive feedback leads them to hesitate and delay the counseling conversations. Then, when they find that too much time has lapsed, it actually becomes more embarrassing to address an old issue so they abandon the effort entirely.

Don't ever let it get that far with your employees. Provide real-time feedback, both positive and negative, to them on a consistent basis and you will prevent minor behavior problems from growing into significant performance issues.

Provide Coaching and Counseling

Most employees respond positively to the coaching process, especially when you incorporate into your process many of the skills and techniques that we've discussed thus far. By setting clear expectations and providing real-time feedback, you can guide your team members' behavior and support their growth and development. But every now and then, you will come across people who do not respond to your coaching. It might be that they are just unable to process the fact that they are making mistakes, or it is a skill issue and they are not equipped to perform the tasks required, or it could be their attitude which prevents them from taking advice even when it is in their best interest to do so.

Your first response to performance issues should be to actively coach the individuals and determine if they need additional training or support. If they are unable to improve their performance after that, yet still have many positive qualities as team members, you might consider exploring other positions within your organization. Sometimes good employees are miscast in jobs that do not play to their strengths, and if you have an opportunity to redeploy a valued employee elsewhere, you should consider it. This does not mean that you should "transfer a problem" to another department, although many managers have tried. Redeployment should only be considered if the employees have the potential to excel in a different role within the organization. If you determine the performance issues would be present no matter what position they held, such as problems with attitude or communication skills, you should not consider a transfer and continue to address the performance yourself. Whatever the case, it is important as a leader to know when to escalate the process and move from coaching to counseling problem employees.

I define *coaching* as that part of the development process that is focused on providing employees with instruction, training, support, and advice. The collaborative nature of the coaching process allows individuals to participate fully in their learning. They are encouraged to ask questions, try new things, and learn from their mistakes without fear of discipline. Feedback is delivered verbally and conversations are typically informally documented. The feel of the coaching process is informal and leaders have a fair amount of flexibility in their choice of communication style.

I use the term *counseling* to describe that part of the performance development process when improvement has stalled or significant problems persist and the tone of the conversation needs to change. Discussions become more formal, and there is an increased sense of urgency to resolve the problem immediately. Patterns of negative behavior or mistakes are identified and overall performance is suffering. While questions are still encouraged in the counseling process, flexibility is replaced by a formalized process and disciplinary consequences are introduced into the discussions. Conversations at this stage are documented in writing and become part of the employee's personnel file. Using the term *counseling* typically indicates that you are farther along in the disciplinary process and consequences could be job threatening.

Coaching and counseling together are important to the overall success of the performance management and development process. There are no hard-and-fast rules as to when you should use one versus the other. With high performers, it is likely that you will never have an occasion to counsel them. With others, you may find that you move between coaching and counseling frequently in an effort to provide them with feedback and help them to resolve their issues. In any case, you should become equally as skilled and comfortable with both the coaching and counseling process.

One note before we move on. There are managers who experience increased anxiety or fear when initiating the counseling process, so they hesitate to make the transition, even when it is appropriate. Otherwise good managers can absolutely sabotage their credibility and effectiveness by allowing a performance issue to continue far too long without moving into the counseling phase.

You should always seek to correct behavior first with coaching, unless the situation warrants a more severe response the first time it presents. But at some point, if the behavior does not change or the performance does not improve, you need to move into the counseling phase in an effort to provide the motivation, urgency or consequences that will help to encourage change. If the performance problem continues to persist even after counseling, the steps of the counseling process will give you the needed structure and documentation to support terminating employment.

Performance issues left unchecked not only do a disservice to the individual, but they undermine productivity and damage your relationship with the rest of your team as well. Team members will question your lack of urgency and they will wonder why you aren't taking action to resolve the issue. You will be viewed as ineffective and incompetent, oblivious to the performance issues right in front of you.

Unfortunately there is no rulebook that can tell you exactly when it is appropriate to move from coaching to counseling. It is different for each individual you are managing and varies by situation. Use resources such as your HR team or more experienced managers to help you develop your discernment so that you can better identify the appropriate point to make the transition.

Document Issues

Let's face it. I'm a human resources manager through and through, so you had to know there was no chance you were getting out of this section without spending at least a little time extolling the virtues of well-written documentation. Counseling without documentation is like a piranha without teeth. It's still a fish—just not that impressive.

As a leader, you should always be documenting positive performances and also noting times when your people miss the mark. There are a number of good reasons you should take the time to document performance, especially by recording your counseling conversations. Here are just a few of them.

- **People have different learning styles.** Some people are auditory (they need to hear it), some are visual (they need to see it), some are tactile (they need to touch it), and some are experiential (they need to do it). When you are communicating with people in the hope that they will learn and retain what you are saying, it's important to use a combination of delivery methods that touch on all these styles to ensure your message is heard and understood.

When you

- *tell* people what you want them to do,
- give them a set of *written* instructions or a *written* summary of what you are asking them to do,
- then allow them to actually *do it* while you are watching so you can praise them for executing it correctly and make adjustments if necessary,

you significantly increase their ability to understand and retain that information. Some managers buy into this concept when it comes to training new hires, but forget its effectiveness when involved in coaching and counseling situations.

- **Most people have very good defense systems.** Actually, I should say *excellent* defense systems, which have been honed over a lifetime of shutting out negative emotions and avoiding unpleasant information. When an employee is called into her manager's office for a conversation, chances are very good that her defense system will immediately go on high alert. Even if the conversation turns benign, it will take her a while to lower her shields far enough that she can take in what you have to say. When you put your message in writing, you give her that second chance to hear you.

  By providing your feedback in writing, you give employees the opportunity to review your message at a later time when they are more open and your point has a better chance of being received. Being heard correctly is especially important during counseling meetings with employees when their continued employment may be contingent on their understanding your message and altering their behavior. In these types of meetings employees often feel threatened and their defenses never really come down, so it is essential that they have the opportunity to review your message again in writing after the meeting.

- **You create a paper trail.** Up until this point we've focused on how documentation helps your employees. There is also a reason to document that helps to support you and your organization. Today more than ever it is important that you, as a representative of your company, limit your legal exposure. When it comes to performance management, that means having excellent documentation of your conversations.

While I am not a legal expert and you should always use your company's resources for legal advice on individual situations, I can tell you from my many years of experience in human resources that well-written documentation helps to limit liability and protect the company against false claims. Written summaries of your conversations and formal written warnings, signed by the employees, confirm that you provided them feedback when there was a problem, that you gave them an opportunity to correct it, and you told them what was going to happen without corrective action. At the very least, documentation limits the effectiveness of the "no one ever told me" excuse. We'll talk more about the specific elements of good documentation in a later chapter.

Hopefully you can see that ongoing documentation of performance pays huge benefits for both the employee and the company. Keeping these records does take time and sometimes you may struggle with finding the right words. Crafting effective documentation is a skill like any other that can be developed with practice.

By summarizing your conversations in writing to employees you significantly increase the chances that they will accurately hear your message, you can easily recognize and document any performance patterns that start to emerge, and you will help protect yourself and the company if legal action is initiated down the road. All in all, it is an important skill for leaders to practice.

Follow Through

I have seen numerous situations where managers screw up their courage enough to have a tough conversation and then drop the ball after the fact, by failing to follow through on commitments they made during the meeting. This is an instant credibility killer. You absolutely must follow through on everything you commit to during a performance discussion.

For instance, during a counseling session with an employee you state that profanity is not tolerated in your workplace and the next time he uses foul language in the workplace, you will place him on a final warning, which could lead to the termination of his employment. Then two weeks later, the employee uses profanity again in front of you and others in the department. This time though, you are in the middle of a deadline and you don't feel like you have the time to deal with it, so you just verbally tell him to knock it off.

That shortsighted decision, made in a busy moment, makes it very difficult for your words to carry any weight going forward. How is your employee supposed to know you mean what you say? And if you make a habit of this practice—threatening dire consequences and then pulling back the next time the situation presents itself—your words will carry little meaning with the individual or the rest of your team. Your disciplinary warnings will be seen as exactly what they are, hollow threats.

When it comes to performance coaching and counseling here's the golden rule:

Don't say it if you don't mean it.

Don't promise to send employees to a class to increase their skills during their annual review and then later say you can't afford the expense. Don't say you will terminate their employment if they do a certain behavior again and then let them off the hook the next time. Don't say they will see their salary increase in their next paycheck, then drag your feet and fail to submit the paperwork.

You need to be prepared to follow through with everything you commit to as a leader, but in the area of coaching and counseling, the consequences can be particularly devastating if you don't. I've said a number of times that you should treat people fairly and with respect, and that includes following through on what you say you will do even if it means terminating your favorite employee's employment because she can't get to work on time. Any positive created by initiating a tough conversation and addressing an issue head on, can be totally undermined by a lack of follow-through on the back end.

KEY LEARNING POINTS FROM THIS CHAPTER

- You should be engaged in the five major activities of the development process every day with each employee: set clear expectations, provide timely and consistent feedback, provide both coaching and counseling, document issues, and follow-through.

- Articulate your standards and expectations frequently and in a variety of ways. Verbally draw people a picture of what success looks like to you.

- Whether positive or constructive, the most effective time to provide feedback is immediately after the behavior so individuals can remember exactly what they did.

- There is tremendous power in praising people for a job well done. Don't always focus on the negative: catch people doing something right!

- Most people will correct their behavior once a problem is pointed out to them, but there are those that won't. Don't be afraid to move from coaching to counseling when the situation warrants it.

- Be as quick to document positive performance as you are to document a problem.

- Some people need to see their issue documented in a memo to completely understand the concerns and fully appreciate the urgency for them to change.

- Follow-through is critical to maintaining your credibility as a leader. Never make a promise to an employee and then fail to deliver on it.

7 Chapter

The Progressive Discipline Process

As I grow older, I pay less attention to what men say.
I just watch what they do.

Andrew Carnegie

Unfortunately, there are times when the performance development process does not achieve the desired results and you have to move to the more formal progressive discipline process. Each step in the progressive discipline process is designed to escalate the consequences for failing to change and to formally document the urgency for the employee to correct the issue. Most people tell me that they don't like this process, that it feels confrontational and adds a level of formality that forever changes the relationship with their employees.

Actually, I really can't argue with that thinking. The progressive discipline process certainly adds a heightened level of formality, and some employees will get confrontational as it is a clear sign to them that the fun and games are over and there are very serious consequences on the table. So in some cases, it does change the dynamic of your relationship with your employees.

But I also say, "So what?" Just because an employee perceives the process to be confrontational doesn't mean that you have to initiate the confrontation or even respond in kind. And the formality of the language in the written documentation doesn't mean that you can't communicate the message verbally in your own style, making the same points as the written warning without all the legalese. As for your relationships with your employees, as much as you might want to have amiable relationships with all of your employees, you have a job to do and sometimes doing your job will put you at odds with them. You are there to lead them, not to be their friend.

Your attitude regarding the progressive discipline process is critical to its success. Let go of any belief that once you begin this process that all roads lead to termination, each and every time. It's just not true. People who are placed on performance probation frequently work through their issues and go on to have successful careers, and a final warning doesn't mean they will never earn a promotion. If you are committed to helping your people grow and develop, you can create a supportive environment where people who enter the progressive discipline process not only survive, but can go on to thrive.

Of course, there are many folks who are unable to adapt, who choose not to change their behavior, or fail to do what they need to do in order to improve their performance. For these people, the process is a way to inform them of the consequences of their continued bad behavior or poor performance and effectively manage them out of the organization.

A formal progressive discipline process is effective when addressing almost any behavior and performance issues you will encounter as a leader. Only in the most severe cases would you want to skip the process and go right to termination of employment. While the philosophy behind the progressive discipline process itself is the same for behavior and performance issues, the way the process is structured is a little different for each. To better understand these differences, let's go through each so you can understand how they work. What we will cover here is an overview of a general progressive discipline process. Your company may have a different process so it is important to know what that process is and you should absolutely follow your organization's policy.

Addressing Behavior Issues

It is my experience that when it comes to addressing behavior issues, in most cases it is very reasonable for you to request that employees *immediately* change their behavior. Whether you are asking them to initiate a behavior, alter their current behavior, or cease a behavior, they can usually make the change quickly. It is also reasonable for you as their leader to ask that they never repeat a behavior. Because of people's ability to alter most of their behavior quickly, there is no need to give them a long period of time to make the improvement.

So rather than identifying a period of time during which your employee needs to show you improvement, behavioral issues are usually addressed using a step process of progressive discipline such as the following:

First Offense: Written Verbal Warning

Second Offense: Written Warning

Third Offense: Final Written Warning

Final Offense: Termination of Employment

Behavior situations addressed through the progressive discipline process are most often instances where employees need to stop demonstrating a negative behavior or need to begin demonstrating a specific positive behavior immediately. The problem is not with their overall performance; it is specific to a behavior. Additional training or skill development is typically not required to correct the issue, just commitment, self-discipline, and execution.

Each failure to correct the behavior issue moves employees a step further along the progressive discipline path. Feedback and documentation should include a description of the desired behavioral change and the consequences for failing to make the change.

Some examples of behavior issues that are best handled by a progressive discipline process like the one outlined above are

- Use of profanity in the workplace.
- Anger or aggression.
- Gossiping about coworkers.
- Attendance issues.
- Harassment issues.
- Rudeness to a customer.
- Negativity or poor attitude.
- Insubordination.
- Failure to follow a policy or procedure.
- General misconduct.

In this model, disciplinary steps may be skipped depending on the severity of the offense. For instance, your company may have a zero-tolerance policy for harassment or aggression of any kind, so an employee demonstrating these behaviors would likely be taken directly to the final warning stage or even termination of employment depending on the severity of the situation. In this case you would enter the process at a more critical and urgent step as you would not want to give the employee three more chances to harass another team member or show aggression in the workplace. This is often called a first and final warning to indicate that the offense was serious enough to go right to the final warning step in the first warning.

Addressing Performance Issues

Performance issues differ from behavior issues in that they are usually more complex and require a longer period of time to correct. Because of this, the simple warning progression used for behavior issues would not be appropriate. Since performance issues tend to take quite a bit longer to resolve than behavioral issues, you need to set aside a period of time for the employee to demonstrate improvement to you. This span of time is typically called a probation period.

Because of the complexity of job responsibilities and the difficulty involved in evaluating performance, employees are often given an action plan as part of the documentation process, to assist them in making the necessary improvement. Performance problems are rarely limited to only one behavior or job-related activity, so the action plan outlines all the behaviors and activities an employee is expected to demonstrate during his probation period. You can find some examples of action plans in the sample documentation provided in the Additional Resources section at the end of this book.

Like the process used when dealing with behavior issues, each step of the progressive discipline process escalates in urgency and severity of potential consequences. A typical progressive discipline process for performance issues would look something like this:

First Step: Performance Warning (documenting issues and prior coaching conversations)

Second Step: Performance Probation with Action Plan

Third Step: Final Performance Probation with Action Plan

Fourth Step: Termination of Employment

Using progressive discipline to address performance issues is a time- and labor-intensive process for a leader. While behavioral issues can often be corrected with one or two conversations, performance issues usually require a heavy commitment from the leader to provide ongoing feedback and support to employees throughout the entire process. In some cases, that could mean several months of focused activity. This time and energy commitment is why some managers shy away from initiating this process, but the potential to grow and develop your employees is well worth the investment. I would even argue that providing this level of feedback and support is one of your primary functions as a leader, so to avoid it is to abandon your people at a time when they need you most.

Probationary Period

Choosing the length of time for a probationary period when addressing a performance problem can be subjective and may vary by situation and between leaders. My philosophy when dealing with performance issues has always been that employees deserve a sufficient period of time to demonstrate to you the improvement you are requesting and to resolve their issues. Most performance problems are complex and may involve additional training or retraining, which can lengthen the process and make progress harder to evaluate. Typically performance probation periods are 30, 45, 60, or 90 days in length.

To determine the appropriate length of time to give an employee to demonstrate improvement in his performance, you should consider a couple of things:

- **Is additional training required?**

   You might find that an employee did not receive appropriate training when he first started the job or that although he was properly trained in the beginning, many years have passed and frequent changes in procedures have left your employee unclear as to the current policies and standards. Sometimes you have to dig a little with the employee to uncover whether it is a training issue or something else, such as a lack of organization or focus. If you find a lack of training to be part of the problem, the period of time you choose for probation should include enough time to conduct the training (or retraining), plus an appropriate period of time for him to demonstrate to you his new skills or knowledge.

- **What is a reasonable time frame to see results?**

This is a concern in positions where the results are not immediately obvious or easily tracked. In sale positions, for instance, depending on the product or service being sold, the closure time for new business could be fairly short (a day to a few weeks) which is easy to track for performance management purposes. Or it could be several months to over a year, which makes demonstrating progress on sales performance in a 30- or 60-day time period challenging. You want to select a time period that is fair for the employee and use an action plan to help build in measurable activities you can track during the probation period.

- **How essential is the skill or activity to the overall job?**

I'm sure most of you have encountered this situation before: an employee does the major part of his job very well but drops the ball on less essential activities. Part of your thought process in determining length of time for improvement should be how critical the issue is to his overall performance and success.

For instance, if your employee is great with customers and that is the essential part of his job, but he is late when completing his paperwork, you may want to give him a longer period of time to show improvement since his poor performance is in an area that is annoying, but not critical. If the situation were reversed, you would want to give him a shorter period of time to improve because, realistically, how long would you want him to perform poorly in front of your customers, potentially driving away business?

- **What is the employee's length of service in the job and with the company?**

Consideration should also be given to the employee's performance history in the job and with the company. There are times when employees with outstanding performance records are transferred or promoted into positions that are just not a good fit for their skills and, as a result, their performance suffers. You would probably want to give a good performer with a good track record a longer time frame to improve than you would someone who had a history of poor performance or was new to the company.

If you are dealing with a long-term employee, one who has been loyal to the company, you should take his length of service into consideration when determining the length of a probationary period; but only up to a point. I am not suggesting you live with a problem employee just because he has tenure, but you may opt for a 90-day probation period rather than a 30- or 60-day one in recognition of his loyalty and service to the company.

Determining the Next Step

Realistically, one of three things will happen at the end of a probation period:

1. The employee significantly improves his performance and is taken off probation.
2. The employee makes some progress but not enough, so the probation period is extended to give him additional time to succeed.
3. The employee fails to demonstrate the necessary improvement and moves to the next phase of the disciplinary process.

In the first scenario, if at the end of the probation period your employee's performance has significantly improved, you want to celebrate his success and officially take him off probation. It is only fair that you be as quick to document success are you are to document concerns. Craft a memo to the employee that congratulates him on his success, noting specifically the areas where he showed improvement. This memo will serve two purposes.

First it documents for his file that he was in fact successful and demonstrated significant improvement in his performance. The employee will feel good that you documented his success as formally as you documented concerns. Second, it gives you an opportunity to include language that informs the employee what will happen if his performance drops again, preventing the "roller-coaster effect."

The Roller-Coaster Effect

Some of you may have had a team member whose performance improves every time you start to get serious and document his problems and then once the pressure is off, his work performance backslides again. I call this the roller-coaster effect because if you are not careful, you will be forever watching this employee's performance go up and down, just like a roller-coaster. In your final memo to the employee that documents the end of probation, you will want to include language that indicates he must maintain this current acceptable performance level or he will find himself quickly back on probation and maybe for a shorter period of time next time.

Here is a sample of the language I might include to help prevent the roller-coaster effect:

You are currently performing at a satisfactory level. However, should your performance drop to an unacceptable level in the future, further disciplinary action may be taken up to and including the reinstatement of your performance probation and/or an escalation to the next level of the disciplinary process, final performance probation.

By discussing this possibility directly with the employee and adding language similar to what I suggested above to your documentation, you inform the employee that you will not tolerate a roller-coaster ride with his performance. If his performance should drop again, depending on the length of time between the end of the current probation and the reemergence of the issue you could: reinstate the same length of probation; shorten the length of time for the next probation; or move him right to the next level in the process—final probation or termination of employment.

In the second scenario, if your employee shows some improvement, but not enough or in all areas to warrant taking him completely off probation, you could extend the current probation period. I would recommend extending the probation period only one time with an employee; otherwise, it can feel like he is on perpetual probation, and that is not fair to him. Document your decision to extend the time period, making sure the employee understands that the expectations and potential consequences from the original probationary period are still valid and in effect.

I have seen some managers put an employee on probation for 30 days and then continue to extend the probation repeatedly in 30-day increments. That is just stringing the employee along and requires too much time commitment on your part to effectively manage the process and maintain your energy and commitment. No one should ever be on perpetual performance probation. The reality is that his barely average performance, average enough so that you feel you need to extend his probation period more than once, is an indication that you need to make the decision to escalate the process or terminate employment.

At the end of the one extension period you should either take employees off probation because they were successful, or move them to the next level in the disciplinary process. If they still aren't showing significant improvement at this point, you need to set a boundary and escalate the process.

In the third scenario, if at the end of the probationary period, he fails to show you the significant improvement you require, then move him to the next level of the disciplinary process or terminate his employment.

NEVER leave employees who have been placed on performance probation hanging at the conclusion of the time period, wondering about the status of their employment. Bring closure to the situation. If you start the process, you have an obligation to follow through and finish it by closing the loop.

Keeping the Right Attitude

Your ability as a leader to maintain a positive attitude about the progressive discipline process is a critical factor in determining whether or not employees who enter the process will ultimately be successful in changing their behavior and performance. If you view it as a hateful process that takes too much of your time and is necessary in order to work your problem employees out of the organization, then that is exactly what it will become. Your attitude will set the tone in each meeting and it will leak out in all of your documentation, making it impossible for your employees to view the process as anything short of them being walked out the door.

Instead, I encourage you to see the process for what it can be—a positive method of providing employees with very specific feedback and support that will allow them to change their behavior and improve their performance. If you see it as a process to help them to grow, thereby investing in their development and potentially saving their employment, you will enter each conversation with a hopeful attitude. With this belief, your language will communicate a feeling of support and promise and the percentage of people who successfully move through the progressive discipline process will dramatically increase.

Even when I suspected that an employee was unable or unwilling to change, I always tried to remain positive and hopeful for the employee's sake. It is a sad truth that there are people who have never had anyone believe in them before, and you as their leader will be the first. Your willingness to invest time and energy into their development, even when they have made a mistake, could be life changing for them. There is nothing more rewarding than the knowledge that you have made a significant difference in someone's life.

Too often these moments may be few and far between, but when you experience one, it refuels your energy and optimism and helps you to keep investing in people even when they don't succeed in the end. For that reason, it reminds me of golf. You can spend a whole afternoon digging out of sand traps and looking for lost balls in the tree line, but on the 18th tee, one great shot straight down the fairway will keep you coming back for more. One amazing shot that feels perfect and effortless will help you to forget all the ones that missed. Success in managing performance issues is very much like success in golf; the key is to approach each opportunity with the belief that it will be successful and amazing rather than a slice into the woods.

KEY LEARNING POINTS FROM THIS CHAPTER

- Your attitude regarding the progressive discipline process is crucial to its success. If you believe it is a one-way road that leads to the termination of employment every time, people will sense this and it will become a self-fulfilling prophecy.

- It is critical that you establish a good relationship with your HR department and follow your company's policies to manage performance issues.

- An effective, well-written progressive discipline policy allows you, as a leader, to skip steps based on the severity of the offense.

- Performance issues usually require a period of time (probationary period) for the employee to demonstrate the required improvement. In contrast, with most behavior issues, you can often ask that the employee correct his behavior immediately.

- Action plans include a list of specific behaviors or areas of responsibility where the employee needs to demonstrate improvement in his performance.

- The roller-coaster effect is when an employee improves his performance each time he is placed on probation, but then lets it slip again once he comes off. Include specific language in the memo formally ending the probation that will allow you to effectively manage the inconsistent performance.

8 Chapter

Sensitive Conversations

Honesty is the first chapter in the book of wisdom.

Thomas Jefferson

Sensitive conversations feel very different from traditional behavior or performance conversations because of the delicate and often very personal nature of the subjects addressed. Most people avoid having them because they are uncomfortable with the topic and they feel like they don't know what to say. But these conversations don't need to be as difficult as we make them in our imaginations, and they can be effectively handled like any other tough conversation. Once you get past the awkwardness and embarrassment, you can address any sensitive issue using the same processes we've already discussed: the development process and progressive discipline process.

I understand firsthand how uncomfortable some of these conversations can be and I too wanted to avoid having them when I was a young manager. But in the end, being able to resolve the issue or problem is more important than avoiding your discomfort. Moreover, sensitive issues rarely just go away and resolve on their own. In fact, your avoidance often fuels the problem making it harder to eventually address. Here's how I learned this lesson early in my career.

Barbara's Story

I was 24 years old and two years into my first management position. I had 30 people reporting directly to me and I was quickly learning through trial and error (emphasis on the error part), what I needed to do to be a good manager and an effective leader. When I was promoted to the manager position I had inherited Barbara, a long-term employee who periodically had a severe, dare I say overwhelming, body odor issue. It was so offensive that when it flared up, it was a significant distraction to the team leaving them unable to focus on their work. Often I would find them gathering in small groups discussing Barbara's odor issue.

In the interest of full disclosure, I will fully acknowledge here that I did not aggressively address this problem in the beginning. I was young, inexperienced, and *very* uncomfortable talking with someone about such a personal issue. To make matters worse, the problem wasn't just your run-of-the-mill unpleasant bad BO, it was a very specific and pungent female type of odor that made it even more embarrassing to talk about.

I knew the issue needed to be addressed with Barbara formally, but I was too embarrassed to speak to her honestly and directly. I hinted at the problem in general terms and avoided being specific at all. I hoped she would "read between the lines" of my feedback and correct the issue. Sometimes after these conversations the issue would disappear for a while, but eventually it would always return. I asked my department manager for help, but he wanted nothing to do with it and told me I was on my own. He was even more intimidated to have the conversation than I was because of the extremely personal nature of the problem. The more I avoided the conversation with Barbara, the greater my fear and insecurity grew and the longer the problem persisted.

Over time, the frustration and discontent among the rest of my team grew to the point where they even tried to resolve the situation on their own, in some not-so-subtle ways. One morning I came in to find they had decorated her workspace with those little green pine tree fresheners, strung across her cubical from wall to wall like festive Christmas garland. I immediately removed the fresheners and admonished the team, but they continued to hide a few in her cubical out of my sight. If Barbara found them, she did not react, and if she understood their meaning she gave no indication, as the odor issue continued to present itself. Eventually, the team reached their breaking point and they rebelled.

On one particularly hot summer afternoon, I came back from a meeting to find that my entire department, except for Barbara, had left work early and gone home. All twenty-nine of them! I asked Barbara where everyone was, but she didn't seem to know. When I got back to my desk, I found a note folded in half with my name written on it. The note said that Barbara's odor was so offensive that afternoon they had collectively decided to go home, as they could no longer work in such an unpleasant environment. They insisted that I address the issue and resolve it for good. Needless to say, they now had my attention and I realized I could not dodge the conversation any longer. I finally realized that it was not just Barbara's issue, but I now owned a piece of it for failing to effectively manage it.

That afternoon I spoke with Barbara. To this day, that meeting stands as one of the most uncomfortable conversations I have had in my entire career. I started by explaining the situation to Barbara and letting her know why her coworkers had left early that afternoon. I reminded her that this was not the first time I had mentioned a problem with her personal odor, and I apologized to her for not addressing it more directly.

At first, she responded as she had before, resisting my feedback and offering several reasons why my feedback was not entirely accurate. She said that she showered every day, her clothes were clean, she used deodorant, and no one else had ever even hinted that she had a body odor issue. She suggested that other people had bad body odor as well and she insisted that she really didn't understand what the problem was; maybe it was just that her coworkers didn't like her. Clearly, she was not going to make this easy for me. So I decided, as uncomfortable as it was to say, I was going to have to be *brutally* honest and direct with her.

"Barbara," I said, "this is not a typical sweaty body odor. I believe it is more of a "female" odor."

Barbara again resisted and pushed back, forcing me to provide even more specifics.

"It is what I believe to be a vaginal odor and it is so unpleasant that it is negatively impacting the productivity of your coworkers. You need to accept my feedback that there is a real problem you must address here. Maybe there is a medical issue causing the odor," I offered.

I think at that point I physically stopped breathing. I sat absolutely still and waited for her reaction. She sat there for a moment, deep in thought, absorbing what I had just said. My heart was beating so loud I was sure she was going to ask about the noise.

Finally she responded and in a small voice said, "It's trench foot. My father gave it to all us girls in the family."

I believe this is the very moment I acquired my "HR poker face." I was caught totally off guard by this explanation and all my energy went to maintaining an expressionless face, lest I actually display any look of shock or humor on my face. My mind raced and all I could think about was World War I soldiers getting trench foot when fighting in France. It made no sense to me, and I tried to think of what to say next. I guessed that she had picked up on my suggestion of a medical explanation and offered trench foot as an option.

Doing my best to maintain my demeanor I said, "Well if that is in fact the case, then this is clearly a medical condition that you can control, as after each of our prior conversations you were able to take steps to alleviate the problem for a period of time."

I continued, "At this point, since you are allowing it to reoccur, you will need to bring me a doctor's note stating that you are receiving treatment for whatever is causing the offensive odor and that there should be no further instances of this problem in the future."

Knowing that Barbara took tremendous pride in her perfect attendance each year, I also told her that any further incidents of this type would result in her being sent home and charged with a sick day, which would mean she would lose her perfect attendance for the year. I was hoping this would be enough incentive to help her maintain control of the issue. I further warned that if the problem continued she would be sent home each time it occurred and eventually, her employment could be terminated under the company's attendance policy.

As awkward as that conversation was with Barbara, the situation did improve. She came in a few days later with a note from her doctor saying the situation was under control and it was. I had to send Barbara home early only once a few weeks after our conversation, but the issue never returned again after that. I believe to this day that by being absolutely honest with her about the specifics of the situation and linking her continued behavior to potential job-threatening consequences, I was able to get through Barbara's defenses, past her embarrassment, and she was able to correct the issue.

I learned a valuable lesson with Barbara that stayed with me throughout my career. When you tiptoe around bad behavior, performance problems, or awkward conversations in the workplace, you can almost always count on them escalating, making them even harder to eventually address. As uncomfortable as it was for me to be that brutally direct with Barbara, it was necessary as the issue was negatively impacting team performance, and Barbara had become the topic of cruel comments and jokes by her coworkers. Barbara's ability to resolve the issue quickly, once directly confronted, proved to me that I should have faced my fears and been that direct and honest with her even sooner. My reluctance hurt Barbara, the team, and ultimately, my credibility.

Stories of my conversation with Barbara eventually made their way to our human resources manager. A couple of weeks later, she called me down to her office and offered me a position in her department. She told me if I had the courage to say "vaginal odor" directly to someone in a conversation, then I could probably say just about anything else that needed to be said. This suggested I had the makings of a good HR manager. A month later I started my career in human resources.

Addressing Sensitive Topics

In general, when addressing sensitive issues, you should start with the steps of the development process: set expectations, provide honest and frequent feedback, and coach the individual towards success. If the behavior or problem continues, you will need to move to the progressive discipline process and begin issuing warnings and documenting your conversations as you would with other behavioral issues. Eventually, as difficult as it may seem, you may have to terminate the employee's employment if she is unable to successfully resolve her issue. Sometimes, as we saw with Barbara, out of embarrassment people will not take feedback seriously until it is addressed honestly and directly, leaving no wiggle room for interpretation, and the consequences of not changing the behavior become clear and very real to them.

In addition to several feedback tools which we will learn about later, here are some general guidelines to consider when addressing sensitive issues.

- Maintain the employee's dignity *at all times*. Choose a quiet setting for the conversation and protect her privacy and confidentiality.
- Demonstrate your compassion and appreciation for how uncomfortable or embarrassing the situation might be for her through your tone of voice, word choice, and body language.
- Be direct and specific in your language. You need to be very clear what you are talking about. Don't leave it up to the employee to read between the lines.
- Make sure you articulate how the sensitive issue relates to a specific performance concern. For example, if your receptionist is wearing outfits better suited to a night club than to your professional office environment, you need to make it clear that her wardrobe choice is negatively impacting the customers' perception of the business

as well as her credibility rather than just stating that you think her blouses are cut too low.

- Be clear as to whether you are just sharing concern on a personal level or if the issue has begun to negatively impact performance. For example, someone who loses a spouse may be distracted and depressed for some period of time. You need to make it clear when you have moved from expressing compassion over the loss to concern that the employee's extended lack of focus is now detracting from performance.
- Coworkers who initially are very supportive and protective of team members who are experiencing personal issues will eventually grow tired and intolerant of them and their troubles if they are left to pick up the slack for too long. Be mindful of this potential shift in attitude and support.
- Use your resources so that you completely understand potential legal issues involved with addressing any medical, mental health, or substance abuse situations. For example, those found to be under the influence of alcohol at work can have their employment terminated for violating policy, but depending on their circumstances, if they have an addiction and are seeking rehabilitation they may be protected under the Americans with Disabilities Act. Seek legal advice as appropriate.
- Know when conversations need to move from expressions of concern to the disciplinary process. Even if the issue is as sensitive in nature as body odor, if it continues after being addressed and negatively impacts performance—the employee's or the coworkers'—it needs to be documented and dealt with using the company's progressive discipline process. Again, be aware of any extenuating legal concerns in pursuing termination.
- Follow proper procedures to investigate, document, and respond to any claim of harassment, especially sexual harassment. Maintain confidentiality to the best of your ability and protect individuals from retaliation. Because of the sensitive nature and potential legal exposure involved in claims of harassment, they are often diverted to human resources for investigation and handling.

KEY LEARNING POINTS FROM THIS CHAPTER

- Sensitive conversations can follow a similar format as other performance conversations even though the subject is often embarrassing and very personal in nature.

- Start with the steps of the developmental process by providing employees with feedback and coaching to help them make the necessary changes.

- Use your company's progressive discipline process to address the sensitive issue if the required changes in behavior are not demonstrated.

- Embarrassment often gets in the way of the employee accurately hearing your feedback and taking the issue seriously when initially addressed, so be aware of this dynamic and demonstrate empathy for the individual.

SECTION FOUR:

PREPARING FOR THE CONVERSATION

9 Chapter

Assemble Your Dream Team

*If I had six hours to chop down a tree, I'd spend the
first hour sharpening the ax.*

Abraham Lincoln

As with many situations in life, when it comes to having tough conversations, the Scouts got it right: "Be prepared." My experience is that you can eliminate much of your anxiety and increase the odds of having a successful conversation if you are well prepared going into it. That means do your homework to make sure you have all the resources you need, have accurate information, create an appropriate environment for the conversation, and involve participants who are fully aware of their roles during the conversation.

Creating Your Own Dream Team

Whether you are new to counseling or a seasoned veteran, you will benefit from creating your very own dream team of support. No leader can succeed going it alone, nor should you have to. You have a wealth of resources around you that can help you to process a situation and determine the best course of action. The smart leader knows when to reach out and ask for help; the wise leader knows the right people to ask.

Your dream team should be a group of people who bring a variety of experience and expertise to the table to help you evaluate your counseling situations and decide the appropriate actions to take. Each member of your team brings a unique perspective and with the team's assistance, you can ensure that you are covering most of your bases before you even enter the room to have the discussion.

Although you are the best judge of who is qualified to be a part of your dream team, I do have some suggestions of people to consider. All of their perspectives can be valuable to you, some vital depending on the situation you are handling.

Mentors

A mentor can be someone from within your organization or from the outside who you trust to give sound, objective advice and guidance. The best mentors are those who are not afraid to provide you with some tough love when needed. They can point out when you might be overreacting, taking something personally, allowing a bias to influence your decision, or suggest when you are missing a key piece of the puzzle. If they have more leadership experience than you, you can benefit from their firsthand knowledge handling similar situations.

If you do not currently have at least one mentor (it's a great idea to have several), identify some individuals you admire and invite them to lunch. While some companies offer a structured mentoring process as a benefit to their team members, most successful mentoring relationships develop organically, so don't get hung up on feeling like you need to formalize the process and have someone "assigned" to you. As long as they are willing to share their knowledge and time with you, use them as a resource and learn what you can from their wealth of experience.

Experienced Leaders

Whether these leaders are peers of yours within the organization or are further up the food chain, there is probably a tremendous amount of experience and knowledge residing within members of your own leadership team. Too often managers work in silos and are reluctant to seek advice from members of their peer group for fear of acknowledging a weakness or admitting a lack of experience. This is one of those times that I need to burst your bubble; if they are working with you—they already know your weaknesses!

Using your fellow managers as a resource does a couple of things for you:

- You build deeper relationships when you ask them for help and advice; everyone wants to be needed.
- You get a broader perspective on the issue.

- You tap into communication styles other than your own that help you to round out your leadership skills.
- You demonstrate humility by acknowledging that you are open to continually learning from others.

Obviously there needs to be a mutual understanding that what is shared between managers for the purpose of effectively addressing a situation is confidential and goes into the collective "vault." To use the information as fodder for gossip is absolutely inappropriate and will destroy your credibility and the trust you've built between you and your team members if it becomes public. You can subtly remind another manager of this expectation of confidentiality by starting the conversation saying, "I have a confidential situation and I could use your guidance."

Human Resources Manager

I am going to keep this brief, as I can easily crawl up onto my soap box without even realizing it. In most organizations, your HR manager can be your greatest resource and one of your best allies. Where your experience is limited to involvement with only the performance issues within your team, the HR manager is usually advising several managers and is actually involved in all the issues for a department or company. This gives the HR manager a broader perspective and a greater understanding as to how other leaders within your organization have dealt with similar situations in the past. This knowledge can help you shorten your learning curve and better prepare you for situations that you've yet to experience firsthand. It also helps to maintain consistency across your organization.

Since the HR role is to act as both an employer and an employee advocate, HR managers can often provide insight into what employees might be feeling or how they might react in a given situation. If you do not have a good working relationship with the HR professionals responsible for your area, I suggest you reach out to them and commit to building a strong relationship.

The Boss

Very few organizations are democracies, so it just makes sense to have the person carrying the biggest stick as part of your dream team. You don't want to handle a touchy employee situation in a vacuum, only to have your disciplinary decision overruled by the person in the corner office. More than once I've seen managers have to swallow their pride and rehire someone after firing him in a very dramatic and public way, because they forgot to loop in their boss first and she disagreed with their decision.

Save yourself the time and embarrassment of executing a decision your boss will overturn. Bring him or her into the discussion on the front end so that the boss has input into the process and you are aware of any strong feelings he might have about the type of the discipline that should occur. Such input may be as simple as "Do what you feel is best," or the boss might say that the department is not prepared to fire your employee at this point, even if you are. Either way, wouldn't you rather know this before having the conversation with the employee? While there are some bosses out there who, unfortunately, don't add much value to the conversation when it comes to performance management, include them anyway. Not every manager is fully competent when it comes to handling employee relations issues, but I haven't met many who are really comfortable being excluded from the process entirely, so include them up front.

Mental Health Professional

I was fortunate to have worked for organizations during my career that invested in an employee assistance program (EAP) as a benefit for their employees. These programs provide employees with a free and confidential place to seek help in dealing with stress, depression or other mental health–related issues. They are also a great place for you as a leader to get advice on handling issues that you believe may be outside of your comfort zone. If you are one of the lucky ones and your organization does offer EAP services, introduce yourself to the local representative or call the 800 number and find out how the process works. You will want to know exactly how to access them in case of an emergency situation with a team member.

If your company does not provide EAP as a benefit, then establish a direct relationship yourself with a local mental health provider or clinic. Find a counselor who would be willing to provide you with on-call or emergency consulting services for a reasonable fee. I've used EAP counselors personally a number of times in the past to get advice on how to handle employees who were in immediate emotional crisis or facing disciplinary action and I was worried about their potential response. They are experts in human behavior and you will find them to be a tremendous resource when dealing with sensitive issues or volatile personalities.

During one particularly stressful situation, an EAP counselor advised me on how to handle an employee who was behaving erratically and had told coworkers he had recently purchased a gun. On another occasion, a counselor helped me to determine the appropriate response when handling an employee who was seriously depressed and coworkers were concerned he might attempt suicide if he lost his job.

In addition to supporting you, it is comforting to know you can provide employees in crisis with a resource who will immediately support them through a difficult time. You may have a situation where you have concerns about an employee's ability to emotionally process the discipline or termination without support. Having a professional counselor available to refer the employee to will provide you with a tremendous amount of comfort that your people are getting the assistance they need. Most of us are not equipped to provide that level of counseling nor is it appropriate for our position to do so. Know when to call in the professionals.

Do yourself a huge favor and establish a relationship now with your EAP provider or other local mental health counselor, before you need the support. Because mental health is their business, they are an outstanding resource to have as part of your dream team. You probably won't need them for the majority of situations that you handle, but when you have one that you know is beyond your capabilities and training, it is truly a blessing to have that relationship already established so you can just pick up the phone and immediately get the support and guidance you need.

As I mentioned previously, you may not decide to use each of these dream team members to prepare for every conversation, but if you put your team in place now and nurture the relationships, they will be there for you when you need them at a moment you don't have a lot of time to waste.

KEY LEARNING POINTS FROM THIS CHAPTER

- Have your dream team in place now, so that the team is available when you need it and you can access guidance quickly.

- Find mentors who will offer you sound advice and who are not afraid to be completely honest with you, especially when you are in the wrong. Surround yourself with the kind of leaders you want to become and learn by their example.

- Don't be afraid to seek advice from a peer who has more experience or specialized knowledge than you. Your willingness to learn and ask for assistance is a sign of your strength as a leader.

- Your human resources manager can be your greatest ally. The HR manager's role can flex from employer advocate to employee advocate, so this team member can often provide a balanced view of the situation.

- Don't get caught leaving your manager out of the mix. Make sure you understand when he wants to be included in the process and get his or her blessing on any decision that involves termination of employment.

- Access your company's EAP counselor to advise you when you are handling difficult situations and offer EAP support to any employee who might need it. If your organization does not have a formal EAP program, identify a mental health resource locally who can offer you and your employees support and advice.

10 Chapter

Have a Meeting *before* the Meeting

Before everything else, getting ready is the secret to success.

Henry Ford

Often the really important counseling conversations include participants in addition to you and the employee. It is not uncommon for the human resources manager, another line manager, or even your boss to sit in on the conversation with you. With that many people in the room the danger of overwhelming and intimidating the employee is a very real concern. You also run the risk of confusing or diluting your message by having too many people trying to talk.

Whenever there is going to be an additional person in the room during a counseling conversation, either as an observer or to help you deliver your message, it is very important that you take some time before the conversation to review the purpose of the meeting and to clarify roles. In other words, *have a meeting before the meeting*. This pre-meeting will allow you to ensure that everyone is on the same page in terms of the message, that they understand what the desired outcome is, and that they are clear on the role they each are expected to play during the discussion.

Depending on the nature of the issue being discussed with the employee, your meeting before the meeting could be as brief as 5 minutes or a much longer discussion that includes outside resources (such as EAP) and other stakeholders. If you don't take the time to have this pre-meeting, there is a strong possibility that your conversation could hit a few snags, like the one Jason experienced with Sarah.

Sarah's Story

In my role as HR manager, I was asked to sit in on a counseling session with Sarah, a unit manager, who was overheard talking negatively about a fellow manager to one of her line employees. Since Sarah was a member of the management team herself, this was considered to be a serious lapse in judgment. Her manager decided ahead of time that she needed to be given a final warning for the behavior and to be told if she talked negatively about members of the management team like that again, she would lose her job.

Participating in the conversation with Sarah was her immediate manager, Jason, and their department head, Connie. I was asked to join the conversation as an observer. Unfortunately, Jason did not take the time to bring us together as a group before we met with Sarah. Because we did not have a meeting before the meeting, we each entered the room with our individual assumptions of what was going to happen.

Jason assumed Connie would be delivering the message about the final warning during the conversation as she was the senior manager in the room. Connie assumed that Jason would discipline Sarah, as he was her direct manager. I felt strongly that my role was to be supportive and only offer feedback once the message was delivered by either of the line managers. As the HR manager, it was important to me that I not be the one to "say the words" to Sarah so I had no intention of taking control of the conversation.

I knew we were in trouble almost immediately. After Sarah came in and sat down, the four of us looked at each other in awkward silence. No one said a thing. Everyone assumed that someone else was going to initiate the meeting. Finally after several uncomfortable minutes, Connie broke the awkward silence and spoke.

Connie started by providing Sarah with some positive feedback, commenting on a number of things that she had done well lately. The conversation flowed for a few minutes while she highlighted Sarah's positive performance. Sarah thanked her for the acknowledgment and then, another awkward silence. Again we all looked at each other in anticipation.

Finally, Sarah asked, "Is that why you asked to meet with me today?"

More silence and I shifted uneasily in my chair. As I looked around the room, everyone else was looking down contemplating the pattern of the carpet that covered the office floor. The tension was becoming palpable, when Jason finally spoke.

"Sarah, it has come to our attention that you were overheard yesterday saying some pretty negative things about Jeff (her fellow manager) to one of your team members."

Sarah thought about that for a minute and then a look of horror washed across her face. "I know exactly what you are talking about and I am so sorry. I was really frustrated with Jeff and I guess I let my emotions get the best of me. I was only blowing off steam, but boy did he make me mad."

We had tapped into her frustrations with Jeff and now she was on a roll. Sarah continued speaking for 20 minutes relating the sequence of events that led up to her making the negative comments in question. Every so often one of her managers would ask a question about one of the details she had provided, but other than that, she was given free rein to vent her emotions and complain about Jeff.

I kept waiting for Jason or Connie to jump in and take control of the conversation. We needed to get back on track and get to the message point of the meeting, to tell her that no matter what Jeff did to frustrate her, she was wrong to talk about him like that to the line staff. She needed to hear that she couldn't do it again and what would happen to her if she did, but that moment never came.

The meeting seemed to go on forever and Sarah began to cover the same ground again. Someone had to wrap this meeting up and say the words (deliver the message) or we would be there all afternoon. I kept waiting for Jason or Connie to take control but neither did. Even though I did not (and do not) believe HR should deliver disciplinary messages, I had to weigh that belief against the damage of this conversation going on forever without coming to the point, so I sat forward in my chair and took the first opening I saw.

When Sarah took her next breath I jumped in and said, "While I appreciate how frustrated you were by Jeff's lack of organization, do you understand how inappropriate it was for you to complain about him to one of your team members?" She lowered her head and without making eye contact answered, "Yes."

I waited a beat to see if Jason or Connie would jump in, but there was only silence. Clearly they were happy to let me do the talking and to wrap things up.

"This behavior is unacceptable, Sarah," I said. "It damages not only Jeff's credibility with the staff, but yours as well. It is divisive and will undermine the success of the team. It cannot happen again. Given the seriousness of the situation, this is your final warning. If you speak negatively about your fellow managers to a team member again or to anyone outside of appropriate channels, your employment may be terminated. Do you understand?"

Sarah nodded that she understood. We asked if she had any questions and she said she didn't. She explained that she totally understood what she had done was wrong and promised it would never happen again. Jason gave her the final warning document that he had prepared before the meeting and asked her to read it over and sign it. Once she did, she left the room repeating that she was sorry she let us down and that she was going to immediately apologize to Jeff.

A quick debrief of the meeting immediately after Sarah left the room confirmed that we had all entered the counseling session with different ideas of who was going to do the talking. Because of that, no one really took control and directed the conversation, Sarah was allowed to take us off on a number of non-productive tangents and the meeting lasted much too long. A meeting before the meeting could have easily and quickly flushed out the differences in our perceptions saving us from inaccurate assumptions and the result would have been a more effective counseling session for Sarah.

Your Pre-Meeting Meeting

Make having a meeting *before* the meeting a priority with you and your management team. It is a great way to help clarify the purpose for the meeting and to ensure that all participants are working from the same agenda during the conversation with the employee. Here are some points that I recommend covering during your group meeting.

Start with the End in Mind

It is important that everyone participating in the meeting understand and agree on the intended outcome. You need to ask yourself what the ultimate purpose of the meeting is: Is your intent to gather additional information? To help coach the employee to accept accountability and responsibility for her actions? Or is it to warn her that if she repeats a specific behavior again she will lose her job?

Whatever the purpose, it is critical that everyone understand it so that all the participants are driving to the same point. It is frustrating for everyone involved when you come to the end of a discussion and one of the participants introduces a new issue, launching you back into a protracted discussion. Agreeing on the purpose beforehand also helps people to know how to steer the conversation back on point if it gets sidetracked. It is not uncommon for an employee's defense system to try to take the discussion off into unrelated issues and concerns in order to avoid, deflect, or delay hearing any negative information.

Determine Overall Tone

Your ability to set an appropriate tone for the conversation is critical to supporting your message. This is where many managers stumble, especially when they are anxious about confronting an employee. A serious message can get lost or watered down if the tone of the conversation is too light or the language is soft and indirect. I call this "candy-coating" your message; setting a lighter tone for a serious message in the hopes that the message will be more readily accepted and to avoid confrontation with employees. If you candy-coat your message too much, they may dismiss your message entirely or perceive it as being unimportant when in fact that may not be accurate.

When it comes to setting the tone, the opposite problem of candy-coating your message is also a concern. You can unnecessarily "freak out" employees by sending signals that convey a more serious issue than you are actually discussing. The employee becomes so worried that she is about to be fired that she fails to hear the more benign message you are actually sharing.

Make sure in your pre-meeting that you discuss the overall tone you want to convey to the employee and ensure that each participant is supporting that message. Setting the appropriate tone for the conversation helps to emotionally prepare the employee for the message you are about to deliver.

There are several things to think about when setting the tone of a conversation.

- **Formality of language**—You can use formal words when setting up the meeting or your language can be casual and nonthreatening. For example, you can send the employee an ominous email requesting a meeting to discuss "performance issues" or you can stop the person in the hall and ask, "Do you have a minute? There's something I'd like to talk to you about." The method of delivery and language should match the ultimate message you intend to deliver.

- **Body language**—Research shows in face-to-face communications we communicate 55 percent of our message through our body language, 38 percent through our tone of voice, and only 7 percent through our word choice. That means that 93 percent of our message will be received by vehicles other than the words we select. Hopefully now you can understand how important body language is to that equation.

What are you communicating with your body language when the employee arrives for the meeting? Are you sitting relaxed in your chair or are you sitting up straight with such perfect posture the Queen Mother would be envious?

Think about the room setup for the meeting as well. Are participants already in their seats or is everyone milling about with people taking a seat as the meeting begins? Are you sitting across from the employee behind a desk or next to her in a chair?

Be aware of your facial expressions and gestures as well. Eye contact is very critical. Be careful that you do not actively avoid eye contact when the employee arrives or during the meeting as this can communicate that you are uncomfortable with the situation or the message. Many people also associate eye contact with trust, so make sure you are meeting and holding her gaze without staring.

Decide on Participants

The first thing your employee will notice when she walks into the meeting room will be the number of people attending and their respective titles. From this, she will infer the level of seriousness of her situation. So it is critical that you give the issue of who participates in the meeting some serious consideration before the meeting as it also helps to set the tone. If your goal is to keep the employee's defenses down so that you can increase your odds of having a productive two-way conversation, lining up managers behind a desk like a firing squad is definitely not the way to go. You will immediately engage the employee's defenses and shut her down before you've even uttered a word.

There are often several individuals who participate in the pre-meeting in order to provide valuable input and approval for the final course of discipline, but not all of them need to be or should be in the room when you meet with the employee. If they are, it could easily feel like overkill. My recommendation for most situations you will address is that you have no more than two other managers in the room during the counseling session. I know this can be hard to do at times and that there may be several people who desire to be a part of the final counseling conversation with the employee, but there are a couple of good reasons for suggesting you limit the participants.

First, it keeps the balance of power in the room from getting too one-sided. No matter how you slice it, in terms of power, it is going to feel like it's the company vs. the employee. If too many people are stacked up on the company side it will feel like an ambush when the employee walks in. If you feel strongly that you need to have three additional people in the room, then one should absolutely be the human resources manager. Since the HR manager's job is also to act as an employee advocate, the HR manager can be positioned physically near the employee to help her feel that the power in the room isn't quite so one-sided.

Second, most meetings take place in a manager's office for reasons of confidentiality. When you start to cram too many people into an office you get people sitting on window ledges, leaning on walls, or finding other creative little perches. Whenever possible you should try to avoid someone standing during a counseling session. From a body language perspective, it implies a sense of power that can be interpreted as intimidating. Also, when there isn't enough distance between people in the room, personal space gets invaded. This can quickly lead to an increase in room temperature, the employee feeling threatened, and a higher level of anxiety for everyone involved.

So keep these things in mind as you determine who will actually participate in the meeting with the employee. While several people may *want* to be there, ask yourself who really *needs* to be a part of the meeting. Remember the goal is to create a situation where the employee has the greatest chance of hearing and understanding your message. As strongly as I feel that HR should be a part of most counseling sessions, there were meetings over the years where I opted out because one more person would have been overwhelming and I agreed that it was more important, based on the specifics of the situation, for other managers to be a part of the discussion.

Identify Roles

It is critically important in any counseling session to designate one person in charge of delivering the message. I refer to this as deciding "Who's driving the bus?" Someone has to be in charge of opening the conversation, keeping it on track, summarizing what was agreed upon, and delivering the final message that often contains the potential consequences if the situation does not improve. If you don't designate someone to drive the bus before the meeting, your conversation can quickly fall apart and your message might never be delivered, as was nearly the case in the conversation with Sarah.

Typically, the responsibility to direct the conversation falls to the employee's direct manager (one level up), or that manager's boss (two levels up). I know as an employee myself, I wanted all communication regarding my performance or employment status to come from my boss as I felt it was most appropriate coming from him. It's one of the main reasons I feel so strongly that HR should never be put in the position of being the first to communicate negative performance feedback to an employee. Too often the employee's first reaction is, "Why hasn't my manager told me this?"

There can be times when the direct manager may not be the best one to lead the discussion. For instance, if it is unclear whether the manager played a part in issues being discussed, then the manager probably should not be the one to drive the bus. If this manager is very inexperienced and new to the management role, it might be a good opportunity for a senior manager to model the correct way to conduct a counseling session so that the newer manager can observe and learn. Ultimately, the decision of who delivers the message should be made considering what is in the best interest for the company, as well as taking into account the relationships participants have with the employee.

Even if you are not designated as the one driving the bus, your role should be clearly defined as well. My role as the HR manager was often as observer or as the employee advocate, as it was important for employees to know they had someone in the room who could help them communicate what they needed to say. A department head or senior manager might participate as an observer to lend seriousness or weight to the message, or to offer a broader perspective on how the behavior or performance is affecting areas outside of the immediate team. The department head or senior manager could also play a more active role by reiterating the message to make sure the employee understands the urgency of correcting the issue. A peer manager might be asked to participate in the counseling session if the peer has knowledge of the issue being discussed and can offer credible feedback to the employee. In all cases, everyone should be crystal clear as to why each participant is in the room.

Once assigned a role, participants should try to maintain that role throughout the conversation, especially if the leader's style is different from theirs and they are tempted to jump in and take over. There were many conversations where I was in the role of observer/employee advocate and the leaders delivering the messages were doing so in a way that was very different from the way I would have done it. While the managers eventually got to where we needed to be, I was a little anxious we wouldn't achieve our purpose. Even though I didn't agree with the approach the manager used, it was important that I not switch roles and take over delivering the message unless I was convinced that the conversation was in jeopardy, as I did in the meeting with Sarah.

Taking a backseat in a performance conversation is not always an easy task. You need to balance respect for style differences with efficiency should the conversation get sidetracked. Making the decision to take control away from the person designated in the pre-meeting as the "bus driver" is a very subjective and intuitive one; only experience will help you to understand when you are crossing the line between supporting and hijacking the conversation. Sometimes you can provide support by asking a clarifying question that can help the manager get back control, allowing you to remain in the observer role.

Review Signals

In baseball, coaches communicate with players during the game by using hand signals and code words. These signals allow all the players on a team to communicate information and a change in direction subtly so that everyone knows what is going to happen next without stopping the flow of the game. Managers can use similar types of signals effectively in performance conversations as well.

While brushing your finger across the side of your nose like Robert Redford and Paul Newman did in *The Sting* might be a little too dramatic, using head nods and other subtle movements can help you to nonverbally communicate during a counseling session and ensure that all the participants are on the same page. Agreeing on these signals in the meeting before the meeting can help to make inevitable changes in the flow of conversations seamless.

Signals can be as simple as the slight nod of the head or even the agreement that the person driving the bus will go forward with communicating the message or discipline unless a code phrase is said by one of the other participants in the room. For example, one signal that I've used is asking the other managers present in the meeting if they have "any further questions" before communicating the discipline. The use of the phrase "any further questions" can be pre-arranged to indicate that the leader of the conversation is satisfied with where the discussion has gone and is ready to bring the conversation to an end and proceed with the predetermined discipline. Participants' silence means that they are all in agreement. If there is a question in someone's mind as to whether the conversation should proceed as planned, she can use my next suggested signal and call a "time-out."

Time-outs are exactly what they sound like—a formal break in the flow of the discussion. Often managers go into counseling sessions with a specific type of discipline in mind that they intend to communicate to the employee. If there is no new information presented during the meeting and they feel the discipline is still appropriate given the facts, they should move forward with communicating that discipline. But what happens when the employee presents new information or it becomes clear that there are more questions that need to be answered before discipline can be communicated? That's when it is important to agree during the pre-meeting that if there are any questions about going forward with the discipline, the manager feeling uneasy should call a time-out.

During a counseling session, before the group proceeds to the discipline portion of the conversation, the manager leading the discussion should check in with the other managers in the room to make sure everyone is still on the same page. This is typically done by asking, "Is everyone good to move forward?" or "Does anyone have any further questions before we move forward?" As long as there are no objections, you can then proceed with the remainder of the message as planned. But if anyone has a question as to the appropriateness of the planned discipline, they should call a time-out. I've actually directly asked, "Can we take a quick time-out?" to put the conversation on hold. This quick check-in with the other decision makers in the room is especially important when terminating someone's employment, since you don't want to have to retreat from that decision once it has been communicated to the employee.

You might as well get comfortable that there is *always* a chance that new information may be presented during a meeting that might change the way you feel about the planned discipline. That isn't to say you need to change your mind about your direction each time, but often there is enough doubt or concern that you will want to confer with the rest of the management team participants before moving forward with the discipline.

Don't be afraid to call a time-out at any point in the conversation. It is only fair to the employee that you be open to reconsidering your decisions if the facts of the situation change. Your time-out can be as simple as asking all the managers to step outside of the room for a moment to confirm that you are still on track, or more extensively, adjourn the meeting for several days as the new information is further investigated. Calling a time-out is not an indication of weakness or indecision in a manager; conversely, it is a sign of strength and integrity.

If you do feel you need to step out of the room to talk in private, simply ask the employee for a few moments to confer with the other managers. You can either have the employee leave the room and wait outside or have the managers involved step outside of the room as a group. When you return to the meeting, thank the employee for her patience and understanding and explain that it was important for you to confer to ensure that you are making the right decision. I have never seen anyone have a problem with managers taking a time-out or postponing the conversation in an effort to make correct decisions.

In a case where you feel there is a need to suspend the meeting until more information is gathered, explain to the employee that she has brought up some information that needs further investigation and that you will be back in touch as soon as possible. Do not make her wait more than 24 hours to hear back from you. In most cases, situations that fall into this type of scenario are usually more serious and are often job threatening. It is cruel and unusual punishment to drag your heels on reconvening the meeting. Wrap up your investigation as quickly as possible and then meet again with the employee. Depending on the outcome of your investigation, the discipline may have changed, so be ready to summarize any new information or your current thought processes before picking up where you left off.

Play "What if?"

Being fully prepared for the discussion includes thinking about what you are going to say and being very clear about the message that will be delivered to the employee. But remember you are dealing with unique individuals and as much as you try to plan and prepare, the actual conversation with the employee can suddenly go off in an unanticipated direction or take an unexpected turn. This is why it is a great idea to explore any "What if?" scenarios that you can think of during your meeting before the meeting.

What if? scenarios are simple to brainstorm. You basically ask the group "What will our response be if the employee says (or does) _____?," and fill in the blank with as many different scenarios as you can imagine. This allows everyone participating to be on the same page if the conversation takes an unexpected turn.

For instance, you could ask the group questions such as these:

- What if the employee were to resign before we could say the words terminating her employment. Would we accept it?
- What if she were to totally deny the behavior she's been accused of?
- What if she admitted to the offending behavior but offered a reasonable excuse?
- What excuses would we accept?
- Is there anything she could say that would change our current decision about discipline?

You get the idea. Clearly you could go on forever with this exercise, but if you work through the scenarios and responses that are the most likely to come up and predetermine what your response will be, you will feel more prepared and confident going into the conversation. Don't forget to explore the possible emotional responses the employee is likely to show you as well and discuss how you will handle each of them.

You can make the What if? exercise even more powerful by role-playing your responses. I hesitate to even suggest this as I can feel you literally cringe at the thought of doing a role-play. But it's a fact that role-playing possible scenarios beforehand will help you to feel more confident during the conversation and this confidence will translate into increased credibility. The more prepared you are, the more relaxed you will feel and the less anxious you will appear. All of which will help to put your employee at ease.

The benefits you gain from having a meeting before the meeting to discuss these issues far outweighs the cost of the time it takes for the group to meet. As you work with the same people over time, you will become familiar with their communication and feedback styles, and the time it takes to prepare will significantly decrease. Eventually, you may be able to go through the entire process in just a few minutes, but it is important that you at least touch on each of the areas outlined above to make sure all of your bases are covered.

KEY LEARNING POINTS FROM THIS CHAPTER

- Whenever you are going to have anyone join a conversation between you and an employee, make sure you have a "meeting before the meeting" to discuss the purpose and to clarify roles.

- Determine the overall tone that you want to communicate to the employee and ensure that everyone's word choice and body language is in alignment with it.

- Select participants carefully. You want to balance including the appropriate individuals in the conversation with overwhelming the employee with participants. Include as few participants as you can while still effectively communicating your message.

- Not everyone who participates in the pre-meeting needs to participate in the actual discussion with the employee.

- HR managers can be perceived as employee advocates as well as employer advocates, so they can often help to balance the perceived power in the room.

- Identify roles and determine who is "driving the bus." This individual will control the flow of the discussion and deliver the final message before the meeting is adjourned.

- Agree on any signals or the use of a "time-out" ahead of time. If anyone is uncomfortable with the direction of the conversation or the final message, she should suspend the meeting by calling for a time-out.

- Role-play any potential responses or reactions the employee may have by going through "What if?" scenarios together so that you are better prepared to respond in the moment.

11 Chapter

Pay Attention to the Details

*Spectacular achievement is always preceded by
unspectacular preparation.*

Robert H. Schuller

In addition to preparing the participants before the conversation, it is equally important that you give thought to some of the logistics of conducting the meeting itself. Making sure these details are planned and executed well might seem like a minor challenge compared to the skill required to facilitate the counseling conversation, but missing any one of these points will cause major problems for you. It is important to ensure that all the little details are ironed out prior to sitting down with the employee.

It's All in the Details

Preparation and planning can help eliminate or at least minimize issues surrounding a difficult situation. It may seem like a lot of extra work, but it will always be worth the time and effort involved to get it right. Ann's termination is a perfect illustration of how even the best-laid plans can sometimes fall short.

Ann's Story

Ann was a long-term employee who had been a satisfactory performer over the years. However, when the company moved to a new computer system, she was unable to make the transition and her performance suffered. Ann was not able to maintain her productivity and her work began to have a high percentage of errors. Even with additional training and support over the course of several months, her work continued to deteriorate and she was unable to regain a satisfactory performance level. Unfortunately, there were no other positions available for Ann in the office and after months of coaching and counseling, her managers were finally forced to make the extremely difficult decision to terminate her employment. I was Ann's HR manager at the time and I gathered her management team together to prepare for the conversation.

During our pre-meeting, we tried to think through the logistics of how best to conduct the termination. We decided to tell Ann at 1:00 p.m. on Thursday afternoon, that way a good portion of the staff would still be at lunch and we could minimize onlookers. It would also allow us to all be available for her at work on Friday if she had any questions about the termination. We completed the necessary paperwork to have her final check available at the meeting rather than waiting until the next pay cycle to pay her out. We felt it was important that she leave with her money in hand.

We also discussed an issue related to Ann's personal life that troubled us. Coworkers had shared concerns that Ann might be the victim of domestic abuse. We spoke to her a couple of times about it and offered her the support of our EAP counselor, but she insisted that there wasn't an issue. Although there had not been an incident in the last year, her managers still had lingering concerns so I arranged for the local EAP counselor to be in the office at the time of the termination and available to Ann immediately afterward. I wasn't sure Ann would agree to talk to her as she continued to deny that there was physical abuse occurring at home, but I believed our concerns were valid enough to arrange it anyway.

We also knew that Ann took the bus to and from work every day and we didn't want her sitting in such a public place after what we expected to be a very emotional conversation. To avoid this I arranged for a car service to be waiting outside the office to take her home that afternoon after our meeting.

It was decided that we would not tell Ann about the meeting beforehand as we didn't want her to worry about it all night. Her managers and I really tried to plan every detail so that this very difficult conversation would go as smoothly as possible and we wanted to maintain Ann's dignity throughout the process, as we all genuinely cared for Ann.

Finally it was Thursday morning, the day of the meeting, and Ann arrived to work early as usual. She sat down at her desk and tried to log into her computer, but she got an error message and her password was denied. She tried multiple times to log in, but kept getting the same error message each time. This confused her and she had to wait over an hour for her manager to arrive at work.

When Ann's manager arrived, Ann told her about the error message. "I keep getting this error message when I try to log in, 'Employee Not Found'. Can you help me fix this?" Ann asked.

Knowing what was in store for Ann later that day, her manager was obviously horrified. She understood immediately what had happened. The company's IT department had already deleted Ann from their system and disabled her password.

"I'm sorry for the confusion; I'll take care of this right away for you," Ann's manager apologized.

It took a few phone calls, but Ann was finally granted access to the system. Needless to say, we learned to manage that process better for future terminations.

As if we weren't already off to a rocky start, at 10:00 a.m. Ann called her bank as she always did on payday to confirm that her direct deposit was in her account. On this day, her bank informed her that her deposit had not arrived. Again Ann became frustrated and called me to find out what was wrong.

"I will look into this right away and get back to you Ann," I said, but the truth was I already knew what had happened. When I put through the paperwork for the termination the payroll department canceled Ann's direct deposit so they could issue a hard check to send to me. Her money wasn't missing; it was sitting in my desk drawer as her final paycheck that we would give her during the meeting. I felt bad about putting Ann off, but it was important that we held all the information about the termination for the meeting at 1:00 p.m.

The missteps of the morning put everyone, including Ann, on edge. But our care and concern for Ann and our efforts to support her helped the rest of the day to go as well as it could in these situations.

When we finally met with Ann, her managers took her back through the conversations that had led to this meeting, reviewed the performance plan she had been given three months ago, and spoke about her failure to improve. When that was complete, Ann was informed her employment was being terminated. We gave her the paycheck I had prepared and the final benefits paperwork, then allowed her to ask any questions she had. It was clear she was overwhelmed and emotionally in shock. Even though she had been warned that she could lose her job, as with many employees, Ann never believed it would actually happen.

After allowing her a few minutes to process the information, I explained, "Ann, we've arranged for a counselor to be available here in the office to speak with you now. I hope you will consider meeting with her, even if it is only for a few minutes." Ann looked concerned. I tried to ease her fears and said, "I think it is important for you to speak to the counselor as the next couple of days will be a time of transition and she might have some suggestions to help you. She might also be able to provide you with some advice on how to share the news with your husband."

I wasn't sure how Ann would react to my bringing up the possible issue with her husband again, even as an aside. Ann was hesitant at first, but she finally agreed and I took her to the adjacent office where the EAP counselor was waiting for her. Before leaving I asked Ann, "How would you like to handle the personal items at your desk? Would you like to pack them up yourself or would you prefer that I do it while you speak with the counselor?" "I would appreciate it if you could do that for me," she whispered. "I'm not sure I am up to talking to a lot of people right now." I agreed, then left the two of them alone.

Although she was initially reluctant, Ann spoke with the counselor for over an hour. She left with an appointment and several numbers to call in case of emergency. Ann and I walked downstairs to the waiting car. Her items had already been placed inside so she didn't have to carry the box out as she said goodbye to her coworkers. She was very grateful that we had thought about the bus ride and had made the arrangements for her to be driven home that afternoon. I gave Ann my business card and told her to call me if she needed anything or had any questions.

I checked in with the EAP counselor a week later and was told that Ann was doing well. She had kept her appointments and she was even taking some classes from the local unemployment office to assist with her transition.

Ann's termination, while heart-breaking, is a wonderful lesson in how you can really demonstrate respect for your employees and help to maintain their dignity even during very difficult situations. As a management team, we learned how to orchestrate some of the administrative details even better so that those mistakes did not happen again. While emotionally difficult for everyone, the decision to let Ann go was appropriate for the business and I am very proud of the way we treated her throughout the process.

What to Consider

To help you manage the logistics of your conversations better, consider these details during your pre-meeting discussion.

Timing

By choosing the best time to conduct your conversation you can often eliminate issues that can unnecessarily complicate the process or compound any negative feelings on the part of the employee. Certainly there are times when disciplinary conversations have to occur immediately as is often the case when the issue at hand involves inappropriate behavior. But for the majority of the performance-based conversations you will conduct, you will have some flexibility in scheduling your meetings. While there is no perfect time to provide negative feedback, there are some things you want to keep in mind.

- Avoid late Friday afternoon discussions if at all possible. Many managers like to have performance discussions on Friday afternoons because the weekend gives them a nice buffer from having to immediately interact with their employee right after an uncomfortable conversation. But by scheduling a serious conversation late on a Friday, you effectively take away any internal resources available to the employee to help him process the conversation.

  People are then left with the option of rehashing the conversation with friends and family outside of work, who are all unlikely to provide a balanced perspective of the situation. Rightfully so, I would expect my mom to believe I was an absolute angel at work and to take my side. And in the case of a termination, this could push your employee to seek outside support such as retaining legal counsel.

  Instead of leaving the employee no alternative other than seeking out a lawyer, you should try to encourage him to use your company's internal grievance process by meeting with HR or appealing the decision with someone higher on the organizational chart than his boss. Try to give employees time in the week after the conversation where they can access these people during normal business hours. If you must deliver bad news on a Friday, schedule it for as early in the day as possible and even consider providing them with the number of someone to call if they have urgent questions over the weekend.

- Watch out for special days. I learned this one the hard way when I allowed a woman to be laid off on the very day she celebrated her 15th year anniversary with the company. She thought she was being called into her manager's office to be congratulated on her service anniversary but instead found out her position was being eliminated. A day or two before or after the special day would still have felt bad to her, but doing it on the *actual* anniversary day added unnecessary insult to injury. While you can't know every special day in someone's life, take a moment to check their personnel file to ensure it is not their service anniversary or birthday at the very least.
- Choose a time of day that minimizes the potential for embarrassment. People do not want to leave a tough conversation with their boss feeling embarrassed and looking like an emotional wreck, and then have to walk into a crowded office space full of coworkers staring at them. I prefer lunch time rather than late in the day as there tends to be fewer people at their desks during lunch. If the situation involves the termination of employment, a noon meeting still allows you time to communicate the departure with the rest of the team the same day and minimizes the effects of the rumor mill ramping up over the weekend.

Location/Environment

As any realtor will tell you, it's all about location, location, location. Put some thought into choosing the most appropriate location for the meeting. The place you select for your conversation should

- Allow for privacy. If your office has glass windows, invest in blinds or find an alternate location you can use for the more sensitive conversations. No one wants to feel they are on display during a vulnerable time when they may not be at their best. Arrange for all phones, including cell phones of the participants, to be turned off, forwarded, or put on vibrate. If your computer notifies you of incoming emails with a little sound, mute it.
- Have tissues available. It's a little thing, but it helps maintain the dignity of the employee when the tears start and the nose begins to run.
- Have enough space. Your location should be large enough to comfortably seat everyone with more than enough room to respect people's personal space. Everyone should have a place to sit; no

perching on window sills or leaning on walls. The employee should not feel physically cornered in the space.

- Support the tone of the conversation. Don't take someone to a coffee shop to have a serious performance discussion. Consider finding neutral ground if you anticipate employees will enter the meeting feeling defensive and you need them to relax and be open to hearing your message. Sit behind your desk only if you want to send a clear message about your authority.

Additional Support

There have been many meetings over the years where I was more worried about what was going to happen after the conversation than during it. The threat of losing a job can be devastating, and some people fall apart to the point that you become concerned about their ability to get home safely or their emotional well-being in the short term. For some, the issues they are experiencing at work are only the tip of the iceberg when compared to the personal problems they are facing at home. Your ability and willingness to provide them with the extra support and assistance needed in these moments is what will set you apart as a compassionate leader.

If you have any concerns about an employee's ability to process the information you are about to give him, provide him with additional support either through your company's EAP program or a local mental health provider/agency. I always had the phone number of our EAP program counselor written on the back of my business card, in my pocket, so that I could easily hand it to an employee if I thought he needed that type of assistance. There were even times when I arranged for the EAP counselor to be standing by waiting for a call, then allowed the employee to use my office so that he could speak immediately to the counselor in private.

Another example of additional support would be to consider arranging for a car service to take your employee home after the conversation as we did with Ann. There is nothing more humiliating than having to sit on a crowded bus or train with your little box of knickknacks on your lap, choking back the tears. Research has consistently shown that how you treat your employees in the last 10 minutes of their employment has more influence on their decision to pursue legal action than anything else relating to their employment with you. Treating your employees with compassion and dignity is not only the right thing to do, it is sound business etiquette and could prevent a lawsuit.

Money Matters

In the case of termination discussions, it is usually a good idea for the employee to receive any money owed as quickly as possible. In fact, some states have laws that require you to present the employee with a check for any money owed immediately upon the termination of employment, so make sure you check your local laws. Even if the state law says you can wait until the next normal pay cycle to give someone a final paycheck, I strongly suggest you consider doing whatever it takes to have a check with at least a portion of the money owed available to hand over during the termination meeting, especially if it is related to a job reduction or poor performance.

The upside of doing this is that employees leave with money in their hands and since they just lost their job, money will be an immediate and important concern for them. The downside is that if you process the checks and then for some reason decide at the last minute to pull back and not terminate their employment at that time, you will have a bit of an administrative mess to clean up with your payroll department, and the employees will probably find out that your intent was to terminate their employment.

Consider the situation where a company planned to eliminate several positions on the following Friday, which was also a normal payday. They put through all the paperwork earlier in the week so that the checks that Friday would include the employees' regular pay, final pay, a payout for unused vacation days, and some severance pay. At some point during the week the organization's managers changed their minds and they decided not to eliminate all of the positions after all. Unfortunately, no one thought to tell payroll and on that Friday, four employees received larger than usual checks.

When the employees investigated the error, they discovered that they had been on the list to have their jobs eliminated and were scheduled to have been terminated that day. Most of them were grateful, of course, that it didn't actually happen, but it did cause them to worry about their future employment and they never really felt secure in their jobs again.

The bottom line is you should be aware of all the pieces that go into orchestrating the administrative part of a termination, even if you are not personally responsible for executing them, so that you can quickly and efficiently reverse the process if needed. If you feel confident ahead of time that the conversation will end in the termination of employment you should take the time to sort through the money side of things so that you can communicate to the employee what money is owed and exactly when it will be paid out.

Security

Another important consideration before conducting your conversation is assessing any security concerns and determining what safety precautions you might need to take. As someone who has participated in hundreds of confrontational conversations over the years, I can emphatically tell you that you need to think about the safety of yourself, the individual you are counseling, and the welfare of all your other employees when conducting any tough conversation. I wish you didn't have to think about such things, but violence in the workplace is a reality and in this area, there is no room for false bravado.

While you can't be totally certain whether someone will become aggressive or violent during or after a conversation, you should always be on the lookout for indicators that might alert you to the potential. Your mantra in this area should be "better safe than sorry," and you need to take the appropriate precautions if you have even the slightest hint of a concern. I strongly recommend that if you are in a position of leading people, you should educate yourself on this topic and build a relationship with an expert in this area who can guide you through any potentially risky situations. I frequently used my EAP contact and local law enforcement as a resource to help determine the threat potential of individuals and to suggest the best course of action to protect myself and our employees.

While profiles and lists of early warning signs are helpful, no one can accurately predict human behavior all of the time. With that said, you can still be vigilant in identifying indicators of an increased risk of violent behavior and err on the side of caution. The Federal Bureau of Investigation's Critical Incident Response Group, Center for the Analysis of Violent Crime has identified risks and indicators of violent crime[1].

Here are some indicators of problematic behavior from that list:

- Increasing belligerence, intimidating behavior, bullying or other inappropriate or aggressive behavior towards coworkers or managers
- Ominous specific threats of violence, either direct or veiled
- Hypersensitivity to criticism
- Recent acquisition of or a fascination with weapons

---

[1] Eugene A. Rugala and Arnold R. Isaacs, editors, *Workplace Violence: Issues in Response*, Federal Bureau of Investigation Publication, June 2002, www.fbi.gov/publications/violence.pdf

- Drug or alcohol abuse
- An apparent obsession with a coworker, supervisor, or employee grievance
- A preoccupation with violent themes
- Interest in recent violent events or incidents of workplace violence
- Statements indicating desperation (financial issues, breakup of marriage, family issues, or other personal problems)
- Outbursts of anger or inability to control emotions
- Extreme disorganization
- Notable changes in behavior
- Homicidal or suicidal comments or threats

Unfortunately, on a number of occasions I have had to arrange for off-duty or plain-clothes police officers to be stationed in the building in response to safety concerns or an actual threat of violence. In dealing with one particularly troubled individual who exhibited several of the indicators above, we were in contact with both our EAP counselor and local law enforcement. On their advice, we determined that the threat of violence was significant and as a precaution, we did not allow the individual back into the workplace and terminated his employment over the phone.

Coworkers are often the first people to see or hear about risky and concerning behavior. It is critical that for everyone's safety you create an environment where your employees are comfortable sharing information with you and alerting you to potential threats.

I remember vividly one incident, where an employee was demonstrating some erratic behavior and over the course of several weeks, his mood seemed to deteriorate as his thoughts and conversations became darker. His marriage was breaking up and as the weeks passed, he became more and more depressed. He told coworkers that he "didn't have anything to live for if he didn't have his wife and kids." He talked endlessly about buying a gun and finally, one day, announced that he had purchased one. It was only then that his coworkers brought their concerns to the attention of management. Even when the situation had been steadily declining, his coworkers had chosen to stay quiet as they didn't want to get their friend in further trouble. They were willing to cover for his being distracted at work and to keep his secrets up to the point he purchased the gun, then their concern for his safety and their own prompted them to alert their manager. By that point, it easily could have been too late.

Once alerted to the situation, we responded quickly. I immediately spoke to EAP, who helped us assess the threat level and helped facilitate getting our employee an emergency appointment with a local counselor. We later learned that he was being treated for a medical condition as well and had stopped taking his medication. Prompt action helped him to receive the support he desperately needed and averted a potentially devastating incident in the workplace.

Everyone experiences loss or hardships in their lives and most people are able to work through it over time. If an employee exhibits one or more of the indicators listed above or you see a sudden negative shift in performance or behavior, you need to take the situation seriously and address it immediately. Get expert advice and take appropriate precautions when counseling this employee. Don't be afraid to use all of your resources, such as involving EAP or a local mental health provider, contacting law enforcement, or even hiring a security company if you believe the situation warrants it. The cost involved with these precautions is far outweighed by the responsibility you have as a leader to maintain a safe work environment.

KEY LEARNING POINTS FROM THIS CHAPTER

- You can eliminate many obstacles that get in the way of executing an effective counseling conversation by attending to most of the logistical and administrative details beforehand.

- When choosing a time for your conversation, make sure you schedule it so there is access to support during working hours afterward to ensure that the employee isn't left to process a difficult message on his own over a weekend. This is especially important when conducting terminations.

- Choose an appropriate location for your meeting that supports the overall tone of the conversation.

- Arrange for additional support to be available for the employee to help him process the message or to help maintain his dignity. This is not the moment to start penny-pinching.

- Do not minimize the importance of money. Make sure all paychecks are accurate and, in the case of terminations, try to arrange for all monies due to be included in the final paycheck.

- Never go into a tough conversation without considering the issue of safety and security. Educate yourself on the warning signs of potentially violent behavior and always err on the side of being overly cautious and well-prepared.

"

SECTION FIVE:

HAVING THE
CONVERSATION

"

12 Chapter

The Opening

One of the best ways to persuade others is with your ears—by listening to them.

Dean Rusk

Once you have completed all the preparations, you are now ready to have the conversation with your employee. In this section we will examine the mechanics of actually conducting effective feedback conversations. While many managers seem to fear this part of the process the most, I have found that there is a structure and method to conducting a tough conversation that when used, will help you to become more comfortable and confident in delivering your message.

In the next chapters I share some of my best tools for providing direct feedback, handling volatile emotions, and communicating difficult messages. We will go into great detail about each phase of conducting a conversation in the following three chapters, but let's quickly get an overview of the process so you have an understanding of how the conversation is structured.

The Three Phases of a Conversation

Most conversations can be broken into three distinct phases:

- The opening
- The feedback phase
- The closing

Each phase has a distinct feel to it based on its purpose in the process. How much time you spend in a counseling conversation will be determined by the topic being addressed, overall tone being conveyed, and the individual being counseled. For example, a conversation to uncover the reason behind recent performance problems and to identify a plan to correct these issues will likely take more time than a conversation to eliminate an inappropriate behavior. Regardless of the topic though, the ratio of time spent in each of these three phases should be about the same.

The opening of the conversation is very important as it sets the tone for the rest of the meeting. Anxiety and defenses are typically highest during the opening so part of your challenge is to help everyone relax and lower the defenses as much as possible. For most conversations, about 20 percent of your time will be spent in the opening, although there will be some exceptions to this which we will talk about later in this chapter.

The vast majority of your time in a counseling conversation— approximately 70 percent—will be spent in the feedback phase. This phase is where you will use all of the skills in your virtual leadership toolbox to engage the employee in a productive discussion. Here you ask open-ended questions to elicit more information, gather details about the situation, and provide the employee with feedback. The feel of this phase in most cases is conversational as there is more give and take. Your conversation has a purpose or message that needs to be delivered, so this is where you will start to set up that message so that there are no surprises at the end. The challenge of this phase is to keep the conversation on track so that the information exchanged supports your ultimate message, which is delivered in the final phase of the conversation, the closing.

The closing should be the shortest part of your conversation. Many people get lost in this phase and, when it happens, they can quickly undo any good that has been developed during the meeting. The closing should be only approximately 10 percent of the total conversation, and it is where your final message is delivered along with the consequences. Any next steps are reviewed and agreed to by the participants, and the meeting is adjourned. Although it sounds simple, a crafty employee can manipulate the conversation so that it seems the closing will never end.

Keeping the three phases of a counseling conversation in mind as you conduct your meeting will help you to stay on track and on topic, identify when you have been stuck in one of the phases for too long, and ensure that you touch on all of your key points before concluding the discussion.

So let's dive in and talk about the first phase of your conversation, the opening phase.

The Opening Phase

All your preparation thus far has brought you to this point. The participants are in place, the preparations are made, and details have been addressed. You are finally in front of the employee. You may have a lot on your mind, but now is the time to really focus and be present. You are the one "driving the bus," and it is time to engage the employee.

During the opening phase of the conversation, you should strive to accomplish these five objectives:

1. Set the tone.
2. Explain the purpose of the meeting.
3. Encourage the employee to talk.
4. Listen more than you talk.
5. Transition to the feedback phase.

Since the opening accounts for only approximately 20 percent of the time allocated for this conversation, you need to make sure you can accomplish each of these objectives quickly and effectively. Let's explore each of them in detail.

Setting the Tone

During your "meeting before the meeting," you should have discussed the type of tone you wanted to convey in your meeting with the employee. In most conversations, the tone is set quickly in the opening phase through your word choice, body language, the location for the meeting, and the participants you choose to invite. The more casual the meeting, the more appropriate it is to use small talk to help the participants loosen up and vent some of the natural energy and anxiety that may be lurking in their bodies. Some brief comments about the weather, current news items, or even asking about the employee's family or personal hobbies are all good icebreakers.

Obviously, if the tone of the conversation is going to be more serious or formal, keep the chitchat to a minimum. If you are about to talk to someone about a claim of sexual harassment, it would be very inappropriate to start out by discussing the chances of the local pro basketball team making it to the finals. The serious nature of the topic dictates that you get down to business pretty quickly.

Explain the Purpose

When employees are informed that they have a meeting with their boss or better yet, several managers, it's like the proverbial first shoe dropping. It sets up a sense of anticipation that will not be released until the other shoe finally drops. Stating the purpose of the meeting is that other shoe. As quickly as you can after initially setting the tone, make a statement that indicates why you are meeting with the employee. This can be as simple as stating, *"The reason I asked you to meet with me is. . . ."* Once you indicate what the meeting is about, her mind will relax and she will focus on the issue at hand. Even if it is bad news, she will at least know what she is dealing with and can begin to emotionally prepare.

Some managers, in an effort to work into a conversation, start with a really general statement such as, *"Are you happy working here?"* when what they really want is to talk about a very specific situation. The employee has no idea where the manager is going with this question, so her anxiety shoots through the roof.

Make sure your purpose statement gives them some indication of what the conversation will be about, such as, *"I'd like to talk about a recent meeting you had with John. Tell me about the conversation you had with him yesterday."* Now she knows the focus of this meeting is her interaction with John the previous day.

Encourage the Employee to Talk

As mentioned, one of the best ways to help dissipate the nervous energy that many employees naturally bring into the room is to get them talking as early in the conversation as possible. Sometimes you can achieve this through your small talk. Other times, you may want to set the stage with an opening remark and then immediately ask a question.

For example, if you are going to counsel an employee on her behavior after hearing about a heated argument she had with a coworker, you might want to start with a question such as, *"I understand there was a situation with Mark yesterday. Why don't you tell me about it?"* As I mentioned in the chapter on basics (see Chapter 4), your ability to get employees talking early in the conversation helps to diffuse their energy and often leads to them sharing information with you long before you've tipped your hand and shared what you know about the situation.

I have always been a big believer in managers holding their cards close to the vest when it comes to conversations regarding specific behavioral incidents. Even though you may feel like you have all the relevant facts regarding an issue, it doesn't hurt to lead with questions that either validate your existing information or unearth new facts. When employees don't know what you already know, there is a greater chance of them sharing useful information with you.

Everyone wants their day in court, so to speak. By allowing them the opportunity to talk right away and give you their version of events, you have provided them with just that. In my experience, it is the individual who feels she was deprived of the opportunity to share her side of the story who tends to reject the disciplinary process, resists moving beyond an event, and, if she is terminated, will initiate legal action. That is the real danger when you skip this portion of the opening and go right into delivering your message. You can appear to have prejudged the employee and be closed to hearing any new information, even if that is not actually the case.

Listen More Than You Talk

Along those same lines, once the employee starts talking, it's time to use your best active listening skills as we discussed in Chapter 4. This will help you to establish a rapport, and you will encourage her to continue sharing information with you.

Although you might be tempted, the opening phase is not the time for feedback. Even if it is clear to you as she is telling her story that she acted inappropriately or made a mistake, just take it in during the opening phase and get as many details as you can about the incident. Your goal is to fully understand her story first, so remain open and noncommittal during this phase. Remember, in the beginning of the conversation, you want employees to lower their anxiety and defenses. That way, when you transition into the feedback phase, they are in a better position to really take in and receive any feedback you need to give them.

Transition to the Next Phase

Your final objective in the opening phase of the conversation is to seamlessly transition into the next phase, the feedback phase. By the end of the opening phase it should be clear to the employee the focus of the discussion and you should have some information ready to discuss as a result of the questions you've asked. You will also have a sense of the employee's attitude because you have been listening to her words and watching her body language for several minutes.

You now need to move the conversation into the feedback phase where you will continue to probe and ask more detailed questions and deliver any feedback that you have. Here are some examples of how you can effectively transition to the next phase of the conversation:

- *"Ok, now that I've heard your side of the story, I'd like to go back and ask you some more detailed questions."*
- *"Thank you for sharing your thoughts with me. What I'd like to do now is talk about how you reacted."*
- *"Some of the information you just shared does not match other feedback I received from several witnesses to the incident, so let's talk about that."*
- *"I feel I have a good understanding of the issue, now I'd like to share some thoughts with you at this point."*

The idea is to make it clear that the preliminary discussion is over and you are now about to get into the meat and potatoes of the issue. And remember, the opening phase should represent approximately 20 percent of your total discussion time, so don't get too bogged down here. Once you start to provide feedback, you have transitioned out of the opening and entered the next phase of the conversation.

A Few Exceptions to the Opening Format

Before we move on, I want to discuss a couple of situations in which you might not want to follow the above format for the conversation opening. These situations are very specific and, as you read through them, I think you will understand why they are exceptions.

Addressing Sensitive Issues

Most of your conversations will follow the format outlined above for the opening phase. But you may find yourself in a situation where you are so uncomfortable about what you need to say that you just don't know how to get the conversation started. Maybe it is personally embarrassing for you to discuss the topic or you believe the employee will be very uncomfortable hearing the feedback. When you sense a high level of anxiety or tension in the room, and, in particular, when you are feeling a lot of anxiety yourself, it is best to skip the small talk and start by acknowledging those feelings.

I call this talking about the elephant in the room. Everyone can feel and sense the anxiety looming large in the middle of the room, but no one wants to actually talk about it. Don't try small talk in sensitive situations as it is nearly impossible and you will end up looking and sounding even more uncomfortable. So acknowledge your feelings of anxiety or discomfort to help release some of the tension in the air. If you decide to try to ignore the tension (the elephant), your employee may make up her own story about why you are nervous, which may be worse than the real issue you are about to address, so avoid being evasive.

In situations where you believe the employee may feel embarrassed by your feedback or you are feeling some discomfort yourself, start the conversation by stating that you are feeling somewhat uncomfortable and that the topic is a difficult one for you to talk about. Apologize for any tension that may cause in the conversation, and then move forward. Discussions involving personal hygiene issues or explicit sexual conduct are situations in which you might acknowledge any discomfort you are feeling up front. Acknowledging your feelings shows that you are human and it in some small way prepares the employee to hear potentially upsetting information.

Here is how I might open a conversation when I am uncomfortable with the topic:

> *"Louis, I have to speak to you about something that quite frankly is a little difficult for me to say, and it might even be a little uncomfortable for you to hear, so I am just going to jump right in with the feedback."*
>
> *"Sue, I understand that there was an incident last night at the staff party that I may need to address. I appreciate it may be embarrassing for you to share these details with me, but it is important that I hear from you exactly what happened. I am uncomfortable having to ask you about it, but it is necessary and I will be discrete."*

Starting with Your Message

There may be situations, although they should be few and far between, in which you are not interested in having a two-way dialogue with your employee. In situations where the path is already set in stone and what the employee has to say won't change the outcome, start with the message first and then give her the opportunity to talk afterward and to share her feelings. Conversations where you are communicating a layoff would be one example of where I would use this technique. In those cases it is all about the message you are delivering and the employee really doesn't have much input into the process, so you might as well get right to it.

Another situation when I would get right to the feedback is when you are delivering the final message that you are terminating someone's employment as a result of poor performance or inappropriate behavior. Often by the time you get to that point there have been a number of conversations as part of your counseling or investigation process. These preliminary conversations are two-way discussions and should follow the five-step format for the opening.

But when it comes time to deliver the termination message, you do not want to encourage further discussion that will belabor the point. Typically you would open the conversation with a lead-in that states the purpose of the discussion and then get right to communicating the termination message. We will discuss terminations in greater detail in Chapter 15.

KEY LEARNING POINTS FROM THIS CHAPTER

- The opening of the conversation sets up the rest of the discussion. You should spend no more than 20 percent of your time in the opening phase.

- Your tone going into the conversation should be in sync with the message you intend to deliver or the employee can feel misled.

- Clearly articulate the purpose of the meeting so the employee can stop spending energy trying to guess what it's all about.

- Get the employee talking early in the conversation to help her release any nervous energy and to provide you with additional information regarding the situation.

- Use good active listening skills to acknowledge what the employee is saying and to move the conversation along.

- When addressing some sensitive issues, it is best to jump right into the conversation. First acknowledge your discomfort or anxiety about what you are going to say and state that the employee might also find your message embarrassing to talk about. This will help to prepare her for your message.

- There are situations, such as with a layoff or with the final meeting for a termination, where you will want to start with your message first in the opening as opposed to waiting until the closing. Understand that doing this does not encourage a two-way dialogue, so ensure that the situation warrants the use of this technique.

13 Chapter

The Feedback Phase

*It is only as we develop others that we permanently
succeed.*

Harvey Firestone

The majority of your time during the counseling conversation will be spent in the feedback phase, so it is critical that you cover all your key points and stay on track or you could find yourself having marathon conversations. This is not always easy as it is in this second phase that your employees will often do their best to challenge your statements, disagree with your decisions, argue your feedback, try to drag you off topic, and play with your emotions. Your ability to stay the course amid the barrage of defensive maneuvers they may launch at you will determine your ultimate success.

There are two parts to communicating any message effectively: what you say and what they hear. Your goal is to deliver your feedback in a way that it is easily understood and then to employ a few simple techniques to verify that it was actually received in the way that you intended.

The Feedback Phase

As with the opening phase of the conversation, there are a number of objectives that you should aim to accomplish during the feedback phase. These are as follows:

1. Flush out pertinent details.
2. Provide feedback.
3. Acknowledge emotions/diffuse energy.
4. Manage defenses.
5. Handle distractions and interruptions.

6. Determine if you are on course.

7. Transition to the closing.

Sometimes you will be handling several of these objectives at the same time, making you feel like that guy on the variety show who used to keep ten plates spinning on top of tall sticks at the same time, trying not to let any of them fall. It is challenging and it takes experience to get proficient in the skills needed to achieve all of these objectives. But when you become comfortable with using the tools we discuss in this chapter, you will be able to make it seem effortless.

Flush Out Pertinent Details

In the opening phase you provided the employee with an opportunity to tell his side of the story, though I am willing to bet he may have left out a few of the specifics, especially if those details didn't help his case. Now that you have a general idea of the employee's state of mind in the conversation, it is time to get more detailed information. Whether you are discussing his performance or addressing a behavior issue, it is a good idea to get as much information as you can from the employee so that you can make a well-informed decision about what action, if any, to take in terms of discipline.

It is important to keep an open mind throughout this phase of the conversation. While you may go into the meeting feeling like you have a good idea of the issue at hand (what happened and what action you anticipate taking), a great leader is always open to considering new information that, when added to the mix, potentially could change the outcome. I know that in many of the conversations in which I participated, the employee was able to offer details or insight in response to our questions that resulted either in further investigation of the situation, the altering of the final discipline we had anticipated, or at the very least, our regrouping as a management team to discuss our options.

The same questioning skills that you use when you are interviewing candidates are equally effective here. Depending on how you phrase your questions, you will get very different results.

There are two types of questions you can use when questioning someone in an effort to solicit more information:

- Closed-ended questions
- Open-ended questions

Closed-Ended Questions

Closed-ended questions are those questions that elicit a yes or no answer. They are restrictive and do not encourage the employee to elaborate with more details so they can impede your search for additional information. If you have ever felt that it was difficult to get information out of someone ("getting them to talk was like pulling teeth"), you may have been using closed-ended questions.

Here are some examples of closed-ended questions that you might have used in a performance discussion:

- *"Do you think you have had enough training to do the job?"*
- *"Is there anything else you think you need?"*
- *"Have you completed all the tasks listed in your performance plan?"*
- *"Do you understand the situation you are in?"*
- *"Can you explain this?"*

As you can see, when the questions are presented in this way it is possible for employees to respond with only a few words, often with just a yes or no answer. Certainly there is the possibility that people could hear these questions and go on to disclose a great deal of information because they are feeling comfortable and understand what you are really after. But if they are feeling defensive, fearful, or threatened, which is often the case in counseling sessions, they will be more inclined to shut down and respond to only what is asked. Because closed-ended questions take less energy to respond to, they do not accomplish the goal of helping to dissipate some of the natural pent-up energy in the conversation.

Open-Ended Questions

What you want to primarily use in counseling situations are open-ended questions. In contrast, they are much broader in scope and encourage employees to be more forthcoming with their answers. By design, open-ended questions require more than a one- or two-word response. They are also perceived as less threatening by the recipients because they don't sound as judgmental, so they help to maintain trust during the conversation.

Because open-ended questions encourage employees to disclose additional information, you are more likely to get the details you need. The employees use more energy in providing you with their response, so open-ended questions also help them to release some of their energy and stress.

In order to help you really see the difference using open-ended questions can make in your conversations, I've taken the closed-ended questions from the example above and changed them into open-ended questions.

Closed: *"Do you think you have had enough training to do the job?"*

Open: ***"What additional training do you believe would be helpful to you?"***

Closed: *"Is there anything else you think you need?"*

Open: ***"How can I help you to be more productive?"***

Closed: *"Have you completed all the tasks listed in your performance plan?"*

Open: ***"What were you able to accomplish during the last four weeks?"***

Closed: *"Do you understand the situation you are in?"*

Open: ***"Tell me your understanding of where you stand regarding your performance."***

Closed: *"Can you explain this?"*

Open: ***"Please explain to me what happened."***

Both types of questions will have a place in your conversation, but you should be able to see how the open-ended questions are more likely to drive the conversation forward and to elicit a greater amount of useful information.

As a reminder, in addition to the type of questions you ask, your word choice, body language, and tone all have a significant bearing on how much information you will be able to flush out. Judgmental or accusatory language and tone will suggest to your employee that the less he says the better. Why should he give you more ammunition when it is clear to him that your mind is already made up? There is nothing more demoralizing than pleading your case to someone who is closed-minded and has already decided you are guilty.

Emotionally charged tone or words may also spark an unwanted emotional outburst from your employee. Once that happens, it will take you additional time and effort to diffuse the reaction before the conversation can again become productive.

And finally, we've talked about the importance of body language before. If you are trying to elicit as much information as you can from the employee before his defenses kick in, you will want to make sure that your body language remains open and nonthreatening, creating a comfortable environment and encouraging him to open up to you. Remember, it is not only important where you sit in the room (behind your desk versus next to the employee), but also how you sit in your chair.

In order to have open body language while sitting, I would typically sit relaxed in the center of my chair, leaning forward slightly, with one arm in my lap and the other on the armrest. Throughout the conversation I would make it a point to check in with my body language to make sure I was not inadvertently showing tension anywhere: no clenched fists or bouncing legs, especially if I knew I was feeling somewhat anxious.

Provide Feedback

Many people struggle with the process of providing feedback to their employees because they don't like confrontation, they want to be liked, or they are afraid of the person's reaction. I've heard all these explanations and more over the years. People who are uncomfortable providing feedback may be able to make it through the opening phase of the conversation, but when it comes to actually saying the words and being honest, they will stop short.

But as we discussed in the beginning of this book, if you are going to be a leader with integrity, if you consider yourself a person of character, and if you value the trusting relationship you have built with your team, you *must* be able to conquer your fears and provide your people with honest feedback on a timely basis.

Feedback Formulas

Because this fear and discomfort can be such a difficult thing for managers to overcome, I believe following a formula in the beginning when you are first learning the skill of providing feedback can be useful in helping you to articulate your message. Once you become comfortable with the process and your skill level increases, you won't even have to think about following the models I'm offering because your feedback will naturally flow from your personal style.

There are two formulas that I have used effectively over the years as tools to help managers to be direct and tactful when providing feedback. I have found that most feedback you will need to give in any situation can be worked into one or both of these formulas. In fact, I used the second formula to help me get over my fear of giving my father feedback, and so these tools have a wide application for both your professional and personal life. Practice each of them, and then determine which is a better fit with your style and the situation you are addressing.

The C.A.R. Formula

The C.A.R. formula is pretty simple and straightforward. It consists of three steps and helps you to clearly articulate feedback in a way that is direct and easy to understand. To use this formula, you describe for the employee the circumstance surrounding the situation, the action he took, and the result. The formula sticks to the facts and helps you to focus on the performance or behavior issue rather than criticizing the person. This formula can also be used to deliver positive feedback as well, although most people don't seem to have a problem sharing good news with their employees.

Circumstance

First, describe the circumstances under which the performance issue, behavior, or decision occurred.

> *"Yesterday was a very busy day for us in the store and we really needed everyone to be there."*

Action

Next, describe specifically what the employee did (or neglected to do), or said that created the problem.

> *"You did not call to tell me that you were going to be absent from work until more than an hour into your shift."*

Result

Finally, what was the impact of their behavior (or lack of action) on people (you, teammates, other employees, guests/customers), or the company's results (missed goals, loss of revenue, loss of reputation)?

> *"While I understand that you were sick, your failure to follow our call-out procedures meant that I did not have enough time to cover your shift. The rest of the team had to work twice as hard as a result of your absence and the customers did not get the level of service we strive to provide."*

The "While I Appreciate . . ." Formula

This next formula is one I learned when I was a young manager. I was not a very secure leader and I had an extremely difficult time providing people with constructive feedback. The following formula was taught in my basic management training course, and although it does sound more scripted and like a formula when you are saying it, it really does work. Here, by filling in the blanks of this three-part formula, you are able to convey your feedback in a structured way.

"While I appreciate _____"

Fill in the rest of the sentence with a statement that reflects your understanding of what the individual was intending to do or accomplish.

" . . . you were trying to be helpful,"

"I have a concern_____"

Complete this sentence with a statement that describes the negative result the other person's actions or words achieved.

" . . . about your tone of voice and the word choice you used. I felt it sounded very demanding and dismissive."

"Might I suggest_____"

Finish this sentence with your advice or recommendation on how it could be done differently in the future to better achieve the intended result.

" . . . that next time you ask if the person needs help before jumping in and taking charge of the situation."

Here is another example of what this formula would look like infused with a little more personal style.

"While I appreciate that you were only trying to be helpful and you did not intend to hurt Carol's feelings, I have a concern that the words and tone you used were perceived as aggressive and disrespectful. Might I suggest that you reflect on the conversation and think about how you could have said that differently so that in the future your suggestions are received as supportive rather than directive."

In the beginning of my career, when I found it really difficult to find the courage to confront an issue, this formula was what I used to initiate conversations. You will find that as your confidence grows, you can abandon the specific words I used in the formula for ones that feel more natural to you, which will help the feedback sound more authentic. If you struggle with finding the words to communicate the feedback like I did, these formulas are a great way to help you find your voice. In fact, I have a friend with whom I shared this formula over 15 years ago, and we still chuckle to this day when one of us starts a conversation with *"While I appreciate . . . ."*

I-Statements

Another tool that is extremely effective when providing feedback is to use "I-statements." I-statements are a way of phrasing your feedback so that it comes from you as an expression of your feelings or your beliefs, rather than a judgment or accusatory statement. I-statements are less likely to trigger the employee's defense system, which will allow you to comment about the specific behavior being addressed rather than using words that make the feedback seem more like a personal attack. They are a little tricky to get the hang of at first, but once you do, I-statements will become an invaluable skill in your leadership toolbox. Here's how they work.

Let's take this example: You overhear a negative interaction between two of your employees, Rod and Henry. You believe that Rod was very rude and dismissive in the way he spoke to Henry, so you call Rod into your office to provide him with some feedback.

Without using I-statements, it might sound something like this:

"Rod, I just overheard your interaction with Henry and I am very concerned. You were condescending and dismissive to him."

What is likely to be Rod's response? What if someone told you that you were condescending and dismissive? Most likely Rod's defenses will kick in immediately and his response will be something like, *"No I wasn't."* Because you stated to Rod that *"you were condescending and dismissive,"* which sounds judgmental, you will now have to argue with him as to whether or not he was actually condescending and dismissive.

If Rod is like most people, he will resist being labeled with those words and will dig in to try to defend his actions. Rather than talking about how

Rod can learn to express himself in a more effective way, you will be defending your having labeled him condescending and dismissive.

Now let me show you how an I-statement can help the situation. Once you sit down with Rod in your office, phrase the same feedback in a way that expresses your feelings, observations, or beliefs.

For example, you could rephrase it like this:

"Rod, I just overheard your interaction with Henry and I am very concerned. I believe that you sounded condescending and dismissive to Henry."

It may seem like a small change, but the effect is huge. By changing the feedback from *"you were"* to *"I believe that you sounded,"* you have offered the feedback as your belief or your feelings rather than a statement of fact. When you do that, you remove some of the finger-pointing that occurred in the first example. For Rod to argue the feedback with you now, he will have to dismiss your right to feel the way you are feeling, and the fact is that everyone has the right to his or her own feelings.

In the end, Rod may still disagree with you, but by using an I-statement you have taken some of the fight out of his argument. After all, this was your feeling after observing the interaction between Rod and Henry and you have a right to feel that way. If Rod does argue your I-statement, what he will have to eventually say in order to win his argument is *"you shouldn't feel that way,"* or *"your feelings are wrong."* Most people, once they hear themselves make those statements out loud, will realize how ridiculous they sound.

Here are some other examples of I-statements:

"In my opinion . . ."
"I feel that . . ."
"My perception is . . ."

As you can see, your I-statement does not technically need to start with the word *I,* but if it speaks to *your* thoughts, feelings, beliefs, and opinions, it will achieve the desired effect. The important point is that you are sharing your feedback from your perspective rather than using words that are accusatory, which helps to keep the focus on the employee's behavior rather than on the words you choose to communicate your feedback.

I have found that even the most defensive people will eventually understand the futility of arguing that someone else shouldn't feel the way they do. I-statements help to take some of the energy out of the argument and help you get to a place where you can more calmly discuss the "why" behind the feedback rather than focusing on the words you used to deliver it.

In this example, the reason you feel this way might have been the tone of Rod's voice, his body language, or his choice of words. In any event, your goal is to help him lower his defenses so that he can hear your feedback and I-statements will help you to do that. You want to help defensive people get past their defenses so that they can take a look at what behaviors created the issues and make a positive change going forward.

I find I-statements so effective that I use them all the time, in all areas of my life. Instead of telling my friend in anger that "You are always late," I say instead, "I feel like you don't respect my time when you are late." The first statement says I'm just itching for an argument. The second statement says, if you care about me, you wouldn't want me to feel this way anymore, and so it promotes problem solving and change.

Acknowledge Emotions/Diffuse Energy

As I have already confessed, since I grew up in a fairly restrained family environment, strong emotions personally unnerved me and were a real challenge for me to deal with in the beginning of my career. To be successful in having tough conversations, you will need to become comfortable, as I did, managing a variety of strong emotions and energy states. Through trial and error, I learned some valuable lessons and discovered several tools that I want to share that will help you to better manage emotions when they crop up during your counseling conversations.

First, it may be helpful for you to hear my definition of a strong emotion. Any behavior or combination of behaviors that demonstrates emotion and distracts you from the natural flow of the conversation or prevents the employee from hearing and taking in your feedback, is a strong emotion that needs to be dealt with right away. A good sign for me that I was encountering a strong emotion was if I found myself paying more attention to how the employee was communicating rather than to the content of what he was saying. When that happened, I knew it was time to step back and acknowledge the emotion.

If you are having a counseling session with someone who begins to show strong emotions, the worst thing you can do is to ignore it. It will only make the situation worse and may cause the person's emotions to escalate. You need to deal with the emotion directly and try to dissipate its energy before you can proceed with delivering your intended message. Subtle demonstrations of emotions such as becoming more animated, a rising voice level, or eyes filling with tears are emotions that can be worked through without it distracting from the feedback process. It is usually okay to continue when you see these signs of emotions, but you may want to slow down a bit so the employee can catch his breath.

Strong emotions, however, are a different story. For example, behaviors such as shouting, uncontrollable crying or sobbing, flashes of anger, excessive use of profanity, or total silence—where all systems have shut down—are all showstoppers. You will need to acknowledge and deal with these emotions immediately before you can move on. To try to ignore these strong emotions and continue with the conversation is only flirting with disaster.

It is difficult to generalize the reasons behind strong emotions. We are all complex individuals, and we each bring our own set of baggage into every interaction. Ultimately, I'm not even sure you need to understand what is behind the emotion when you first see it in order to help someone work through it in the moment. After all, you are the person's boss, not a therapist. But I'd like to suggest a couple of ways for you to effectively deal with these situations so you can diffuse the energy that is fueling the emotion and move on with a productive conversation.

Identifying Levels of Emotion

Emotions will present themselves at different intensity levels. In order to help you distinguish between these different levels, I have divided them into four groups, listed here in order of increasing intensity. While I am not a professional counselor, I will provide you with some suggestions on how I would deal with someone who was exhibiting behaviors at each level based on my experience. As always, if something does not feel right to you or you would like support dealing with a specific individual, please consult your company's HR Department, EAP advisor, or a local mental health professional.

Level 1: You Recognize Their Emotions

What It Looks Like

At this level employees are communicating emotion through word choice or subtle physical signs. They are saying "I am angry" or "He hurt my feelings," but they are not showing you their anger or hurt in any other significant way. Their face may flush as they speak, which can often happen when people are expressing their feelings, especially feelings of anger or embarrassment. Their body language may also give clues to how they are feeling: their arms may be crossed or they may literally be vibrating with nervous energy. Their eyes might water or their voice might break as they speak, but at this level, they don't seem to have a problem continuing with the discussion. Their emotions are under control and they are able to appropriately participate in the give and take of the conversation.

How to Manage It

When you see indications of emotion at this level, use your best active listening skills to acknowledge the emotion you believe you are seeing and to check to see if you are correct. For example, you might say,

"I can understand why you might feel angry because of that" or *"that could have been very embarrassing for you to hear."*

By stating the emotion you are seeing out loud to him you help to validate his feelings so he can move on in the conversation. Additionally, if you are off in your assessment, he has the opportunity to correct your perception. If possible, try to communicate back to him using words that he has already used with you. For instance, if he says he was "hurt," you reflect back to him that you understand that he "feels hurt."

If you have read the signs correctly and your statement is accurate as to how he is feeling, you will be demonstrating to him that you hear him and that you get what he is saying. Sometimes this simple acknowledgment is enough for him to release the emotion and drop into a much calmer and more receptive state for receiving feedback. Acknowledging his feelings also helps you to build trust and will encourage your employee to share information with you in a deeper and more honest way because he trusts that you understand where he is coming from—you get him.

There is great power in showing someone that you get what he is feeling, especially without him actually having to specifically tell you. Sometimes people aren't even aware they are giving off clues as to how they are feeling, so verbalizing what you perceive is a good way to validate their feelings, particularly since the same clue could mean several things and you don't want to make assumptions.

For instance, are they avoiding eye contact with you because they are ashamed, scared, or maybe even feeling intimidated? Have they crossed their arms because they are feeling defensive or anxious, or because the room feels cold to them?

This is why it is dangerous to make an assumption based on one clue and why you should never acknowledge feelings as a statement of fact, such as *"You are clearly angry."* Phrase your acknowledgment in a way that allows him the room to correct your assumptions, even if you think you are right. You can even phrase it as a question, *"So I'm hearing that made you very angry, is that correct?"*

Level 2: The Emotion Is Unmistakably Part of the Conversation

What It Looks Like

Here, the emotion is spilling out into the conversation in very obvious ways. Employees are not only telling you how they feel but are clearly showing you with behaviors associated with those emotions. For example, they may start to use strong language or profanity, which may be inappropriate or out of character; or they may raise their voice, show agitation, their face or neck may flush and become red, or their body language may become very animated with larger than normal gestures.

At this level, while they are still able to articulate their point or position, their emotions are clearly flavoring how they are delivering their message. You are still able to hold a discussion, but you may need to allow them a few moments to vent so that you can move on with your conversation. You know you are at a Level 2 because you can easily see that their venting is helping to release the energy associated with the emotion and that you will be able to resume the conversation in a few minutes. At Level 2, emotion is only a temporary distraction. In other words, the more they talk or cry, the calmer they get.

How to Manage It

As with someone at the first level, acknowledge the emotion so that you demonstrate that you are listening and that you understand. It may sound silly, but people will question (even if it is subconsciously) whether or not you understand how they are feeling if you don't actually state it for them. Again, use all of your active listening skills here. Sometimes in an agitated or anxious state, people lose their train of thought or their point will become muddled as they vent the emotion. By paraphrasing what you are hearing back to the employee, you will help him to clarify his points and confirm that you are following his story.

In most cases, people just want their feelings to be validated, to be "heard," and once they feel that happens they will calm right down. If they don't believe you are getting how they are feeling, they may escalate the emotion and behavior in an effort to get through to you. Again, acknowledging the emotion should help to validate for them that you are listening and letting them vent will help to physically drain some of the energy from their body.

This is also a great time to practice the essential skill of being silent. As much as you want to show your employee support and get to problem solving (and the feedback portion of the conversation), it is usually best for you to sit back and let him vent for awhile once the emotions appear. You can demonstrate your support and show that you are following the conversation with your body language (head nod, leaning forward slightly) or short phrases of support ("That's too bad," or "I understand."). Try not to interrupt the venting too much, even if you have questions.

If your employee is really on a roll, you should periodically help him take a break by paraphrasing what you have heard so far. It gives him a chance to sit back and assess how he is feeling and by listening to you paraphrase what he has already said, he can see if he's gotten sidetracked in his storytelling. After a brief break, you can then kick it back to him by urging him to "go on" or by asking an open-ended question so he continues.

Your goal at this level is to allow employees to vent the energy associated with their emotions because in this stage you can clearly see that talking is helping to bring them into a much calmer state. And once they are there, you can then have a more productive conversation as they will be better equipped to participate and listen to what you have to say.

Level 3: It's All about the Emotions Now

What It Looks Like

People who have escalated to this level in a conversation have moved well beyond concern over communicating in a professional manner. Their body language is aggressive and full of gestures (pointing, exaggerated arm movements). They may even stand up and pace the room as they speak. Their communication can better be described as ranting rather than the venting described at the previous level, and it may seem they are just barely hanging onto their self-control.

Their verbal message can consist of personal attacks directed at people, decisions, or the situation. They are often defensive and unwilling to accept responsibility for their comments or behaviors at this point. It is not uncommon for them to go on the offensive and aggressively attempt to shift blame or attention elsewhere. They may express feelings of injustice or paranoia. Sometimes they will start to cry and this can escalate to a point where they go into, as Oprah calls it, the "ugly cry." It is obvious the issue has tapped into a much deeper well of emotion than they are capable of handling in the moment. Whether angry or sad, their level of emotion is at a point where you must abandon any thought of proceeding with the conversation.

How to Manage It

Before you can proceed with your intended message, you must deal with the emotions being presented to you and, if you can, you should help your employee get to a calmer state. When an employee has entered this level of emotion, you may need to become assertive in your tone and language to get him to hear you and to take back control of the conversation. If he is presenting behavior that is inappropriate or of concern to you (e.g., profanity, yelling, any aggressive behavior), assertively tell him that he needs to stop that behavior and that the conversation will not resume until he does so. Make sure your tone is assertive without being aggressive, as matching his intensity note for note may feel like a threat to him and escalate his behavior.

At this level, using a firm, calm tone of voice and keeping your body language open is important. My experience is that people in this situation ultimately want to be heard and understood, so you can use that as leverage to help the employee ramp down his emotions. You might say something like,

Bob, I'm going to need you to lower your voice and stop using profanity before we can continue with our conversation.

You might also reiterate that you want to help him but that his point is getting lost in emotion. You might say,

Bob, I really want to understand what you are saying, but I am having a hard time right now. I think it would help if you could calm down so you can better explain your point to me.

You may also warn him that you will end the conversation if he is not able to continue in a professional manner.

Do not try to press on with the conversation when employees are in a highly emotional state. There have been many times when I have adjourned a conversation so that an employee could regroup after an emotional outburst or have sat there quietly with someone who was crying and needed several minutes to calm down enough so that we could resume the conversation.

You never should lose control of a conversation. Whatever the situation, you need to be confident and assertive enough to rein employees back in when they step over the line. If you do not address the concerning behavior immediately, it will likely continue, possibly escalating into more inappropriate and aggressive or violent behavior.

Watch your emotions as well. Sometimes when an employee's comments feel like a personal attack, it can be difficult to keep your cool and not get dragged into a shouting match. This is why it is helpful to have someone in the room with you when you are going to have a difficult conversation. If you ever get surprised and find yourself alone with an employee and the situation is deteriorating quickly, don't be afraid to call a time-out and adjourn the meeting. It shows more professionalism and leadership for you to walk away from an escalating situation than for you to stay in there and bang heads.

The key to understanding the emotion at this level is that you are ultimately able to calm the employee down. You may need to take a break to regroup, but eventually the employee listens to you and you are able to maintain control of the conversation.

Level 4: Show Stopper

What It Looks Like

At this stage the intensity of the emotion is preventing you from continuing with the conversation or you are at a point where you are concerned about your ability to maintain control. Safety begins to be a real concern. Employees do not respond to your requests to calm down or are unable to get control of their emotions enough to proceed. Their behavior during the conversation is so aggressive or inappropriate that it might actually result in your immediately terminating their employment.

I have been in conversations where the intended message was not job threatening, but the employee's response during the conversation was so inappropriate that it resulted in termination. In any event, there is no way for you to salvage the conversation or get it back on a productive track once it has reached Level 4.

How to Manage It

In this case, you manage the conversation by ending it. At Level 3 you would have already warned the employee that you will end the conversation if he does not get control of his emotions. Here you follow through with that warning and adjourn the meeting. Don't spend a lot of time and energy trying to explain your reasoning; he isn't listening now anyway. Tell him that you believe the conversation is no longer productive and that it is not in his best interest to try to continue. Let him know that the meeting is over for now, and that you will be in touch with him soon to discuss the next step.

Depending on the behavior demonstrated, you may want to consider involving other people after the meeting for support, such as contacting EAP or HR. If the behavior has been at all aggressive or threatening, you will need to deal with that as well. Ultimately you need to ensure your safety and the security of your workplace. Instances of aggressive or violent behavior, even if not directed at an individual, should not be tolerated and need to be dealt with quickly and decisively.

In the end, effectively handling emotions in the workplace can be one of the hardest skills for a leader to master. Although challenging, you should never avoid a conversation because you are worried about managing the employee's emotional reaction. Get the support you need and move forward. Some employees actually count on their managers being intimidated by emotions and will use this as a defense tactic to avoid receiving critical feedback, which leads us to our next objective.

Managing Defenses

The next objective in the feedback phase will be to manage the employee's defenses to receiving your feedback. Tough conversations come in all shapes and sizes and, while dealing with emotions is certainly a skill you need to develop, effectively maneuvering through the minefield of defenses that many employees set is a common challenge. While some defenses are not loud or emotional in nature, you can rest assured that their purpose is to protect the individual and to stop you from delivering a message the employee is afraid of or unwilling to hear.

While I believe most people are somewhat unaware in the moment that they are being defensive, I do believe that there are individuals who are expert manipulators who have learned how to purposely use these defensive behaviors to try to derail you from your intended message. Their goal is to distract your attention; to get you talking about something else off topic or to shift blame elsewhere. If they can control the situation and the conversation, their hope is that they can change your mind or distract you from your purpose. Some employees push back so hard that you wonder if, at some level, they believe that the discipline or feedback is invalidated if they do not accept it.

Be on the lookout for these common defensive behaviors the next time you are having a tough conversation; don't fall into their diversion trap. Remember, your goal is to take employees through the entire counseling process, which includes you delivering your intended feedback and any disciplinary message before the conversation concludes. Defenses are like quicksand, and if you get sucked into any of these, you might not be able to pull yourself out before the end of the conversation.

The Blame Game

In the blame game, employees try to shift the blame for their behavior or the performance in question to someone or something else. For every point you make, they counter with details and facts that support why they are not at fault. Sometimes they will even point the finger of blame at you in an effort to evoke feelings of guilt and insecurity. Their message is clear; they are not to blame but rather they are a victim of circumstance. Their goal is to avoid accepting the responsibility so that they can ultimately avoid the discipline.

If you encounter this defense I suggest trying to move the employee out of victim mode by helping him to identify specific behaviors, actions, decisions, or choices he's made that contributed to the issue at hand. Do not accept his excuses. Ask him, *"What actions could you have taken that would have brought about a different result?"* or *"What part of this do you own?"* If you try a couple of times to get him to own his behavior and he still won't, it may be a situation that has roots deep into his self-esteem and you are not going to get him to accept responsibility. In that case, let him know that you are disappointed he is not taking ownership for his behaviors and move on with your message. You can always circle back another day to see if he is more receptive to accepting responsibility.

The Stonewall

In a stonewall maneuver, employees totally shut down and minimally participate in the conversation, if at all. Their answers are short and do not provide much in the way of information or understanding. They may even go completely silent. Physically they may be avoiding eye contact, looking down at the floor, or shifted in the chair so that a portion of their back is facing you. It is hard to tell exactly what they are feeling because they are not communicating much of anything. Their silence could be based in fear or anger, but you don't know for sure. Their behaviors and lack of interaction are a defense intended to block the conversation from moving forward.

My suggestion here is to address the situation head on. Say to the employee, *"I noticed that you are not making eye contact with me and that you seem to be upset. What are you thinking about right now?"* Let your employee know that your intention is to have a productive two-way conversation with him and ask him to participate. If the behavior continues, tell him that you would prefer it if he would participate in the conversation, but you will proceed even if he chooses not to engage. If the resistance to interacting with you persists, deliver your feedback and explain any consequences and then end the conversation.

Taking the Offensive

They say the best defense is a good offense, and some employees use this as their strategy to control the direction of the conversation. Their goal is to grab control of the conversation from the get-go. Once they start talking, you will not be able to get a word in edgewise.

In an effort to get you off their scent they will throw anyone and everyone under the proverbial bus. *"I don't understand why you are talking to me about this when you have people doing things ten times worse right under your nose."* I've heard that reasoning more than once. And it's tempting; what manager wouldn't want to hear about what else is going wrong? And that is when they suck you in.

The challenge with managing this defensive maneuver is to stick to the subject at hand and not let the employee sway you from the issue you want to discuss. If he brings up other subjects that peak your interest, tell him that you would like to hear more about that in a minute, but first you need to finish discussing the issue that specifically relates to him. You may need to say multiple times during the conversation, *"But we are talking about you right now."* That's okay, say it as many times as needed to bring the conversation back on track. If his efforts to control the focus of the conversation really start to prevent forward progress, then stop the discussion and address the behavior directly. Once identified openly as a defense, you should be able to neutralize its effectiveness and proceed with the conversation.

Playing on Your Emotions

We discussed dealing with emotions at length in the previous section, but let's add one more thing here as it relates to emotions as a defense. Some people become very skilled at identifying when their manager is uncomfortable dealing with a certain emotion, and once they figure it out, they go right to that place as quickly as they can in every tough conversation.

I have heard a number of male managers confess that they fall apart when a female employee cries during a conversation. Others are intimidated by raised voices or signs of anger. These managers quickly abandon their message when the emotions they are sensitive to are brought into the mix. Unfortunately, employees in a counseling session will use this knowledge to their advantage to take control of conversations and attempt to sidestep discipline.

You may also come "predisposed" if you will, to be more sympathetic to certain life situations because of your background. Personal situations such as someone struggling with cancer, being a single parent, or going through a divorce can really tap into a well of sympathy and compassion in you if you have experienced similar situations in your life. In some cases it can cause you to have a blind spot, to tolerate bad behavior or poor performance longer than you should, or lead you to make allowances and exceptions that you wouldn't normally make.

I have seen employees overplay the sympathy card many times in an effort to pull on the heartstrings of their manager and avoid discipline. To be clear, I am not saying you shouldn't show compassion for someone struggling with a difficult life situation, but I am suggesting that you should be cautious and not let your emotions prevent you from taking appropriate action. Increase your awareness of when your emotions can cloud your decision-making process. If you are dealing with an employee whose situation hits a little too close to home, make sure you use your support team to ensure that your decisions are fair and equitable and don't adversely impact the rest of your team.

If you do find that a conversation has triggered any of these defenses, bring the discussion back on track as soon as possible. Even the most experienced managers can find themselves caught up in one of these defenses temporarily, but the really good leaders can identify what has happened quickly before too much time is wasted and get back on to their intended message.

Handle Distractions and Interruptions

If you have managed the details ahead of time you should be able to effectively eliminate or limit the amount of disruptions you will encounter while conducting your conversation. You've done this by choosing an appropriate location for the conversation, turning off or forwarding phones and email, and letting a trusted employee know you are about to have a private conversation so you should not be interrupted. But even the best planning cannot totally prevent something from happening in the moment so you need to be aware of your surroundings and be prepared to deal with situations as they arise.

For the best results, you want everyone's attention to be focused on the conversation, not drifting off to other areas of concern. This might mean suspending a meeting in order to deal with a more immediate issue that is distracting you or your employee. Here are a few examples of distractions I have encountered over the years. In each of these examples the manager did not suspend the meeting or acknowledge the distraction, which only aggravated the situation.

Inclement Weather

At certain times of the year, in many geographical locations, the weather can be a very real distraction. I observed a manager attempting to continue a performance discussion with an employee while she watched heavy snow falling outside the window and the rest of the office packed up to leave for the day. In the Midwest a manager tried to finish a discussion during a tornado warning (we could see it from the high-rise window), and in my hometown of Orlando, it was an approaching hurricane.

In all of these situations the employees were no longer listening to the managers' feedback because of the focus on the approaching severe weather. Inclement weather conditions worry employees. They worry about their own safety going home and the safety of family members. Their children may be home alone or on their way home from school as the storm moves in. Don't try to fight it. Acknowledge and appreciate severe weather conditions as a distraction and suspend or postpone meetings accordingly.

Loud Noises

It may sound like common sense, but you should suspend a meeting or find another location if there are noises outside your location that are loud and distracting. Don't be like one manager who was so focused on finishing a difficult conversation that he attempted to continue it while the building fire alarm was sounding. Needless to say, he lost the attention of the employee as soon as the alarm went off. Loud construction noise, noise from a meeting in the next room, or background noise from people suddenly gathering in the hall outside your quiet conversation nook all need to be acknowledged as distractions and dealt with immediately.

Time of Day

If you anticipate a lengthy discussion, don't start your meeting just before noon or at the end of the employee's shift unless it is absolutely necessary. Hunger will distract anyone. If you are going to meet over the lunch hour give the employees prior notice so they have the option of eating early or arrange for lunch to be brought in.

Also, don't assume everyone has flexibility in their work schedule. Some people have family obligations that require them to be home at a certain time and holding them past their normal departure hour can be very upsetting to them. Be cognizant of this and ask permission first from employees if you need to schedule a meeting that may fall outside of their traditional working hours. That includes early breakfast meetings. If a meeting is running long, show consideration and ask if they need to leave or offer to suspend the meeting and reconvene at a more convenient time if possible.

People Interruptions

There may be times when even though you've asked not to be interrupted, a minor (or major) crisis erupts and someone determines it is important enough to disrupt your meeting. If this happens, excuse yourself and step outside of the room for a moment to deal with the interruption. If the crisis can be handled within a minute or two, do so and then return to the conversation quickly. Apologize for the disruption and pick up where you left off.

If you determine it is going to take more than a few minutes of your time to resolve the problem and it takes priority over your meeting, return to the room, apologize for the interruption, and suspend the meeting. If you can offer some sort of general explanation for suspending the meeting, try to do so; it will help ease any hurt or slight the employee may be feeling. Do not leave him hanging there not knowing when the meeting will resume. If possible, give him a sense of how long the interruption will be or, better yet, confirm a new meeting time.

Determine If You Are on Course

Now that you've effectively handled any interruptions, you need to determine if there was anything brought to light during the course of your discussion that leads you to reconsider your final message. Again, often new information will be offered that either requires more investigation or somewhat alters your final message to the employee, so be open to making changes if appropriate.

Your ability to remain open during a counseling session allows for this type of last minute change in direction. As the driver of the bus, it is your responsibility to determine if you are still on point with your intended message or if you need to suspend the meeting so that additional investigation or conversations can take place.

As we discussed before, sometimes this determination is as simple as looking around the room to the other managers present and getting silent confirmation that you can move forward as planned. Other times, you may need to call a brief time-out so that you can quickly huddle up outside of the employee's presence to confirm your direction and understanding. You also may choose to suspend the end of the conversation in order to gather more information and have additional conversations. All of these scenarios can and should be discussed in your pre-meeting so there is not an awkward lull in the conversation when you come to this point.

Transition to the Close

Once you've decided you can move forward, it is time to transition to the closing phase. The closing is where you will deliver your final message to the employee. At this point, the majority of the give-and-take of the conversation has ended. It is important to make it clear to the employee that the feedback portion of the conversation has ended and to set the tone for the closing, which is often more directive than conversational in nature.

This transition can easily be accomplished in a couple of sentences. Start by thanking the employee for his participation and for his input. Summarize any key points that were made during the feedback phase and specifically cite any areas of agreement or commitments that were made during the conversation. Then, move into the closing where you will cover any disciplinary actions being taken and articulate possible future consequences should the issue present itself again.

KEY LEARNING POINTS FROM THIS CHAPTER

- The majority of your time during a counseling conversation will be spent in the feedback phase, approximately 70 percent.

- To help you flush out the details of a situation, ask good open-ended questions that naturally encourage the employee to provide you with more details.

- Ensure that your word choice and body language do not inadvertently send a negative message to the employee and shut down the discussion.

- Use one of these formulas to provide feedback when you are feeling anxious about the process and do not feel like you can find the words.

  - C.A.R. Formula: Circumstance, Action, Result

  - "While I Appreciate . . ." Formula:

    - "While I appreciate. . . ."

    - "I have a concern. . . ."

    - "Might I suggest. . . ."

- Use I-statements to phrase your feedback in a way that speaks to your feelings, beliefs, and opinions. I-statements help to keep defenses down and tend to sound less accusatory to the recipient.

- You need to actively deal with any emotion in a conversation that distracts you from proceeding with your message or gets in the way of the employee accurately hearing and understanding what you are saying.

- Identify when an individual is allowing a defense to get in the way of taking in your feedback. Bring the conversation quickly back on topic and do not get distracted by the defense.

- Effectively handle distractions or interruptions to your conversations, suspending the discussion if necessary so that you have the employee's full attention.

14 Chapter

The Close

The truth will set you free, but first it will make you miserable.

Mark Twain

As an HR manager, I would routinely follow up with employees after they finished an important conversation with their manager to make sure they understood the feedback and to gauge their emotional state. Too often when I asked them to articulate the one important message they heard in their conversation with their manager, they were at a loss. The message the manager was confident had been delivered and understood was actually missed entirely. In the end, the employee walked away unclear of the purpose of the meeting, but more importantly, did not fully understand the consequences of repeating the behavior or failing to change.

Before every conversation you should ask yourself, "What is my message here?" While it varies with the specifics of each situation, I would generally define your message as this—the one thing you want the employee to understand most when she walks out of the meeting. Is her job in jeopardy? What happens if she repeats the behavior? Where does she stand in terms of her performance? You know you've done a great job delivering your message when your employee can accurately sum up the entire conversation in one or two sentences.

The Closing Phase

In a counseling conversation, the closing is where you deliver or reinforce your message. Here you will make it crystal clear to the employee exactly where she stands and what you think about her behavior or current performance. It is also where you will let her know the consequences of not changing her performance or repeating the behavior again in the future.

The closing has a much different tone from the opening and the feedback phases. It is typically more direct and one-way rather than conversational and engaging. Your job in the closing phase is to:

1. Deliver your message.
2. Explain the or-else clause.
3. Check for understanding and answer questions.
4. Discuss follow-up meetings.
5. Introduce documentation.
6. Close the meeting.

While you can make mistakes in the first two phases of your discussion and still have a productive conversation in the end, it is critical that you are at the top of your game in the closing phase to ensure you hit all the key points effectively. If you don't, you can undo any of the good foundation that was laid earlier in the conversation. Let's take a closer look at each of these closing objectives individually.

Deliver Your Message

Here is where the rubber meets the road. Up until this point you and your employee have been discussing the details of an issue, but you may not have been entirely clear about your final message yet. It is absolutely essential at this point that you say the words directly and clearly, with no beating around the bush. If you stop short now, your employee may totally miss the purpose of the discussion. While it is easy for me to say be honest and direct, I do understand how difficult the reality of that can be sometimes.

If you find this sort of direct and honest feedback uncomfortable to deliver, you still have some internal work to do. Whether you are afraid of confrontation, concerned about hurting feelings, or worried about what the others will think of you, these are all internal obstacles that you need to work through before sitting down with the employee. If you are not feeling confident about delivering the message you will not be able to hide it during the closing.

Sometimes you may not be in complete agreement with the message, but because of your position or office politics, you are asked to be the one to deliver it. This situation is a little different. Because of the power structure of organizations, managers are sometimes asked to deliver messages that they do not personally support. If this is the case, before the meeting with the employee you need to voice your concerns assertively and appropriately to those individuals farther up the organizational chart. In the end, they may make a decision that you do not agree with, but you must execute and support.

I have been in a number of these situations myself over the years and, while I didn't personally like or agree with the message, I owned it while I was in the room in front of the employee. Showing your dissent to the employee during the conversation is a sure way to fracture a team, undermine leadership, or muddy the waters. Most employees can tell if you, as their manager, do not believe in the message you are delivering so if they see any hesitation on your part for whatever reason, they may read it as wiggle room and not take you or the conversation seriously.

Remember the story I shared at the beginning of Dave's termination and how he took every opportunity to see hope in his manager's vague message. This scenario is actually quite common. If you don't state directly and clearly the seriousness of the situation and the possible outcomes if it isn't resolved (especially if his job is in jeopardy), the consequences often don't become real to the employee.

In my opinion, it is in the closing portion of the conversation that you can best demonstrate the kind of leader you are. By saying the words that are uncomfortable, by being honest and compassionate, and by directly stating the reality of the situation, you will demonstrate to your employees that you are concerned for their welfare and you will show them the respect they deserve.

As part of the planning process you should have given significant thought to what message you want to deliver during the closing, but remember to remain open and flexible. Avoid a situation where you plow forward no matter what. Sometimes new information comes to light during the feedback phase that prompts you to rethink your message. For instance, you are planning on giving someone a final warning, but during the discussion she provides you with new information that leads you to believe the final warning might be too harsh an action to take. Be confident enough to reconsider your initial decision and do what is right by the employee.

If that does happen, use a time-out to reconfirm the direction you are taking with your counterparts in the meeting and to rewrite any documentation you prepared ahead of time. If the new information is not significant enough to make you change direction, then you can proceed with delivering your message. It is a mark of a good leader to show that you are confident enough to be open to new input and are not locked into a course of action come hell or high water.

Crafting Your Message

Obviously, the exact phrasing and content of your message during the closing phase will vary with the specifics of the situation, but to give you an idea of what a well-crafted message looks like, some general examples are given below.

For Poor Performance

"It is important that you clearly understand the situation you are in. As we've discussed, you are not currently meeting your performance goals and you need to bring your performance up to an acceptable level immediately. If you do not make the necessary improvements, your job may be in jeopardy. We will review your progress again in 30 days."

"As we've agreed, providing outstanding customer service is our top priority. Bottom line, the way you interacted with our customer yesterday is unacceptable to us. If you feel you need additional training, please let me know immediately; otherwise, going forward, I expect you to follow the established guidelines for handling customer complaints."

For Behavior Issues

"While I now have a better understanding of the issues that lead up to the disagreement, it is never acceptable for you to use profanity in the workplace. Please refrain from using it again and find a more professional way to communicate your feelings."

"Thank you for explaining your thought process to me. It helps me to put your actions into context. But that does not change the fact that going into a restricted area after hours is absolutely prohibited. In the future, please come see me if you have a need to access an area that is off limits and I will assist you."

As you can see, each of these statements articulates clearly what the problem is and what needs to change. These statements are good examples of what you might say when you need to let employees know that their behavior or performance is unacceptable but there are not yet specific or immediate consequences if they were to continue with the current performance or repeat the behavior again. You could use these general messages early in the disciplinary process, when the issue is being addressed for the first time.

But what if you've already warned the employee several times and the performance or behavior still has not improved? At that point, her window of opportunity to change is growing short (or nonexistent). The stakes are much higher, and there are usually serious and often job-threatening consequences to not making a change or doing the offending behavior again. As tough conversations increase in urgency and seriousness, there is a second and absolutely essential element that you need to include in your message in order for it to have greater impact, and that is the or-else clause.

The Or-Else Clause

Simply put, the "or-else" clause is the statement of what will happen next if the employee does not improve her performance or demonstrates the behavior again. In other words, the or-else clause outlines the consequences for the employee. All conversations should have a message, but not every message needs to have an or-else clause.

To determine if you need an or-else clause ask yourself, *"What is it that I am prepared to do if the behavior repeats or the performance does not improve?"* If it is not critical that the employee immediately change her behavior, and by critical I mean job threatening, then you may not need an or-else clause in your message. But if your intent is to formally discipline her in any way, especially if you might consider terminating her employment at some point, you absolutely need an or-else clause so that you clearly and directly tell her what those potential consequences will be.

There are many ways to communicate the or-else clause. I typically use a version of the following in my written documentation:

"Failure to correct this issue (or improve performance) may result in further disciplinary action up to and including the termination of your employment."

I appreciate that this is somewhat formal language and it definitely has a legal ring to it, but it seems to fit the tone that is used in documentation when you are in the later stages of the disciplinary process. When you are speaking face to face with someone, you may prefer to use more casual language that clearly states what will happen next. This is okay, just be careful not to water down or candy-coat the consequences with your word choice. Remember, the temptation to soften the blow with your language is strong for some people, so be aware if you find you are pulling back from your intended message out of insecurities.

So how do you know exactly what you should say? Determining the or-else clause is a fairly simple process. Based on the situation you are addressing, ask yourself one of the following questions:

Performance

"If they do not demonstrate improvement in their performance, what will I do next, how long will I give them to improve, and could they lose their job?"

Behavior

"If they do this again, are there consequences and would I terminate their employment?"

We will speak in more detail about the documentation process in a later chapter, but for now, to begin to give you a better idea of how to build consequences and time periods into your messages, I have changed the messages used as examples in the section above to include an or-else clause.

Examples for Poor Performance

"It is important that you clearly understand the situation you are in. As we've discussed, you are not currently meeting your performance goals and you need to bring your performance up to an acceptable level immediately. If you do not make the necessary improvements, your job may be in jeopardy. We will review your progress again in 30 days. **(or-else clause) If at that time you have not demonstrated and maintained significant improvement in your performance, further disciplinary action may result, up to and including you being placed on final performance probation or termination of your employment."*

"As we've agreed, providing outstanding customer service is our top priority. Bottom line, the way you interacted with our customer yesterday was unacceptable to us. If you need additional training, please let me know. Otherwise, going forward, I expect you to follow the established guidelines for handling customer complaints. **(or-else**

clause) You need to immediately improve your performance in the area of customer service. If you have another negative customer interaction, further disciplinary action may be taken, up to and including being placed on final performance probation or the termination of your employment."

Examples for Behavior Issues

"While I now have a better understanding of the issues that lead up to the disagreement, it is never acceptable for you to use profanity in the workplace (or-else clause) and it is totally unacceptable behavior. Should you use profanity again when speaking with a coworker or customer, you may receive a final written warning or depending on the severity of the situation, your employment may be terminated."

"Thank you for explaining your thought process to me. It helps me to put your actions into context. But that does not change the fact that going into a restricted area after hours is absolutely prohibited. (or-else clause) In the future, if you go into a restricted area without proper authorization, further disciplinary action may be taken up to and including the termination of your employment."

Leaving Yourself Options

A quick comment before we leave this section about language and the difference between stating you **"will"** be terminated versus you **"may"** be terminated. I fully understand the argument behind telling someone that you *will* absolutely fire them if they repeat a behavior if that is your intention. It's full disclosure, right?

But I have been around the block enough times to know that quite often what seems like a certainty today may turn into a situation where you would like some flexibility tomorrow. Even though you may feel absolutely certain today that you would terminate employment, I am a strong supporter of providing managers with the ability to use their discretion at a later date without feeling unnecessarily boxed into a corner by an or-else clause they uttered months prior.

In this case, being a little less specific can actually help from a legal perspective as well. Whatever you say you will do in documentation you need to follow through with in action. Let me say that again:

Whatever you say you will do in documentation you need to follow through with in action.

If you don't, you can end up weakening your position in the event of legal action down the road. So while it might feel right to accentuate your message by telling your employee that you "will" fire her if she behaves badly again, I am suggesting that you adopt as your standard the less absolute language that you "may" fire her instead.

By using "may," you don't compromise anything in terms of seriousness or urgency in your message by leaving the door open, as terminating her employment is still very much on the table as an option. But by backing off a little in your language, you will allow yourself the flexibility to discern the appropriate severity of discipline down the road given the length of time between occurrences and the specific circumstances of the situation, without feeling like you were exaggerating in an earlier conversation or making idle threats.

We've talked a lot about the importance of articulating the or-else clause, but sometimes as we all know, situations can get away from us in real life. We think we are being honest, but we end up pulling our punches in order to spare employees' feelings or to avoid scaring them. To help illustrate this, let me tell you about Wayne.

Wayne's Story

Wayne worked in the sales department and his performance had been less than impressive for some time. Because he had not achieved his annual sales goals the prior year, his manager had been meeting with him formally for the last several months to track his progress on this year's goals.

It was now the beginning of May and while Wayne's sales numbers were not terrible, they were still well below his goals for the year and Wayne was definitely struggling. In contrast to Wayne's performance, the rest of the sales team was doing very well and they were all on target to reach their mid-year goals.

Wayne's manager, Sue, was very concerned that his performance was not improving, and she was getting a lot of pressure from her boss to either correct the situation or to cut Wayne loose. Sue liked Wayne and did not want to see him lose his job, but her boss had given her until the end of June to manage the situation or he threatened to step in and take care of things himself. Obviously Sue did not want to appear to be an ineffective manager to her boss, so given the seriousness of the situation for both her and Wayne, Sue asked me to sit in on her next conversation with Wayne.

We met Wayne in a conference room later that day and once the pleasantries were out of the way (the opening), Sue pulled out the most recent production reports and started to go through them with Wayne. Wayne seemed to understand what his goals were and that his numbers were not where they needed to be. He offered several excuses as to why his sales numbers were sluggish. During the exchange Wayne looked very relaxed. He didn't appear to be defensive as they talked, but generally concerned about the situation.

Sue took out the action plan she had given Wayne a couple of months prior and the two of them had a very productive conversation about his daily activities and what things specifically he could do to possibly improve his results (feedback phase). Overall, their interaction was light and productive.

It seemed clear that Sue was winding down the meeting when she began to pack up her papers. I took that opportunity to ask Wayne how he felt about the plan and his current production levels.

"I really wish I could be doing more," he said. "I feel like I am dragging the team down right now. I hate that everyone has to pick up my slack."

His response made me feel comfortable that he understood where his performance stood and how his lack of sales was impacting the rest of the team. That was good, Wayne seemed to understand the problem.

Although I felt the conversation had been productive, I had not heard Sue specifically speak once to the urgency of Wayne needing to improve his results, or for that matter, the consequences if he failed to improve. Knowing his job was on the line if he didn't improve by the end of June I asked Wayne an important question.

"Wayne," I asked, "what is your understanding of where you stand with regard to your current performance?"

He hesitated for a moment, and then answered speaking more to Sue than to me. "I know I have to get my numbers up. Sue has been a great support and it helps to know your boss has faith in you. I know I should be doing a lot more of the prospecting activities listed here in this plan, but it is so hard to find the time to get out and drive around. We have some big accounts that need my attention in the next couple of months, but I think that I will be able to kick it into high gear in the fall and finish the year on target."

There it was. He did not understand that his current performance was job threatening. On top of that, he had no idea that he would not be employed past

July 1 unless he showed significant improvement. While Sue was providing Wayne with tremendous emotional support and she was clearly communicating that his sales production level was a problem, she had not said the words to Wayne that he most needed to hear. She had not delivered the all-important message with the or-else clause.

I wasn't sure why Sue had not been totally honest with Wayne about the urgency of his situation, but I suspected she was reluctant to deliver such a serious message to someone she believed in and was trying to support. I knew we needed to finish the conversation and move into the closing phase, so I provided Sue with some prompting. I asked her very directly, "Sue, just so Wayne is clear about where he currently stands, is his job in jeopardy?"

Sue immediately looked down at the table and Wayne shot her a panicked look. Sitting physically taller in her chair I could see Sue gathering her courage. Finally she said, "Wayne, you are in real trouble here. You have struggled to hit your sales numbers for almost a year now. You are at a very serious point and you need to start improving immediately."

Wayne sat back, taking in the message. I sensed Sue needed a little more help to deliver the rest of her message.

"Okay" I said speaking directly to Sue, "so we are at a point where Wayne absolutely needs to make significant progress toward his goals. How much time does he actually have to show you this improvement?"

"He has until the end of June, about another seven and a half weeks," Sue said. I could see her body relax now that the truth was out in the open.

I kept going. Again to Sue I said, "Just so everyone is really clear here, what will be the consequences if Wayne is not able to show you significant improvement by the end of June?"

Sue had finally found her voice. She turned directly to Wayne and said, "I am very sorry Wayne, but if you can't get your numbers up to where they need to be by the end of June, you will lose your job."

Wayne's eyes got big and he looked like he had just swallowed a bug. As her message started to sink in, he began asking Sue questions about exactly what he needed to show her to keep his job. They talked for another thirty minutes and when Wayne left the conference room, there was a new sense of urgency and purpose in his steps.

Afterward, I asked Sue why she hadn't been that clear before with Wayne. She said that she was afraid to be too honest with him, that the truth might even de-motivate him, and she hesitated to add the extra pressure of potentially losing his job to the equation. She wanted him to stay positive and focused so he would keep trying to hit his goals.

As manager of the department, Sue absolutely had a vested interest in Wayne's success. She had communicated to him that the situation was important, but had stopped short of telling him specifically that it was job threatening and that his time was running out. She was not only hurting Wayne by candy-coating the message, she was hurting herself.

This story does have a happy ending. Wayne really ramped up his efforts and he made it successfully past the June deadline. Now that he clearly understood the reality of his situation, he was able to make better decisions with his workload and give his sales-generating activities top priority. In this case, Wayne's fear of losing his job became just the motivation he needed to improve his performance.

Check for Understanding and Answer Questions

Before you leave any feedback conversation, it is vital that you check to make sure that the employee has accurately heard what you said, that she fully understands the message you intended to deliver, and she appreciates the implications of the or-else clause. This not only ensures that employees receive your message, but that you accurately delivered it as you had intended. Remember, communication is a two-way street. You are only successful when you are accurately heard.

After you deliver your message and explain the consequences of a repeat offense (if applicable), ask the employee if she has any questions about what you've just said. Allow her to ask questions to clarify her understanding of your message or the consequences, but do not allow her to launch back into a discussion of the issue. Some people will take this opportunity to try to argue the points again in an effort to change or soften the consequences. Try not to let that happen.

By the time you are in the position of delivering your message, you should be very confident that it is accurate and appropriate for the situation at hand, so at this point do not engage in further discussion about its validity. You may have to hold a hard line here and politely shut down your employee's desire to argue or negotiate. Keep the conversation focused on questions relating to her understanding your message and the potential consequences.

Once your employee has exhausted all her questions, you should ask her to summarize in her own words your message and the or-else clause. This will allow you to determine if you effectively articulated the message you wanted to communicate and to confirm she accurately heard what you said. If there is a disconnect anywhere, you have the opportunity to tweak your message or correct any misunderstandings before adjourning the meeting.

Remember, people have a lot going on during difficult conversations; intellectually and emotionally. They are trying to process what is happening, attempting to maintain control of their emotions, and trying to manage their defenses which could be working overtime to filter out the scary parts of your message. Consciously or unconsciously, they could have edited out important information. That is why it is so critical that you take an extra minute to confirm they received the intended message.

Here is an example of how I might check for understanding:

> *"We've discussed a lot during this meeting and*
> *I just want to make sure that we are all on the same*
> *page before we walk out of this room. Could you share*
> *with me, in your own words, your understanding*
> *of the important message I gave you today and the*
> *consequences to you if your performance does not*
> *improve (or 'if you repeat this behavior')?"*

Discuss Follow-Up Meetings

The next step in the closing is to determine if the situation warrants scheduling a follow-up meeting to continue the conversation or to review the employee's progress. Some situations only require additional conversations if the issue or behavior presents itself again, such as with inappropriate behavior (aggression, use of profanity, insubordination, negative comments about coworkers or customers) or attendance issues. The hope is always that once you've addressed an issue, the employee will make the appropriate changes and the undesirable behavior will not repeat itself.

In the case of performance issues, the opposite is actually true. It is almost always appropriate that you schedule at least one additional follow-up meeting to review progress, especially if you are placing them on a formal performance probation. These additional meetings should be scheduled regularly during the probationary period and are intended as a formal opportunity for you to provide the employee with concrete feedback regarding her progress. As unnerving as it can be to be placed on probation, it is even more stressful to never hear feedback regarding your progress. Keeping your employee in the dark regarding her progress undermines her confidence and can mislead her into thinking her performance is acceptable when it is not.

As a leader, you want to ensure you are providing your employees with all the feedback and support they will need to correct any issues and reach their full potential. Frequent positive feedback helps them to build confidence and momentum so they can overcome their performance issues. Timely constructive feedback lets them know exactly where they stand in the process. If they are not meeting expectations and the improvement is not significant, your honest assessment of their progress can help them to mentally prepare for losing their job. Either way, with regular feedback meetings, they have a timely and accurate understanding of their current performance and you minimize any surprises at the end.

And when you commit to meeting with the employee to review her progress weekly—DO IT! I can't stress this point enough. Failure to hold up your end of the bargain is unacceptable and it damages your credibility. It indicates that you are clearly not committed to the success of this employee as you cannot even be bothered to follow through on what you agreed to in your meeting and in writing. Even if there hasn't been enough time to evaluate the performance or to observe any improvement, if you agreed to a weekly follow-up meeting, keep the meeting and share whatever feedback you do have. At the very least, it is a great opportunity to connect with your employee and to motivate her to work harder.

Too often I see managers have long emotionally draining conversations with employees about their performance and at the end, they commit to doing whatever they can to be supportive. Then a few days later, they cancel or postpone indefinitely the follow-up feedback meetings. This type of behavior sends conflicting messages to employees, leaving them wondering how committed you are to their improvement and if they can trust what you say.

The ultimate responsibility to improve performance should fall on each employee, so if she fails in the end, she is the one who is accountable. When you do not provide the support you commit to, in the way you've committed to do it, you are giving the employee someone else to blame for her failure, and you've shifted responsibility from her to you. You do not want to put yourself in that position. It weakens you as a leader and it undermines your legal position should you terminate the employee at the end of the performance probation period. The message here is simple: whatever you commit to, follow through without exception.

Introduce Documentation

One of the questions I get asked the most is "Do I need to document this conversation?" The answer is almost always yes. Unfortunately in our challenging legal climate, it's usually not good enough to just know you've had a feedback conversation; you need to be able to prove you've had it. Documentation provides you with a certain level of proof. It leaves a written trail of the conversations you've had with your employees that others can follow.

Depending on the situation you are addressing and its level of seriousness, you will make a decision regarding the use of documentation and if appropriate, what type you will use. Documentation can take a variety of forms depending on the seriousness of the discussion and overall situation. It can be prepared ahead of time and produced at the end of the meeting or it can be created after the meeting using the content from your discussion and offered for signature during a follow-up meeting.

While I strongly believe in documenting most performance conversations with employees and providing them with a copy, I don't believe that all documentation requires an employee's signature. We will discuss documentation in much greater detail in a subsequent section, but for now, know that at this point in the conversation, this would be the time for you to address the topic of documentation with the employee.

Close the Meeting

You are now at the point where it is time to wrap up the conversation and conclude the meeting. Your message has been delivered, you've answered any questions, and if appropriate, you've scheduled a follow-up meeting.

During the closing phase it is also important that you thank the employee for her participation. You should thank her in a way that is sincere and honest; in some cases, depending on the tone of the meeting and the employee's attitude, this might be a little tricky.

Some meetings just don't go well and employees get emotional or conduct themselves in a way that is not flattering. Look past any momentary outbursts or emotional defenses and find something to thank them for that is sincere. Thank them for their time, for being honest, for listening so well, for participating, for sharing their point of view, or for just being open to hearing the feedback.

This is an area where you can quickly cross over from genuine sincerity to an appearance of condescension, so be careful to choose something that you honestly appreciate about her role in the meeting. Counseling conversations can be stressful and if the employee has behaved in a professional and dignified way even while hearing unpleasant feedback, acknowledge that professionalism and maturity so you reinforce that behavior for future conversations. Thanking her also allows the conversation to end on a somewhat positive note.

When the meeting has concluded, stand up as a nonverbal signal to the employee and anyone else who participated in the discussion that the meeting is adjourned and that they can leave. I have been in meetings where the employee was so focused on processing the information she just received that she did not get up to leave when the meeting was over. The manager leading the meeting never got up from his chair, so everyone just sat there in awkward silence, wondering who was going to be the first person to move. Avoid this situation and either get up yourself to leave the room or have someone else in the room get up to open the door for the employee.

There may be times when the employee is not fully in control of her emotions at the end of the meeting and she may need a few moments to compose herself before leaving the office. Be respectful of employees and never do anything to cause them to lose their dignity. If you sense the employee would be embarrassed to go out into the public office space at that moment, let her know that it is alright if she remains behind for a few minutes to compose herself, and then you leave the office.

This is often where it is very helpful to have an HR manager as part of the meeting so she can stay behind to provide additional emotional support and to help the employee process the feedback you have just given her. Over the years I learned to become very comfortable with silence, allowing distraught employees to pull themselves together before walking out of the room. If you do stay with an employee, be very careful of what you say in that moment. It is human nature to want to make people feel better. It would be tempting in an effort to provide comfort and support to start talking and undo or negate some of the earlier messages, so refrain from launching back into the conversation.

Now that you've adjourned the meeting, the hard part is over and you are through with the process of preparing for and conducting a difficult conversation with an employee. Once you get comfortable with the format, you can use this process to conduct almost any feedback session or counseling conversation. In fact, the tools we discussed in this section for providing feedback and handling emotional responses can easily transfer to situations in your personal life. By practicing these skills and using the tools and formulas presented, you will build your confidence and take the fear out of feedback.

KEY LEARNING POINTS FROM THIS CHAPTER

- It is essential that you deliver your message and any or-else clause during the closing phase of the conversation. Employees have a right to know the problem (your message) and if there are any consequences to their behavior or performance (the or-else clause).

- Be clear, direct, and honest when delivering your message. Vagueness and candy-coating of your message only compound the issue. Remember: You have to say the words.

- In your message, clearly state the problem or issue, the effect it had on others or the company, and what needs to change.

- Your or-else clause is a description of what you are prepared to do in response to the employee behavior repeating or the performance not improving, in other words, the consequences.

- Your most formal or legal language is usually found in the or-else clause, so make sure you use your resources (HR, attorney) to help you craft the language.

- Use the word may instead of the word will in your statement of consequences. You need to follow through with action whatever you say you will do in your documentation, so the less absolute wording of may offers you future options.

- Before you adjourn the meeting, make sure you ask the employee to repeat what she's understood as the message and the or-else clause to check her comprehension. This allows you to clarify any misunderstandings.

- Schedule a follow-up meeting if appropriate. If you do schedule another meeting, make sure you follow through and have it. You will undermine the effectiveness of your conversation and your credibility if you do not keep your commitments.

- Address the topic of documentation by either presenting them with a memo or stating that documentation is forthcoming.

15 Chapter

Terminating Employment

Recession is when a neighbor loses his job.
Depression is when you lose yours.

Ronald Reagan

No one really enjoys firing people, except maybe Donald Trump. If you are in a leadership position, terminating someone's employment will likely become a reality for you at some point. As much as you might wish otherwise, you will have at least one employee who will significantly underperform or who will make ill-advised choices that will lead you to make the tough decision to terminate his employment. Shying away from the responsibility of making that decision will only perpetuate the problem and damage your credibility with others, as people will question your reasons for failing to act decisively.

The termination conversation can be one of the most difficult to have emotionally, but it is technically really one of the easiest to conduct, if you have effectively handled the progressive discipline process along the way. If you have been consistently providing the employees with honest and direct feedback, documenting your conversations, and warning them of the potential consequences of their continued bad behavior or poor performance, then the termination discussion can be very short. Your goal is to maintain the employee's dignity and cover all your bases legally in those final moments. Your success with this comes down to your ability to be honest and say the words.

To help you orchestrate the termination conversation, you will follow many of the same steps and use the same skills covered throughout this book, although you will be using a very streamlined version of the process due to the nature of the situation. When it comes to terminations, the vast majority of your time will be spent preparing for the conversation rather than executing it.

In most situations, you will be communicating the termination message as a result of one of these scenarios:

- At the end of the progressive discipline process where the employee failed to change his behavior or improve his performance.
- In response to a behavior/performance issue that rises to the level of immediate termination without prior warning.
- As a result of a job elimination or layoff decision.

The Format of a Termination Conversation

Whether you are terminating for bad behavior, poor performance or downsizing, the process of preparing for and conducting the termination conversation will be similar. Many of the steps will look familiar to you as we have covered them already in great length, but I will walk you through the mechanics of the conversation so that you can see how the process works specifically for terminations.

Prepare for the Conversation

More than any other conversation, you will want to make sure your ducks are all in a row when conducting a termination. Before conducting the termination conversation you will want to confirm that your investigation into the issue or situation is complete and that you have all the information you need to make the final decision to end employment.

Have a Meeting before the Meeting

As with other counseling conversations, you will want to have a meeting before the meeting to make sure everyone is on the same page and that everyone knows their role during the conversation. Ensure that you have approval from all stakeholders involved and that you have touched base with anyone in your chain of command who needs to approve the decision to terminate employment. Also make sure you tap into your dream team to help support you through this difficult conversation.

In the case of terminations, it is advisable to designate one person to deliver the message and then have at least one other witness in the room. I do not recommend doing a termination without a witness. This recommendation is for the protection of everyone involved. Typically the person chosen to deliver the message will be the employee's direct manager or the manager's boss. The HR manager is an excellent choice as a witness as she can address final pay and benefit questions as well as support the participants in the conversation. With terminations in particular, it is a good idea to role-play various "What if?" scenarios before the meeting as you want to be very well prepared for any reaction from the employee.

Work Out the Details

As with any tough conversation, you will want to make sure you have arranged all the details for the meeting in advance so that everything runs smoothly with no delays or interruption in the flow of the conversation.

Location

Determine the best location for the conversation. With a termination, you will typically meet in a manager's office or conference room where it is quiet and private. This is a formal meeting so the location should match the tone. Situations involving severe misconduct where the employee has already been suspended may be handled over the phone if there is a concern about bringing the employee back into the work environment.

Timing

Decide the best time to have the conversation. We discussed the concerns with conducting terminations late on Friday afternoons as employees are left with no internal support to help them process the information, especially if the termination took them by surprise. Look for times when a good percentage of the staff is naturally away from their desks to minimize embarrassment and drama as the employee exits the building.

Additional Support

It may be appropriate to arrange for additional support for the employee such as connecting him with EAP or a local mental health provider. Find out if he carpools with other employees or takes public transportation as you may want to consider providing him with alternate transportation home after the conversation.

Final Pay

Money and benefits tend to be of primary concern to employees when they are notified that they've lost their job. Remember to consult HR and review any state laws regarding the disposition of the employee's final pay. Whatever the state law, try to present the employee with a check that includes at least his final wages, if not everything that he is owed, as quickly as possible.

Benefits

Again, your human resources department is a great resource for both you and the employee. Once the termination message has been delivered, you can arrange for HR to take over the lead in the conversation to discuss the final pay and disposition of benefits. If an HR representative is not a part of the conversation as a witness, you can arrange for one to be available to the employee immediately afterward.

Some companies like to present employees with a package during the termination meeting outlining what will happen to their benefits. This is especially important to coordinate if you are laying off or eliminating positions as the people will be caught off guard by the termination, and family members will want to know what is happening with their medical insurance. Other companies prefer to mail the information within the 60-day time period granted by law if it is a standard termination. Either way, at the very least you should know what the company's insurance policy guidelines are so that you can inform the employees verbally if their benefits will end immediately or at the end of the month.

Security

More than any other time, it is during and after termination meetings that you will most likely experience issues relating to security. Take whatever precautions you think are appropriate, even if you feel the threat to be remote. Use the FBI's violence threat assessment list to determine if you should involve outside authorities or have off-duty police officers available at your location during or for a period of time after the termination meeting.

Even if you determine the threat level to be low, you will still want to supervise the employee while he leaves the building. Remember you need to balance your security concerns with your desire to treat the individual with respect and maintain his dignity through to the end. Don't have someone hover over him unless his behavior dictates it. You might arrange to have several members of the management team strategically placed along the exit route from the building so that the employee can be observed as he leaves. That way he is supervised, but not actually escorted from the premises.

You will also want to decide if you need to remove other team members from the environment, especially if they share a common space with the employee being terminated. If the circumstances behind the termination involve other employees as witnesses or complainants, you should think about having these individuals at the very least leave the area until the termination is complete and the employee has left the workplace. Emotions can run high in the final moments, and you don't want to place a witness or victim in harm's way as the employee who just lost his job may feel he has nothing to lose at that point.

Have the Conversation

By the time you are at this point in the termination process you should have nothing more to say to the employee other than to deliver the message that his employment is being terminated. If additional conversation is needed before the decision can be made, then that needs to happen in a separate meeting prior to the termination or in the initial part of the termination discussion. Once you get to the termination meeting, the time for discussion has passed and your goal is to communicate your message clearly and efficiently.

I am also a stickler for language on this point; you should never terminate an employee, you terminate his employment. To reflect this philosophy my language would be something like, "as a result, your employment is being terminated effective immediately," rather than "you are being terminated" or "you're fired." It may be a subtle distinction to most, but I believe keeping your language focused on the job and away from the employee helps to keep it from feeling like a personal attack. I have seen employees react strongly when told "you're terminated." At times when emotions are already on overdrive, it is best to keep your language as neutral as possible.

I believe termination conversations should be short and sweet. If you haven't delivered the message within 5 or 10 minutes you are talking too much. There should be no reason to rehash any of the details of the situation or to reopen the investigation unless something really extraordinary is brought to light at the last moment. Otherwise, you should follow a much abbreviated version of the tough conversation format we discussed earlier.

- **The Opening:** Jump right in. In a sentence or two, summarize the issue and why you are meeting with them.
- **The Feedback Phase:** State again how their behavior or performance was unacceptable or outside of company policy or guidelines.
- **The Closing:** Deliver the termination message and have the courage to say the words. In one or two sentences, terminate their employment.

Once the termination has been communicated, you can ask them if they have any questions. Maintain tight control on this part of the conversation, and do not launch back into a negotiation or rehash of prior conversations. Ask your HR manager to address payroll and benefit concerns or provide the information yourself if HR is not available.

Inquire as to how the employee would prefer to handle gathering his personal items at his desk. Barring any real security concerns, you can consider allowing him the opportunity to pack his own desk, but you may want to steer him to a time when fewer team members are around. You could offer to come in after hours or on the weekend if the packing is going to take some time. You can also offer the option to pack the desk yourself and mail his personal belongings home or meet him outside of the office to bring the box to him. Use your best discretion of how to be respectful to the employee while also minimizing disruption and drama for the rest of the team.

At this point you are done with the conversation. Unless the employee is emotionally unable to leave, stand up and adjourn the meeting. Allow a few minutes for the employee to compose himself if necessary, but encourage him to leave the workplace as soon as possible. Most people will want to leave right away, but a long-term employee may want to say goodbye to his friends and coworkers. Monitor this, as long as it doesn't turn into a lengthy disruption for the team, you can allow him some space to say their goodbyes. If it starts to get out of control or if the employee begins to spread negativity, suggest to coworkers that they arrange to meet with the former employee outside of work. Be compassionate but firm.

With most terminations, you can manage the process so that there is enough time to conduct a pre-meeting and to make all the necessary arrangements before meeting with the employee. There are some occasions, however, when the situation warrants notifying the employee that his employment is being terminated at the end of a meeting that was initially scheduled to investigate an issue. Situations like this are instances where the employee has behaved in such an egregious way that you are clear that you need to end his employment immediately after discussing the situation with him.

In these cases, make sure that there is a noticeable break in the conversation between the investigation portion and delivering the termination message. You may want to call a time-out to step outside and confer with other managers or stakeholders to make sure there is agreement as you will not have had a chance to do that in a pre-meeting. The break in the conversation helps to indicate to the employee that the tone and circumstances of the conversation have changed so that he can make the emotional shift with you. Otherwise you may find him still trying to plead his case and exacerbating the issue.

Since you will not have a check or benefit information in hand because of the urgent nature of the situation, inform the employee that someone will contact him within 24 hours to discuss his final pay and to answer any benefit questions.

Communicating the Termination to Others

You will want to be very sensitive when communicating the departure of an employee to the rest of the staff and to customers or clients. The reasons for the departure and the specifics of the situation should be kept confidential in order to respect the former employee's privacy. In the case of frequent bad behavior or a long-term performance situation, most of the internal team members will have a good idea why their coworker is no longer there, but you should say or do nothing to confirm the specifics of the situation.

It is important that you communicate with the rest of your team as soon as you can after the employee leaves. You can do this by email, by meeting with your team as a group, or through one-on-one conversations. Communicate that the former employee is "no longer with us." If the person who left was a long-term employee and added value over the years, you might say something like, *"John Smith is no longer with us. We appreciate his contributions to our company over the years and we wish him well in his future endeavors."* People don't like feeling left out of the information loop and you don't want the news of a departure to spread through your employee gossip hotline if you can help it. Let team members hear the news directly from you as soon as possible.

You demonstrate your leadership skill and integrity in these situations by your professionalism when you communicate a termination. If you gossip or disparage the individual after the fact, it will reflect poorly on you, and if it gets back to the former employee, he could be prompted to initiate legal action. The remaining team members need to know that the employee is no longer coming to work and how they should handle any of the workload in the short term. Clients and customers need to know who will be handling their business and that you value them. That's all. Expounding anymore on the situation could make matters worse and escalate emotions.

Documentation

Most companies I have worked with do not provide the employee with documentation in a standard termination. Asking the employee to sign paperwork that terminates his employment is salt in the wound. You should still prepare documentation of the termination conversation for the personnel file and have the manager sign it, but nothing needs to go to the employee.

The exception to this is typically with a job elimination or a layoff. In these cases, the employee is usually provided with a letter stating that it was either a layoff due to lack of work or that the position was eliminated due to organizational restructuring. The employee can then use this letter to apply immediately for unemployment and to demonstrate to prospective future employers that the separation was not due to poor performance.

While terminating the employment of an employee can be very stressful, you can take pride in planning the process efficiently and conducting the conversation with compassion and respect for the individual. I remember the first person I ever let go and, to this day, I feel bad about it. It was the right decision for the business, but he was such a nice guy it broke my heart. I went home that night and cried. I knew this would not be my last termination as a leader and my despair fueled my desire to learn how to manage the process more effectively.

As strange as it may sound, I have had a number of people over the years come back to me and thank me for the compassion I showed them during their termination process and to tell me that losing their job was the best thing that could have ever happened to them. Other leaders have told me similar stories. For some people, behavior or performance issues are just a symptom of their unhappiness in their job. The termination forces them to take action which often leads them to a career that gives them greater success and satisfaction.

In the moment, losing your job can seem devastating, but with time and distance comes clarity and people sometimes realize after the fact that it wasn't the right place for them to be anyway. Treat people with respect and dignity during this traumatic event and they can look back and remember you with appreciation for how well you handled the difficult and emotional process.

KEY LEARNING POINTS FROM THIS CHAPTER

- Preparing for a termination meeting follows a similar format to feed-back conversations, although the meeting tends to be more condensed and less conversational.

- Always have a witness in the room when terminating an individual's employment. Your HR manager is usually an excellent choice.

- Be consistent in how you handle matters of final pay and benefits.

- Never terminate an employee, terminate the employment.

- How you treat people in the last 10 minutes of their employment greatly influences their decision to pursue legal action.

- Do not disparage former employees when you communicate the termination to the rest of the work team or to clients. Treat them with respect after they have left your employment, even if they have behaved in a manner that you feel doesn't deserve your respect.

- Asking the employee to sign a document that says he's been terminated can feel to him like you are putting salt in a wound. Document the file instead with a summary of the conversation.

SECTION SIX:

AFTER THE CONVERSATION

16 Chapter

You're Not Done Yet

*I've learned that people will forget what you said,
people will forget what you did, but people will
never forget how you made them feel.*

Maya Angelou

Follow-through is essential to building trust with your employees and your ability to maintain credibility as a leader, so make sure you don't lose focus after the conversation. While the conversation itself may be emotionally draining, the process does not end there. You will need to regroup with the people involved, including any stakeholders, to gather feedback on the process and to determine the next steps. Your employee will often be anxious about the recent exchange and will be waiting to gauge your attitude the next time you interact with her. This is especially true if the conversation was at all confrontational. You will also have some documentation to create and you may need to meet with the employee again to get that signed.

After the Conversation

Losing focus on the following issues can really undo any progress you've made with the employee up until this point. Here is a list of activities to consider after each tough conversation to ensure that you follow through on the process and prevent anything (or anyone) from slipping through the cracks.

Debrief after the Meeting

Immediately after the meeting when the conversation is still fresh in your mind, gather everyone involved (other than the employee) and any stakeholders who were not present and debrief the conversation. Whether you call it a wrap up, debrief, or postmortem, the purpose is the same, for participants to share their feelings and opinions about how the meeting went and to provide each other with real-time feedback.

This can be an incredible learning tool, especially for managers who work as a team and for less experienced managers. Understand that experience is not the greatest teacher, as we can make the same mistake over and over again and never really learn anything from it. Evaluating your experience is where true learning takes place. When we take the time to evaluate what was done well and what needs to improve for the next conversation, we are taking our skills to an even higher level. And when the leaders involved in the conversation feel comfortable enough to provide each other with honest and specific feedback as peers, it is a powerful learning experience for everyone involved.

The format I use for conducting the debriefing session is to go around the room to each participant and ask:

- What was your overall impression of the conversation? Was it a success?
- What do you feel went really well in the conversation?
- What could we have executed better?
- Is there something we missed?
- What are our next steps with this employee?

Once your leadership team becomes used to this process, you will not have to formally facilitate the discussion, it will happen organically as part of the debriefing meeting. Less experienced managers who are new to counseling employees have the opportunity to ask questions and to understand the thought processes of their more experienced leaders. It is also a way to help provide feedback in a nonthreatening way to senior leaders who might still need to refine their skills. Since everyone is giving and receiving feedback, it takes the focus off any one individual.

Check in with the Employee

Whether or not you have agreed to meet again formally to monitor the employee's progress, you will want someone to do a quick informal check-in with the employee within 24 to 48 hours of the meeting. Sometimes managers feel that when the discussion is uncomfortable or emotional, the best thing to do is to give the employee a lot of space after the meeting. While some space is good, too much will start to feel awkward and begin to strain the relationship, and the employee will start to believe you are avoiding her.

An informal check-in can be as simple as stopping by her desk (as long as it is private) and asking how she is doing. Depending on her response, you might continue to probe about how she is feeling now that she has had a chance to digest the feedback. If all seems well, you can move on.

You can also have someone else, such as the HR manager, check in with her. This was something I did on a regular basis for managers. If I knew a manager had just communicated a difficult message to an employee, I would make it a point to find that employee within a day or two to see how she was doing. If I wasn't involved in the original conversation I could get a very good sense of whether the employee understood the manager's message by what was shared with me.

Doing a check-in also allows you to confirm that your intended message was received by the employee and it gives you an opportunity to gauge the employee's attitude. Very few employees succeed when they harbor anger or resentment toward their manager as a result of negative feedback. If it looks as if the employee is not working through her negative emotions to a more productive place, you may need to revisit the conversation again more formally to try and help clear the air.

Keep Scheduled Follow-Up Meetings

One of the best ways to sabotage your progressive discipline process is to not follow through on any commitments you made during the conversation. I see managers fall into this trap time and time again. They have a wonderful conversation with an employee filled with meaningful dialogue and a commitment to change and then as soon as the conversation is over, they let the employee and the situation fall completely off their radar. Worse, if elements of the conversation were uncomfortable at all, they actively avoid making eye contact with that employee later on.

You absolutely must effectively close the loop on your difficult conversations and follow through with any and all commitments you made. This is especially important when addressing performance issues when you have asked the employee to demonstrate improvement to you over a given period of time. Typically, you would schedule a meeting every other week, or weekly, depending on the overall time frame being used in the performance plan, to provide feedback on progress.

Progress meetings are very important as they provide employees with formal feedback on a consistent basis and keep goals and activities from the performance plan in the forefront. They also allow employees the opportunity to ask questions or to express concern about the process. By keeping these meetings, you demonstrate your commitment to your employee's success through your investment of time and support in the process.

One of the worst things you can do as a leader is to commit to meeting with your employees to review their progress then continually reschedule or outright skip those meetings. Think about the message you are sending when you cancel meetings essential to your employees' efforts to keep their job.

If you commit to meeting with an employee on a weekly basis, then meet weekly, whether you feel you have any significant feedback to provide or not. The damage you will do by skipping those meetings far outweighs any concerns over "wasting time." Aside from your moral responsibility to follow through on your commitments, your failure to keep up your end of the bargain will also significantly weaken your position in any subsequent legal actions.

Provide Follow-Up Documentation

Sometimes you will find that your conversation starts as a fact-finding discussion, but moves into a counseling session. You did not prepare your documentation ahead of time because you did not have all the facts and needed to meet with the employee to fully understand the situation in order to determine the appropriate discipline. In these cases, you may want to verbally inform the employee immediately during the counseling session that she is being placed on a written or final warning so she understands what will happen if she behaves that way again, and let her know that you will get back with her shortly with a document summarizing your discussion for her to review and sign.

As crazy as it seems, some managers drop the ball here and never get the discipline or the or-else clause documented in writing. Maybe they believe the employee is aware of what will happen and they feel awkward reopening the issue for discussion again just to get the paperwork signed. While I can understand the resistance, following up with the written documentation is absolutely essential even if it feels like you are reopening an old wound. If you don't follow through with the promised documentation, it will undermine and weaken the entire progressive discipline process.

If you have a conversation that needs to be documented after the fact, let the employee know that they will be receiving a written document summarizing the conversation and you will be in touch with her shortly to review it. Do not let more than one business day pass before reconvening with her and presenting her with the document. In fact, if possible, do it the same day.

Closing this loop here needs to be a priority for you. When too much time passes between the conversation and when you give them the documentation summarizing the conversation, you run the risk that in the meantime they will repeat the behavior. Having your warnings documented in writing places you and the company in a better legal position.

When having the follow-up conversation to review the warning document, briefly summarize the key points from the previous conversation, give the employee the document, and allow her the opportunity to read it before signing. As long as the verbal conversation and written documentation are in sync, you should have no problems in getting the employee's signature. We will go into more depth about crafting your documentation in the following chapter.

Find a Reason to Interact

Over the years I have discovered that almost as important as effectively having the difficult conversation is making sure your first interaction after the conversation is a positive one. Counseling sessions often churn up a variety of emotions for both you and the employee. It is common for the employee to leave feeling embarrassed, upset, or angry. She may be harboring some hurt feelings and could use a positive interaction with her manager to help her move on.

To break the ice and get everyone through this awkward "are we okay" moment, find a reason to have a positive interaction with your employee soon after your counseling session. It doesn't need to be anything earth-shattering, just a reason to interact so that she can see that you do not harbor any negative feelings, even if she still does. It is separate from the check-in part of the process in that you are not going back into the content of the conversation in any way, just reestablishing your connection and clearing any lingering awkwardness between you and the employee.

Here are a couple of do's and don'ts to help you through this critical time.

Do:

- Make eye contact with the employee when you speak.
- Find something to appreciate and thank them for.
- Be genuine with your comments.
- Smile at them.

Don't:

- Avoid their looks or duck a chance meeting with them.
- Share information about their situation with their coworkers.
- Carry any negative emotions from the conversation into the next interaction.
- Act like they don't matter anymore.
- Punish them in addition to the discipline.

This last bullet point is really very important. Your responsibility as a leader is to coach and counsel, discipline as appropriate, but not to punish. Too often managers let their personal feelings slip into the mix and employees who misbehave not only receive the formal written warnings, but they also receive a little informal punishment from their management team as well.

Informal punishment might take the form of a loss of additional privileges, harsh treatment, sarcasm, an undesirable work schedule, or the cold shoulder from the boss. Rise above the temptation. Doling out informal punishment is immature, unprofessional, and says more about your leadership than it does about the person you are attempting to punish.

KEY LEARNING POINTS FROM THIS CHAPTER

- It is essential that you follow through on any commitments or items left unresolved after the conversation.

- Adopt the habit of immediately gathering all managers together who were involved in the conversation for a debriefing session to share feedback and overall impressions of how the meeting went.

- Check in with the employee within 24 to 48 hours to confirm the intended message was understood and to gauge her attitude. You can do this yourself or ask someone like the HR manager to do this on your behalf.

- Keep all scheduled follow-up meetings. Your employees will often interpret canceled meetings as a sign of your disinterest in helping them and your lack of confidence in their ability to improve.

- If you do not have documentation ready to deliver during the meeting, make sure you create it within a day or two, meet again with the employee to review it with her, and ask for her signature acknowledging receipt.

- Find a positive reason to interact with the employee following your conversation. She will want to see that you are okay with her and that you will be treating her appropriately afterward, especially if it was a heated or confrontational conversation.

- Seek to discipline, not punish. Avoid reinforcing your message with subtle forms of punishment such as giving them the cold shoulder or taking away privileges not related to the issue being addressed. Doing this gives the impression that you are vindictive and have a personal agenda.

SECTION SEVEN:

THE WONDERFUL WORLD OF DOCUMENTATION

17 Chapter

What Is Documentation?

*While the spoken word can travel faster, you can't take
it home in your hand. Only the written word can be
absorbed wholly at the convenience of the reader.*

Kingman Brewster

There is an old Chinese proverb that says, *"The palest ink is better than
the best memory."* While the Chinese may not have had performance documentation in mind, I think it is important to our discussion. It is generally
accepted that in the minefield known as employment law, some documentation, even if it isn't written perfectly, is better than no documentation at all.
Well, I should say in *most* cases.

I am sure there are several corporate attorneys who might argue that if
you are going to do something outside of company policy or against the law,
it's best not to document it. But for our purposes we will assume that your
intention is pure and you have only the best interest of the employee and the
company at heart. So given that understanding, documentation is not just a
good idea, it is an essential part of the disciplinary process.

I know for many managers this is where the wheels can come off the
wagon pretty quickly when they don't follow through and document their
performance discussions. Great conversations can be undercut by a leader's
failure to properly document the issue that was addressed, the feedback
given and in particular, the consequences discussed (your or-else clause).
As a general rule, when an issue rises to the level that it might put the
employee's job in danger, you *absolutely* should have documentation of
your conversations, preferably signed by the employee.

Leaders are taught to inspire and motivate their employees, to be honest
with their feedback, and to coach their people through any rough edges in
their performance. Obviously you would like to maintain the best relationship that you can with your employees. If you do not already know from

direct experience you can probably guess that introducing formal documentation, with its legal language and signature lines, can significantly change the tone of your coaching. It is at that exact moment that some employees make a shift from a cooperative to an adversarial attitude.

When to Document

So what does documentation look like and how do you know when it is appropriate to move from strictly coaching the employee, to documenting his behavior or performance as part of a progressive discipline process? To answer that question, let's take a look at the reasons why you would want to formally document an issue in writing.

You Start to See a Pattern

It is very common for an employee to have an issue that when first addressed, does not rise to the level of needing formal documentation. He is late to work, misses a deadline, fails to check out with the supervisor before leaving, does not achieve his monthly goals for the first time, or his traditionally flawless attire does not conform to your company's dress code one day. As one-off instances or first-time offenses, these issues are worth documenting in an informal way, but probably do not rise to the level of the first step of a progressive discipline process. In that case you would provide coaching and support and hope the employee is able to correct the issue.

If the issue does not correct itself and it repeats or if the performance continues to decline, a pattern is developing, and it is time to add formal documentation to conversations and move from coaching to counseling. Providing employees with written documentation helps to raise the importance of the situation and hopefully increases their sense of urgency to correct the problem.

The Problem Is Already Serious

Some behaviors and performance problems present themselves for the first time at a serious and urgent level so you will need to document the issue immediately. Maybe your employee has a verbal argument with a teammate, is rude to a guest, makes a mistake that costs the company repeat business, or forges some paperwork. The problem is already serious enough that you might choose to address it by going directly to the progressive discipline process and issuing a warning.

As we have seen, some problems are so serious that you may want to skip a step or two in your stated progressive discipline process to reflect the more urgent and critical need for the employee to change his behavior and correct the situation. Addressing an issue at the most serious level, where it is appropriate to give a final warning without having issued previous warnings, as I mentioned, is called giving a first and final warning. This indicates that it is the first and last warning the employee will receive on this issue. Make sure your company policy is written in a way that allows for this deviation and that you are consistent with your exceptions. In other words, don't give one employee a final warning for a behavior and the next employee who does the same thing a written verbal unless the circumstances warrant disparate treatment.

You Have Concerns about Legal Action

There are occasions where you just want a written record for your files of an issue, conversation, or action you took, in case of a legal action being initiated at some later date. For example, you might want written documentation of your investigation into a claim of sexual harassment, summaries of your interviews regarding a theft, notes of sensitive conversations when you did not have a witness available, or times when you want a historical record of issues or interactions that didn't feel quite "right" to you. Trust your instincts. If you feel there might be a need at some point to have an accurate record of a conversation or incident, document it and put it in your files in case something does flare up and a written record is needed.

Remember, not all documentation is given to the employee, as is the case of your interview notes from a sexual harassment investigation. In that case, only the written or final warning would go to the employee who has been accused of inappropriate behavior. Your notes documenting the interviews would typically be kept in a separate file, usually by human resources.

An easy way to document something which you feel is not quite appropriate to copy to an employee is to send yourself an email with the subject, "Summary of (incident or conversation) on (date)." In the body of the email, type the notes that you want to save as a written record. Send the email to yourself, print a copy of it, and save it in a secure location.

I had a file in my desk labeled "Miscellaneous Documentation." Documentation that I wasn't ready to put in the employee files went there. If something happened later on and the written record of a conversation or investigation were needed, I could always retrieve it from that file and make it a permanent part of the employee's file at that time. If nothing further happened, the document stayed right where it was safe and sound.

As a side note, this file is usually subject to subpoena so you are not hiding it from anyone or keeping it away from prying legal eyes. The purpose is to document concerns when they may be in the very early stages of development. Once something is presented as a credible issue that needs to be dealt with formally, you move the documentation into the employee's permanent file.

The Issue Is Job Threatening

As we've discussed before, conversations with employees informing them that their behavior or performance is at a point where it may be job threatening are laden with stress and anxiety. Employees' defenses get triggered and many actually emotionally shut down and can no longer comprehend what you are saying to them.

When it gets to that point, for the employee's sake, you will want to deliver your message a number of times in a variety of formats. A written document that can be reread later will help employees to absorb your message, and will help to ensure there are no misunderstandings about the nature of the problem and the consequences if it is not corrected.

When all is said and done, as an exceptional leader you must be prepared to become proficient at creating effective written documentation and incorporating it into your coaching and counseling routine. It's true that introducing documentation into the mix may end up escalating your employee's anxiety and could strain your relationship, but there are very sound business reasons that make it essential that you execute this step.

Types of Documentation

When I speak of documentation, most managers immediately think of the most formal type: the kind with the intimidating legal language that threatens jobs and requires a signature from the employee. But that, by no means, is the most common type of documentation. I'd like to ask that you expand your definition of documentation to reflect more of a continuum, with the very informal and less intimidating type on one end of the scale, to the more formal, legal-sounding kind at the other end.

The following graphic illustrates the various types of documentation you can use and the progression from informal to formal.

Least Intimidating

Most Intimidating

- Informal
- General
- Written Verbal
- Written Warning
- Performance Probation
- Final Warning

These different types of documentation also correspond to the various stages of a typical progressive discipline process that organizations might use. Here are the differences between each type of documentation and how to effectively use it.

Informal

Most performance management processes require leaders to review their direct report's performance on at least an annual basis. In order to accurately remember a full 12 months' worth of performance highs and lows, most managers need to keep some sort of informal record of their employees' performance. This record would be considered informal documentation.

Informal documentation can take the form of handwritten notes of general conversations you've had with your employees, emails to yourself confirming conversations and recapping major points, or entries into an Excel spreadsheet that summarize an employee's positive and negative performance on a daily basis. Since the employee does not necessarily see or confirm receipt of informal documentation, it is best used to keep a general record of positive performance and coaching conversations and as a way to identify potential patterns in performance going forward.

And remember, just because the employee hasn't seen the documentation doesn't mean that it can't be used as part of a legal action. ALL documentation is traditionally subpoenaed as part of the discovery process in a lawsuit and that includes any little scraps of paper you may have hidden away in a file in your desk drawer that pertains to your employees. So use the same standards of professionalism when writing informal documentation as you do when writing the more formal type. To be safe, I always assume whatever I write will be seen one day by the employee or a lawyer and craft my thoughts accordingly.

General

Unless the employee is having behavior or performance issues that need to be documented, most interactions and correspondence fall into the general documentation category. This would include general conversations regarding work product and expectations, email communications between you and the employee, notes of thanks for a job well done, memos that give the employee instruction and direction, and copies of department or company policies. This documentation represents 90 percent of the day-to-day communication you have with your employees and as you can see, it can be verbal or written.

What separates this type of documentation from the informal type is that it is actually shared with the employee in some way. It can be used to acknowledge and address either positive or negative performance or behavior. When relating to coaching negative behavior or substandard performance, general documentation answers the big question, "When did you first inform the employee that there was a problem?"

Written Verbal

When I first heard this term I had to scratch my head a bit. It sounded like an oxymoron, like jumbo shrimp. It certainly struck me as counterintuitive at the very least: How could it be a verbal warning if you were documenting the warning in writing?

Actually the purpose of this type of documentation is pretty straightforward. A written verbal is a written record that documents a verbal warning that you gave to an employee. Written verbal warnings have a more formal and serious feeling than the first two categories and are usually the first step in a company's formal progressive discipline process. Written verbal warnings go one step beyond the general documentation category in that you not only are telling the employee that there is a problem, but you are documenting that you told him and giving him a copy of that documentation.

I recommend at this point in the continuum that you begin to have the employees sign the documentation as well (we will talk more about signatures in a later section). The increase in formality should help to indicate to your employees that you are not fooling around, something about their behavior or performance needs to change or it could become job threatening.

With this level of documentation, you are traditionally no longer talking about documenting positive performance. From this point on, the focus of each type of documentation is to help correct unacceptable behavior and substandard performance and create a paper trail of your conversations. Written verbal warnings typically are forwarded to the HR department and kept in the employee's personnel file as part of the official employment record.

Written Warning

A written warning escalates the progressive discipline process to the next step. Your employee has now received a second formal warning about his behavior or performance. Your language in the written warning should clearly indicate the seriousness of the situation and the potential consequences if the behavior repeats or if there is not significant improvement in performance.

While the termination of his employment at this point may not be the actual next step in the process, I recommend that you clearly indicate that the situation could become job threatening if not corrected. While it might feel like it is too soon in the process to talk about termination, it is important to make that link for people very clear. If termination is a real possibility at some point on this path, it is your responsibility to be honest and inform them of the potential consequences.

Sometimes an individual's defense system will work overtime to downplay the seriousness of the situation or to protect him from the thought that there is the potential he could lose his job. Give your employees every opportunity to understand exactly where they stand and to take the appropriate action to eliminate the problem early in the progressive discipline process. As with a written verbal warning, I would ask the employee to sign the document to indicate that he received a copy and send the original to HR for inclusion in his file.

Performance Probation

Remember, it is reasonable to expect someone to correct a behavioral issue immediately, but with performance problems it makes sense to give employees a longer period of time to improve their performance and to show you progress. This is especially the case with individuals in higher level professional or salaried positions. With these employees, use of performance probation with an action plan is very effective.

As discussed, the duration of the probation period is somewhat subjective and is usually determined by considering the employee's tenure with the company, length of time in the position, the need for additional training, the nature of the work being evaluated, and his ability to demonstrate improvement to you quickly. A typical probation period would start at 30 days.

The performance plan document for the probation usually includes a brief description of the areas where there is substandard performance and provides an action plan to help the employee demonstrate improvement to you. Since the duration of the plan is often several weeks, it is a good idea to build in weekly or biweekly check-in meetings between you and the employee so you can provide him with regular and timely feedback on his progress.

As with other types of documentation, the performance plan document for the probation should have a final paragraph that outlines the consequences to the employee if he does not improve his performance. This would include the or-else clause and language indicating that loss of employment was a possible, if not a probable, outcome if changes are not made. The plan should be signed by the employee and sent to HR to become part of the permanent record.

Again, at this stage in the progressive discipline process I would urge you to consider having a witness present during your conversations. Appropriate choices would be the employee's direct manager or supervisor (if you are a level or two removed), your manager, or the HR manager. As you know, I am partial to including the HR manager for this purpose.

Final Warning

Final warnings are often the last step in the progressive discipline process and are most often issued to address behavioral issues. The language in this type of documentation needs to be very clear; if the behavior occurs again you may immediately terminate employment. It should be signed by the employee and I strongly recommend that you have a witness.

Final warnings are very strong pieces of documentation to have when defending your actions in legal proceedings or during an unemployment hearing. They tend to be written in a straightforward, no nonsense style and use the most formal, direct, and serious sounding language. With that being said, as I mentioned earlier, I do recommend that you use "may result" or "can result" in your or-else clause, as you may want the option to not follow through with the stated consequences based on the situation.

Remember, giving yourself options within the language of your documentation does not necessarily weaken your legal position; in contrast, failure to follow through with something you commit to doing in your documentation absolutely does.

KEY LEARNING POINTS FROM THIS CHAPTER

- Make a commitment to praise in writing as quickly as you document negative performance and behavior issues.

- By documenting coaching conversations informally you can easily see patterns as they develop and identify when it is time to move from coaching to counseling.

- As long as your company policy allows it, you can use a first and final warning for issues that present themselves at the serious or urgent level by skipping steps in the progressive discipline process and moving right to the final step.

- If you are at all concerned about potential legal action concerning the handling of an issue, make sure you have good documentation in place. Issue the appropriate warnings and document investigations by summarizing discussions with a note to file.

- Documentation is a critical part of any progressive discipline process as it reinforces your message to the employee, outlines the consequences, and creates a paper trail of your conversations.

- Documentation can range from informal handwritten notes to very formal memos that state the employee will lose his job if changes are not made. Choose the most appropriate format for the issue you are addressing.

18 Chapter

Crafting Your Document

___

To be persuasive we must be believable;
to be believable we must be credible;
to be credible we must be truthful.

Edward R. Murrow

Since the first two types of documentation (informal and general), are typically nonthreatening and are most often positive in nature, I will leave you to use your own good sense when creating documents that fall into these categories. Because of the seriousness and legal concerns involved, I am going to concentrate on the types of documentation that you will need to create when you move into the progressive discipline process.

Writing Your Documents

Creating the memo that documents an employee's unacceptable behavior or performance does not require the same effort as birthing a baby, although I certainly understand how some people might feel that way. It can be labor and time-intensive when you first start learning how to create your documentation. If you are not used to confronting issues head on, verbally or otherwise, the direct and somewhat blunt nature of the writing style can make you feel very uncomfortable and unsure of yourself.

I have found that the majority of people tend to write in a way that mirrors how they speak, so if you are predisposed to beating around the bush when delivering negative performance feedback in person, you will be inclined to do the same when you create documentation that addresses behavior and performance problems. Unfortunately, at this level in the documentation process you really can't afford to sidestep issues. If you give in to the temptation to be vague or to candy-coat your message, you will render your documentation toothless, perpetuate confusion, and leave your employee in the dark as to where they stand with their performance.

As you know by now, when it comes to delivering performance feedback I believe in full disclosure or as close as you can appropriately get to it. Employees have a right to know if their behavior could result in further disciplinary action or if they could even pay the ultimate price of having their employment terminated. To that end, when it comes to written documentation, the style should be clear, direct, succinct, easy to understand, and totally forthcoming about any potential disciplinary actions that may be taken.

Your documentation should also be appropriate to the situation at hand. For example, a written warning to an employee after his first tardy stating that he may lose his job probably would feel a little heavy-handed. As a leader you need to be able to find that line between reminding your employee about a company policy and bringing out the big guns and threatening his job. Employees don't want to work for someone who threatens them with termination each and every time they have a conversation.

The Format

So where do you start? I have found that most well-written documentation follows a similar format:

The Introduction

This includes a brief summary of the problem and any pertinent details of the situation being addressed. It describes the circumstances that brought you to this point so everyone is on the same page. Sometimes this section is combined with the next section in the same paragraph if it is very short.

The Issue

In this section you get into the meat of the issue. You elaborate more about why the behavior is unacceptable, the impact the behavior has on the business or the team, and reiterate any company policy that pertains to the issue. In the case of performance probation, the issue section of the memo would contain the action plan, which outlines how the employee is expected to bring his performance up to an acceptable level.

Consequences

This is where you get down to it—what is happening as a result of the unacceptable behavior or poor performance. For example, is the employee being given a final warning, being placed on performance probation, or having certain privileges or benefits suspended? You need to be clear about what the employee needs to do to resolve the issue (your expectations) and include, if appropriate, the time frame being given to demonstrate improvement.

Or-Else Clause

The importance of the or-else clause was covered in detail in the "Having the Conversation" section of this book. As a reminder, the or-else clause is a straightforward statement of what the employee can expect as the next step should the behavior repeat or the performance fail to improve. This is the section where the language tends to take on a more noticeable legal tone.

Statement of Support

I feel it is important to end your documentation memo with a statement of support whenever possible. Here you would reiterate your commitment to support the employee in his efforts to improve, your belief that he is capable of resolving the issue, or your trust that he will eliminate the unwanted behavior and act accordingly from now on. You can also indicate in this section if you will be meeting with him on a regular basis to review his progress.

Depending on the issue you are documenting, these steps could be covered very briefly with a number of well-crafted sentences, or as in the case of performance probation, the performance plan document including the action plan could end up being several pages long. I have found that 95 percent of the formal written documentation that I created over the years followed this format.

So now that you know the format you just need to plug in the specifics and you will have your documentation crafted.

Let's walk through an example or two so you can see the format in action.

Scenario 1: Written Warning for Missing Deadlines

Your employee, Sam, is a very hard worker most of the time. But you have been noticing lately that he has missed a couple of critical deadlines with his projects. Over the past six months he has been late with assignments on a number of occasions. His communication about his lateness was sporadic at best. During the last two months he has been late with his month-end reports to you, and just this week, he missed a deadline with a project that you needed to give to your boss. Once again, there was no communication from Sam beforehand that you were not going to have the information on time. His lateness certainly didn't make either of you look good to your boss.

You spoke to Sam informally after each missed deadline and he promised that he was going to try harder. Then, after last month's report was late, you gave Sam a written verbal warning that his failure to meet deadlines was negatively impacting his performance and that he needed to address the issue immediately. You also told him he needed to do a better job of communicating the status of his reports to you. You gave a copy of the written verbal warning to Sam and asked him to sign it. Now with this most recent missed deadline, you feel it is time to escalate to the next step in the progressive discipline process and give Sam a written warning.

Here is how you might craft the written document following the format.

Memorandum

[Date]

To: Sam Smith

From: [Your Name]

Subject: Written Warning *(put the name of the warning in the subject line)*

(Introduction)
On a number of occasions during the past 6 months we have spoken about your failure to meet some critical deadlines with your assignments. During our last conversation on [Date], we specifically discussed how important it is that you communicate any anticipated delays to me well in advance of the deadline being missed. During our discussion, you committed to resolving this issue and improving your communication with me.

(The Issue)
Since our last discussion you missed yet another assignment deadline and failed to inform me prior to the deadline being missed. You were assigned a project that was due yesterday and you failed to turn it in on time. This prevented me from meeting my deadline. This type of behavior reflects poorly on our entire department and raises concerns about your reliability and sense of urgency. As a member of this team it is absolutely critical that you meet all assigned deadlines and communicate any problems to me immediately.

(Consequences)
Because your ability to meet assignment deadlines is so important to your success, I am giving you a written warning for this issue. You are expected to take whatever steps necessary to correct the problem and ensure that you do not miss another deadline. Additionally, your communication with me needs to significantly improve. If there is a situation that will prevent you from completing your work in a timely manner, you need to bring it to my attention immediately. I do not expect you to miss any more deadlines.

(Or-Else Clause)
Should there be another instance where you fail to meet an assignment deadline, further disciplinary action may be taken up to and including a final written warning or the termination of your employment.

(Statement of Support)
Sam, I believe you are very capable of correcting this situation. As always, I am available to support you in any way that I can so you can be successful. If you feel you could benefit from additional training or my assistance in any other way, please let me know how I can help.

---------------------------------   ---------------------------------
Employee's Signature   Manager's Signature
Read and Acknowledged

(We will discuss getting signatures in the next section.)

As you might expect, the more complex the issue, the more sentences it will take to document all the pieces. Here is an example that is short and sweet and gets right to the point.

Scenario 2: Final Warning for Unprofessional Behavior

You are sitting at your desk when outside of your office you hear two of your employees arguing and they are starting to raise their voices. While both employees are clearly agitated, one employee, Greg, seems to be doing the majority of the yelling. Just as you approach, you hear Greg say in a loud and angry tone, "F*$k you!" to the other employee, while pointing his finger in the other employee's face. You observe that Greg is acting in a very threatening manner and you quickly step in to break up the incident.

You investigate the situation and after speaking with both employees and several coworkers who witnessed the argument, you determine that Greg instigated the altercation and was the one whose behavior was unprofessional. He allowed his emotions to get out of control and he used profanity. While the other employee, Frank, said he never really felt physically threatened by Greg, you were not comfortable with the level of aggression Greg showed during the altercation.

You decide this is behavior that cannot be tolerated in the workplace and while you considered terminating Greg's employment, based on his exemplary performance record otherwise, you decide to give him a final warning instead.

Here is how you might write this final warning using the format.

Memorandum

To: Greg Smith
From: [Your Name]
Subject: Final Warning

(Introduction)

Yesterday you were observed arguing with your coworker, Frank. The conversation became loud and witnesses reported that you lost your temper, spoke in an angry manner, adopted a physically aggressive posture and used profanity shouting "F*$k you" at Frank.

(The Issue)

The way you interacted with Frank is completely inappropriate and unprofessional. The situation was exacerbated by your use of profanity and perceived aggression. This type of behavior is totally unacceptable and will not be tolerated.

(Consequences)

As a result, you are being given a Final Warning. In the future, you need to conduct yourself at all times with the utmost professionalism, maintain control of your emotions, and demonstrate respect for your coworkers. Your ability to communicate concerns with your teammates in a professional and appropriate way is essential to your building influence and positive relationships with them. Failure to do so negatively impacts your performance.

(Or-Else Clause)

Aggression and profanity of any sort is not tolerated in our workplace. Any additional instances may result in further disciplinary action up to and including the immediate termination of your employment.

(Statement of Support)

Greg, I am confident that you will take the necessary steps to ensure that this type of behavior does not happen again as it negatively impacts your credibility and detracts from your otherwise exceptional performance record. Please let me know if I can assist you in any way to resolve this issue.

_____   _____
Employee's Signature   Manager's Signature
Read and Acknowledged

                                                       _____
                                                       Witness's Signature

As you can see in this example, you can handle each section in two to three well-crafted sentences. This will not always be the case, some situations will require more narrative, but you should strive to document the critical facts as briefly and clearly as possible.

When creating documentation, I suggest creating a first draft and then letting it sit for a couple of hours, then come back to it with fresh eyes. As you read what you've written over again, place yourself in the shoes of someone from outside of the company. Would they be able to understand the issue and the discipline being taken from what you have written? If not, edit, add more facts or eliminate flowery narrative as necessary so that your message is direct, clear, and easily understood.

In the Additional Resources section located at the end of this book, you will find more examples of documentation including a sample performance probation memo that illustrates how that type of documentation differs slightly with the inclusion of the action plan. Create your own templates to use so that you don't have to recreate the wheel each time you have to craft another memo.

Bridging Gaps in Documentation

Sometimes you will find yourself in a situation where you have had verbal conversations with your employee regarding an issue during which you verbally informed him of the consequences if his behavior or performance did not improve, but you did not formally document those conversations in writing. In other words, you have the employee at the appropriate step in the progressive discipline process verbally, but there is no documentation in his file to confirm the conversations ever occurred or that he was put on notice that his job might be in jeopardy. Obviously, this is not a best practice when it comes to counseling employees, but realistically it does happen so we should talk about how to minimize the damage if it does occur.

Scenario 3: Wrapping in Verbal Conversations

For example, let's say you have a manager named Diane. Over the past several months you have had a couple of conversations with Diane about her communication skills. You spoke to Diane about how she can come across as condescending in her written communications and how she has put people on the defensive at times with her word choices; now one of Diane's direct reports just met with you to complain about the way she speaks to her team. You realize that the situation is not improving and, in fact, it seems to be getting worse.

While you coached and verbally counseled Diane about the need to improve her communication skills as each situation presented itself, you now realize that things are not improving and you will need to give Diane a written warning for the way in which she communicates with others.

Even though you have not formally documented the previous coaching and counseling conversations, you can still cover your bases by documenting them now and wrapping them into the "Introduction" portion of the written warning. You might start the "Introduction" of Diane's written warning like this:

"Over that last several months we have met a number of times to discuss the quality of your communications with others. On March 5th, we discussed how the tone of an email you sent to Sue Smith was perceived to be condescending. On June 1st, we met to discuss feedback I received from a number of your coworkers regarding how you were communicating with them. Specifically, we discussed the need for you to avoid using words that can be emotionally charged and offend people. During these previous conversations I expressed concern that this issue, if not resolved, could seriously impact your performance, and you committed to improving your communication skills. Today, I received additional feedback from members of your team that indicates your communication style continues to be ineffective. Specifically they said. . . ."

By specifically documenting the previous conversations in the introduction to the written warning, you have in effect bridged the gap in formal documentation and you are now caught up. While it is always best to document real-time as the conversations occur, there are times when it just doesn't happen and when that is the case, you should do what you can to wrap any undocumented conversations into the next formal memo you write.

You can use this method to bridge gaps when addressing most behavior and performance issues. Again, it's not the best-case scenario, but I have even used this method in a final warning where the manager had been seriously lax in formally documenting his conversations and now was in the final stages of the progressive discipline process with an employee without any documentation in the employee's file.

Legally and ethically you are in a much better position if you follow your progressive discipline policy and have the employee receive timely written warnings, which they sign, as you progress with your counseling. It gives the employee the greatest opportunity to take corrective action and it protects the company in future legal matters by formally documenting all of your conversations as they occur.

KEY LEARNING POINTS FROM THIS CHAPTER

- Most written documentation follows a similar format:

  - Introduction: summary of events leading to the discussion and current documentation.

  - Issue: description of the problem being addressed, impact on others, any company policy that pertains to the issue and action plan, if appropriate.

  - Consequences: what is happening as a result of the behavior or performance issue.

  - Or else clause: what will happen if the employee does it again or fails to improve.

  - Statement of support: your commitment to support the employee through this process and any commitments you are willing to make.

- The length of your documentation will vary depending on the issue being addressed. In some cases one to three sentences in each section will suffice; in others, it may take you several paragraphs to adequately document the issue. Action plans will lengthen your document considerably.

- You can bridge any gaps in documentation by specifically noting any previously undocumented conversations in the introduction portion of the memo.

19 Chapter

Signatures and Witnesses

*To effectively communicate, we must realize that
we are all different in the way we perceive the
world and use this understanding as a guide to our
communication with others.*

Anthony Robbins

Getting a Signature

Asking someone to sign a performance document can be a stressful situation. It brings a level of seriousness to a situation that some managers would like to downplay, especially in the initial stages of the progressive discipline process. But signatures on documents are critical to your ability to effectively defend yourself in a legal proceeding. Because of this, they are important any time you believe the situation has escalated to the point where employment may be in jeopardy if corrective action is not taken. To that end, signatures are an essential part of your counseling and documentation process. When it comes to defending yourself in a legal action, more important than what you *actually said* to the employee is what you can *prove you said* to the employee. Written documentation with the employee's signature provides that proof.

Signatures are a part of your counseling process whether you like it or not. Most of the time your employees will sign the memos you ask them to sign without incident. But every now and then, an employee will get his hackles up and refuse to sign your memo. If not handled appropriately, this can really create an adversarial environment between you and your employee, the very person you are trying to help with your counseling efforts.

Refusal to Sign

So what do you do when an employee refuses to sign? I believe the majority of this struggle is the result of confusion over what the employee's signature actually signifies. So let's break it down.

You will notice on the sample memos I've included in this book, the signature line reads like this:

_____	_____
Employee's Signature	Manager's Signature
Read and Acknowledged	

Underneath the line for the employee's signature are the words, "Read and Acknowledged." This means that the employee has _read_ a copy of the documentation and has _acknowledged_ receipt of it, nothing more. It does not mean that he agrees with the content of the memo or with the consequences or discipline.

Many employees believe that their signature indicates that they agree with what is going on and if they don't sign, they can in some way avoid the discipline. Their refusal to sign is an effort on their part to demonstrate their disagreement and to some extent, exert control in a situation where they are feeling powerless.

From the company's perspective, while you would like everyone to be on the same page it is not as important whether or not employees agree with your assessment of the problem or the method of discipline you have chosen. In fact, they often don't agree with either. When they do agree, it usually means that there is hope that they will resolve the situation as they are not fighting the feedback.

But gaining their agreement is not why you are asking them to sign your document. You are asking them to sign the document to prove that you gave them a copy of the memo and they read it. So two things need to happen: you need to ask them to read it in front of you (or go through it together), and you need to give them a copy of the document (usually after they sign it). If you explain this rationale to employees before asking them to sign the document, I have found that almost all employees will agree to sign the documentation with that understanding.

When giving employees a document to review and sign, you should explain the following:

- _Now that we've reviewed the contents of the memo, I am going to ask you to sign this copy._

- *By signing this document you signify that you have read the contents of the memo and you acknowledge that you are receiving a copy of it.*

That's it. Most employees will sign at this point, but every now and then one will continue to resist. If one does continue to express serious concerns about signing the document, share the following as appropriate:

- *Your signature does not indicate agreement, although I hope you at least understand the issue as we've discussed it and the consequences to you.*
- *If you strongly disagree with the content of this memo or the discipline, I encourage you to sleep on it overnight to allow some of the emotion to drain away and look at it again tomorrow with fresh eyes. If you still feel this strongly in the morning, we can talk further or you are welcome to discuss your concerns directly with human resources.*
- *Your refusal to sign in no way alters your current situation. The consequences and potential future discipline if the issue remains unresolved remain in effect as outlined in this memo.*

Again, most people will sign at this point. For that 1 in 100 employee who absolutely continues to refuse to sign no matter what you say, try the following:

- If you do not have a witness in the room, explain to the employee that you would like someone else to join the conversation as a witness. Immediately ask another manager to join the meeting.
- Explain to the witness that the employee has refused to acknowledge receipt of a memo (you do not need to give them any more details than that) and ask the employee if that is still the case so the witness can hear his refusal.
- Explain that you are going to write "Refused to Sign" on the employee's signature line, then do so.
- Sign the document on the manager's signature line and if there isn't already a line for the witness, handwrite one and ask the witness to sign the document on this line.
- If it is consistent with your company policy, give your employee a copy of the memo at this point. Some companies have a policy that employees are entitled only to copies of the documents they sign. I

would want to demonstrate that I believed my actions to be fair and above reproach, so I would give the employee a copy anyway, taking any perceived power or advantage out of the refusal to sign.

I have found the key to managing this situation when it arises is to stay very calm and to treat it in a very matter-of-fact manner, with no heightened emotion or anxiety. If you get upset and agitated with employees, they will perceive their refusal to be a big deal and they will probably refuse to sign anything else you give them from that point on. Remember, their signature on a document indicates only that they read and acknowledged receipt of it. By stating "Refused to Sign" you are still covering your bases as best you can since they did receive the memo and reviewed it and their refusal to sign demonstrates that.

Order of Signature

A final note: once the conversation is over and, if the documentation was prepared ahead of time, you are ready to sign, you should always sign the document in this order:

- Employee
- Manager
- Witness

There is one iron-clad rule when it comes to signing documentation:

An employee should NEVER receive documentation that has already been signed by the manager.

I believe signing the document ahead of time sends all the wrong messages and is most likely to result in the employee's refusal to sign out of spite. Most counseling conversations are just that, conversations where you want to have the employees participate and, at the very least, give you their side of the story. When you sign a document before you give it to the employee you send the opposite message, that his side of the story doesn't matter, that you were not actually open to changing your mind during the conversation, and that the discipline was already a done deal when you sat down.

Again, the most productive conversations will be those where the employee believes you have listened to what he had to say and considered his point of view. Out of respect for the employee, make sure you sign the paperwork after he does, or if he refuses to sign, after you document that refusal and get a witness.

So the bottom line when it comes to getting signatures is this: it is good for you and the company to get signatures on documents when you are in the progressive discipline process with an employee. The employee's signature indicates that he read and acknowledged receipt of the memo. It is not the end of the world if he refuses to sign, so don't make it a big deal. Nothing changes; the process continues to move forward just as if he'd signed it.

By clearly explaining the meaning of the signature beforehand and taking any refusal to sign in stride, you can effectively minimize the impact of requesting the employee's signature on your documentation

Including a Witness

The more confrontational the atmosphere during a tough conversation, the better chance you have of your message being poorly communicated or entirely misunderstood. That is why witnesses can play a critical role in your counseling process. Here are my suggestions for when you might consider including a witness in your conversation:

- The situation with the employee has progressed to the point where termination of his employment is the logical next step.
- Past conversations with this employee have not gone well; either your message was not completely understood or emotions got in the way of delivering the message.
- To protect yourself in case of future legal action, you want a witness to the conversation.
- The situation is highly sensitive, as in the case of sexual harassment claims.
- You believe the employee would be put at ease by having someone else in the room, as is sometimes the case when one participant is male and the other is female.

While technically anyone can act as a witness to a conversation, you will want to use good judgment when inviting a third party to participate. It should make sense to the employee why this person is joining the conversation;

otherwise he may feel embarrassed, worry about confidentiality, or feel as if he is being ganged up on. This could set an adversarial tone from the outset and make it more challenging to get him to lower his defenses enough to hear your message.

With some conversations a natural witness is already a part of the process. Maybe your boss has asked to join the meeting or the HR manager participated in the prior conversations with this employee so it makes sense to continue to include them. Anyone already in a conversation can witness your documentation for you. But what if you are planning a tough conversation and no one else has been part of the process, how do you go about selecting the right person as a witness? In choosing your witness you want to consider two things: the role in the conversation and the balance of power.

The Witness's Role

What role do you need your witnesses to play? Do you need them to just sit quietly and witness the message so they can sign the document, do you want them to participate in the conversation by providing you with details and support, or would you like them to help the employee feel more comfortable? Once you determine their role in the conversation, the most appropriate choice becomes more obvious to you.

In most conversations, your witnesses will play a passive role in the meeting, observing the conversation and witnessing what is said and how the participants behave. They may not take part in delivering the message but may assist other participants by rephrasing what is said for clarity and understanding or asking pertinent questions. Typically witnesses are not seen as having an agenda or an active role in the conversation. If you remember back to the discussion about your pre-meeting conversations, the witnesses should be very clear as to their role in the conversation.

That isn't to say that witnesses can't talk at all. There may be times when you need them to be more active in the beginning, providing facts or details about a situation, but eventually they should take a backseat and allow you to deliver the feedback and your message.

For example, if you are counseling an employee about a situation where his behavior was inappropriate and you did not personally witness the incident but another manager did, you may want to consider including that manager in the conversation. That manager's role would be active in the beginning of the meeting as she provides firsthand observations and details of what occurred, but then she should shift into the background and play a more passive, observational role as you deliver your message.

The Balance of Power

I am always very concerned about the perceived balance of power in any counseling conversation and the addition of a witness who is going to actively participate in delivering the message may tip that perceived power too far in the direction of management. Whenever possible, I like to include a more neutral individual as a witness, such as the human resources manager, so that the employee can feel there is someone in the room who is not directly one of their managers and can support them if necessary.

The person you select as a witness will help you to set the tone in your meeting, but remember, you never want to leave the employee feeling like he is going in front of a firing squad. Take a look at the people you are considering using as a witness and their relationship on the organizational chart to the employee. If you include as a witness your boss, it will definitely add a level of seriousness and urgency to the conversation. Another manager from outside the department can heighten the employee's anxiety; if they do not have a natural working relationship with that manager, as the employee may feel his privacy is being invaded.

Explain Their Presence

Once you have selected your witness make sure she understands her role in the meeting and how she can best support you and the employee. As I mentioned before, in the opening of your conversation you will want to explain why the individual you have selected is participating.

For a general conversation, you might explain it like this:

"I've asked (individual's name) to join us today to provide additional perspective and to lend both of us support, as it is important to me that we are all on the same page."

If the witness is there to provide specific information or details, you could add:

"(The witness's name) has some important information to share that will help us to gain a better understanding of the situation."

The witness introduction doesn't need to be long, but it should explain enough to help the employee put her presence into context.

Witness's Signature

Once the conversation has concluded and the employee has signed the document (if prepared ahead of time), you should sign next as the manager and then ask the witness to sign the document.

This is how I typically prepared the signature portion of the document when a witness is involved:

Employee's Signature
Read and Acknowledged

Manager's Signature

Witness's Signature

It is important that you are able to read the witness's signature. If you can't, make sure the name is printed clearly under the signature. Both your name and the employee's name are on the top of the memo, so it is already clear who you are. Later on you will want to be able to identify who your witness is in case of legal action. Some people make it a practice to make their signature as difficult to read as possible, so don't forget to double-check.

KEY LEARNING POINTS FROM THIS CHAPTER

- Most employees will sign the documentation once you explain that their signature affirms they've read and acknowledged receipt of the memo rather than their agreement with its contents or the resulting discipline.

- If an employee still refuses to sign even after you explain the meaning of his signature, ask a witness to join you if you don't already have one, and write "Refused to Sign" on the employee signature line. Then sign the document yourself and ask the witness to also sign her name. Treat the employee's refusal to sign as a nonissue.

- Never sign a document before the employee; let him sign first. It sends all the wrong messages when you hand the employee a document that is already signed.

- Consider having a witness to any conversation where you believe it will benefit you or the employee to have another person as a part of the meeting.

- Prepare your witnesses as to their role in the conversation so that they don't inadvertently say or do something counterproductive to the purpose of the meeting.

- Be mindful of the balance of power in any counseling conversation. You do not want the employee to feel significantly outnumbered.

- Make sure you can read the witness's signature. The witness's name is often not on the top of the memo so there is no other reference to the identity of the witness. If you can't easily read the signature, print the name underneath.

SECTION EIGHT:

BRINGING IT ALL TOGETHER

20 Chapter

Final Thoughts

The number one reason leaders are unsuccessful is their inability to lead themselves.

Truett Cathy

We've covered a lot of information here and you might be feeling a little overwhelmed, which is totally understandable. When you really break down the complete process of providing people with honest feedback and documenting those conversations, you can see that there are a lot of moving parts. You may even feel it is too much to incorporate into your style all at once, especially when you realize that it takes time to become proficient in many of the skills and tools we've discussed. So let me give you some advice on how you should start.

Work from the Inside Out

In order to become a better leader on the outside, you need to become a better leader on the inside. Trust and credibility are built by leaders who are being authentic, allowing their true values and beliefs to shine through. People will instinctively know when you are acting out of self-interest or personal gain. If you have not yet done so, take the time to identify your personal core values and beliefs and explore the kind of leadership style you want to develop. Start with the qualities discussed in Chapter 4, and then add on any others you believe are important.

Think about the kind of reputation you want to build or the kind of legacy you hope to leave behind, and then work backwards. By articulating what you want to be known for in the latter part of your career, you will be able to identify those qualities, traits, and skills you will need to develop now in order to achieve that level of recognition and success. Does it matter to you that people perceive you to be a forthright, fair, courageous, and trustworthy leader? If so, you will need to develop good character, build trust with people, set high expectations for yourself and others, put the interests of your people above your own, and invest in the growth and development of others.

Set out to align your daily behavior with these qualities so that your actions are in sync with your values. That is what it means to be authentic. If you hold good character and building trust as values, when you are faced with the decision as to whether or not to provide honest feedback, even though you feel uncomfortable, your path will be clear.

In order to remain true to your values, you must overcome your fear and work through your discomfort in order to have that tough conversation. Once you make the decision to become a better leader, the question moves from "Should I have the conversation?" to "How can I effectively have the conversation?" Even if you are not as proficient as you would like to be at first, it is more important that you make the attempt to provide direct and honest feedback to your team and learn from any missteps along the way.

Take the time to become more self-aware. Are there any beliefs or habits that are limiting your success? Self-assessments are great tools to help you to get a better understanding of your style and personality traits. They also help you to uncover any beliefs or behaviors that might be lingering on your "dark side," which could become obstacles to your effectiveness. Solicit feedback from your direct reports, peers, and your leadership team, to provide you with information as to your current strengths and opportunity areas. Treat this feedback as the gift it is and receive it with appreciation.

Practice the Skills

Once you've made the commitment to providing direct and timely feedback, you will need to actively develop your communication skills so that you are as effective as possible. Think about your virtual leadership toolbox, do you have all the skills you need to assist you in having those difficult conversations? Find opportunities to practice your skills in conversations where the stakes don't feel quite as high. Provide people with direct feedback and demonstrate that you are really hearing them by using good active listening skills.

Try flexing your style to effectively interact with people who communicate using a style different from your own. This will give you exposure to other styles of communication and you can learn what works best with each before there is a crisis situation. Practice giving people enough space to speak when they are anxious, allow them to diffuse their energy, and learn to love silence. Be consistent with your level and frequency of communication.

After mastering the basic skills, you can work on adding some of the more advanced skills we discussed to your toolbox. With experience, you will develop a natural intuition that will help to guide you through your conversations. You can move from worrying about the words you are saying to focusing more on directing and guiding the flow of the conversation, making it even more productive.

By keeping your ultimate message in mind, you can ensure that you are thinking several steps ahead and driving the flow of the discussion toward that goal. The ability to maintain control of your emotions, and sometimes even make effective use of a good poker face, will allow you to keep the focus of the conversation directed on the employee. There will be times when you get thrown an unexpected curveball during a discussion, one that you didn't prepare for, but experience and confidence in your skills will allow you to quickly recover from any distractions.

Learn Your Company's Processes

Most companies allow you the flexibility to bring your individual personality and leadership style to the coaching process, but when it comes to more formal counseling, they have a set of guidelines that they want you to use. If you do not already have an excellent working relationship with your human resources department, I urge you to immediately develop one. In most organizations, HR is the keeper of the formal and informal policies and practices and can help to support and guide you through understanding the progressive discipline process.

And if you have a good working knowledge of the company's process—USE IT! It sounds so simple, but too often managers don't make the best use of resources they already have at their disposal. All the tools you need to help you effectively manage performance are most likely already there for you, you just need to become comfortable accessing them and begin to incorporate them into your coaching and counseling style.

As you begin to use the progressive discipline process to help manage your employees' performance and to correct unwanted behavior, be consistent with how you apply it. I have yet to encounter a corporate performance management process that was totally ineffective as written; it is almost always the application of that process by the organization's management team that makes it successful or renders it useless. If you administer the process fairly and consistently, you will go a long way toward creating a positive perception and building trust with your people.

Prepare for Every Conversation

Some of the suggestions that I mentioned in the section on preparing for conversations can be handled once to set them up, if they are not currently in place, and then the hard work is done. Pull your resources together now if you do not already have your dream team in place. Once you develop that network of support, you can easily maintain it with minimal time and effort. Then you can have expert advice at the ready whenever you need to access it.

While the time involved in preparing for an actual conversation may decrease as you become more experienced and your comfort level working with your fellow managers' increases, you should never skip the important step of having a meeting before the meeting. Always insist on gathering anyone who is going to be directly involved in the conversation with the employee together, even if it is only for a few minutes before the actual meeting, to discuss any logistic concerns, confirm the message, and clarify roles. Safety and security should never be overlooked. Always make sure you are in-tune to any behaviors or conditions that may indicate that an individual or situation might turn threatening, and take appropriate precautionary measures.

If you are in the early stages of the progressive discipline process or the situation doesn't warrant additional participants in the conversation, make sure you still mentally go through your pre-meeting checklist and clarify the purpose for the conversation in your own mind. I frequently do a mini version of the "What If?" game on my own before any difficult conversations, just so I feel better prepared. In situations where you are one on one with the employee, it is especially important that you remain focused and follow through until your complete message has been delivered as there is no one else to help you stay on track.

Have the Tough Conversations

Now that you have the skills and tools you need, don't shy away from having the difficult conversations. Follow the framework you learned for each phase of the discussion to help you deliver your feedback in a way that maintains the employee's dignity and demonstrates your respect for them as an individual. Use good, open-ended questions to get the employee talking, to help them release any nervous energy, and to flush out the details of a situation. Practice using the feedback formulas; the C.A.R. formula (Circumstances, Actions, and Results) and the "While I Appreciate . . ." formula to structure your feedback in a way that clearly states the issue and the consequences of their behavior.

Begin to incorporate I-statements into any feedback that you currently provide. They are a perfect tool for any conversation, not just the tough ones. I-statements help you to provide your feedback in a constructive way that avoids any name calling. The more proficient you are with the way in which you state your feedback and concerns, the less likely you are to trigger or escalate the employee's personal defense system. Your goal should always be to provide your feedback in a way that it can be best heard and understood by the employee. Using the feedback formulas and I-statements will help you to maximize the possibility that your message will get through.

Improving your ability to effectively neutralize defenses and emotions during difficult conversations will help to increase your confidence level making you less likely to avoid them in the first place. I believe one of the hardest skills to perfect is the ability to separate emotionally from the situation and to not react to emotional outbursts or verbal attacks. In the moment, it is easy to get carried away and allow emotions to control the direction of the conversation. By recognizing that emotion is often just a defense mechanism and knowing how to diffuse those emotions, you will be able to maintain the professional distance you need to deliver your feedback or discipline. Practice taking the high road when employees try to make it personal and you will have nothing to apologize for later.

And don't forget your or-else clause. You can begin to work it into every conversation now and you will see an immediate improvement in the clarity and impact of your messages. It is a shame to put all this effort into speaking with an employee about unacceptable performance or behavior, only to stop short of informing them what this means to their overall performance or employment. People have a right to know the consequences of repeating an unwanted behavior. If someone is behaving in a way that could jeopardize their continued employment, don't let your discomfort with saying the words prevent you from doing your job. It is your responsibility to be totally honest with them about the situation and the possible outcomes.

Simplify Your Documentation

When I first started creating my own memos to address performance issues and to document my counseling conversations, I would often sit and stare at the blank page, totally intimidated by the responsibility of choosing the perfect words for the situation. Over the years, I learned that I was making the process much harder than it had to be. By breaking the documentation format into smaller sections, you can easily create documents with impact that address all the pertinent points, honestly informing employees of their situation and protecting you and the company in the event of any legal action.

Save every piece of performance documentation you write and begin to create templates that you can use when crafting future memos. No sense in recreating the wheel. When you have a moment of greatness and write something well, use it again. The samples I provide throughout the book and in the Additional Resources section can be used as a starting point.

Documentation is most effective when it is clear, concise, and easy to understand. Don't use unnecessary words and don't belabor your point. Remember the goal is to create a document that can be easily understood by your employee and reinforces the message you delivered verbally. If it is too hard to follow, you have failed.

Over the years, I kept a file with samples of documentation I'd written for every step of the progressive discipline process. As my skill and knowledge increased, I would update my templates with language that was more effective so that I was always working off the best template possible. I recommend that you do the same. Keep samples in a secure location to maintain privacy, especially if they contain information specific to an individual employee. If you use a sample as a starting place when creating a new piece of documentation, make sure you change the names and dates at the top of the memo. I have seen a few managers get caught giving a memo to an employee that is actually addressed to a different employee, because they forgot to erase the information from their template. I usually save my templates and samples without names to avoid accidentally making this mistake.

If you take the responsibilities of leadership seriously, you already understand the tremendous influence and impact you can have on the lives of the people you lead. Outside of family and friends, the relationship an employee has with her boss is the most significant factor in determining job satisfaction and success at work. People want to work for someone who they trust and believe in, someone who lifts them up rather than tears them down, and invests in their growth and development beyond job-related skills.

I've heard that people join a company because of its reputation, but leave it because of their manager. I believe one of the keys to becoming the kind of leader other people want to work for is providing honest and direct communication. Honest feedback helps to build trust, credibility, and positive working relationships. The tools and advice offered in this book can help you to become a better communicator and a more effective leader. I think you will find that by investing in yourself and developing your leadership skills, then by investing in others and having the tough conversations, you will achieve the level of influence and success you desire.

I wish you success on your journey!

Additional Resources

Sample Documentation

The following are examples of documentation which address behavior and performance situations. These samples are intended to provide you with an idea of how to address, in writing, some of the more common behavior and performance issues you may encounter. The author is not an attorney and nothing in this book should be construed as legal advice. Any documentation you create based on these samples should not be used without consulting your human resources department or your legal counsel. Every disciplinary situation is unique and should be addressed accordingly under your company policies and guidelines. Please use good sense and all of your available resources, such as your HR department and legal counsel, to provide you with specific recommendations regarding any situation you are documenting.

Sample: Written Verbal Warning—Behavior

Memorandum

[Date]

To: John Smith

From: [Your Name]

Subject: Summary of Meeting on [Date]

I wanted to take a moment to recap our meeting from Friday. Gregg Brown and I met with you to discuss some feedback we received while conducting an investigation into an incident involving one of your team members. There seems to be concern regarding your conversations with female employees. Specifically, two conversations were brought to our attention.

The first incident occurred several months ago. You were having a drink after work with several employees and they felt that your comments were inappropriate and made them feel uncomfortable, as if you were fishing around for a date. Additionally, they felt that the banter back and forth was not at the professional level that they would expect from a member of the management team. The second incident occurred just two weeks ago. A client told us that she felt you had asked her on a date and that she also felt uncomfortable around you.

During our meeting, you expressed that you had not intended in either instance to make the individuals uncomfortable. We understand that was not your intention, but the perception makes you appear unprofessional and must be dealt with immediately. We suggested that you raise your level of communication with others and refrain from any form of sexual banter with the staff. We also strongly suggested that you avoid drinking with or hanging out with the staff after work.

As a leader in our company, it is your responsibility to behave in a way that maintains your professionalism, credibility and builds strong and effective relationships with our employees and clients. We take charges of harassment very seriously and we will terminate the employment of anyone found to be creating a harassing environment.

We hope that our discussion helps you to see where your behavior needs to change and that this will not become an issue in the future. Please feel free to contact either Gregg or myself if you have any questions or concerns regarding our conversation or this memo.

_____   _____

Employee's Signature   Manager's Signature
Read and Acknowledged

Sample: Written Warning—Behavior

Memorandum

To: Jane Smith

From: [Your Name]

Subject: Written Warning

It was brought to my attention that last Tuesday, during a conversation with other employees, you made disparaging remarks about one of your fellow supervisors. Specifically, you reportedly said that Sally "couldn't manage her way out of a paper bag" and that "She must have dirt on the General Manager to have been promoted."

These remarks are unprofessional and highly inappropriate, and could negatively impact the reputation and credibility of the supervisor. More importantly, disparaging a fellow member of the management team reflects poorly on you and your leadership.

You must maintain a positive, executive presence at all times in the workplace, especially when communicating with other employees. Comments of this type must cease immediately.

If there is another instance of unprofessional conduct or speaking negatively about another employee or manager, further disciplinary action may result, up to and including being placed on Final Warning or the termination of your employment.

Jane, I hope you can move beyond this incident and repair your relationship with Sally. Please let me know if there is anything I can do to assist you in this process.

_____   _____
Employee's Signature   Manager's Signature
Read and Acknowledged

Sample: Final Warning—Behavior

Memorandum

[Date]

To: John Smith

From: [Your Name]

Subject: Final Warning—Behavior

It was brought to my attention that on [Date], you made an inappropriate comment regarding Sally, a female coworker. It is reported that as Sally walked by you in the hall you said "Nice ass." Gregg Brown, the HR Manager, and I spoke with you the next day and you admitted making the comment. You explained that you were only kidding and didn't mean to offend anyone.

This comment was completely inappropriate. It is everyone's responsibility to create and maintain an environment that is harassment free for all of our employees. Inappropriate comments such as the one you made are disrespectful and have no place in our workplace, even if you feel you are making them in jest.

This behavior will not be tolerated. Any further occurrences may result in further disciplinary action, up to and including the termination of your employment. In addition, our company has a nonretaliation policy as outlined in our Employee Handbook. It states, "Retaliation against any individual for reporting harassment or for cooperating in any investigation will not be tolerated and will, itself, subject the individual to discipline up to and including termination." Please conduct yourself accordingly.

John, I know you are remorseful for your behavior and I am confident you can put this behind you. If you have any questions or concerns regarding this issue or this memo, please feel free to see me.

_____
Employee's Signature
Read and Acknowledged

_____
Manager's Signature

_____
Witness's Signature

Memorandum

[Date]

To: Jane Smith

From: [Your Name]

Subject: Final Warning

On [Date], while in the administrative area of our offices, you were observed yelling at another employee in a threatening manner. You've admitted regret for this behavior and while we understand that you feel that you were provoked into the interaction, this type of communication is unprofessional and will not be tolerated.

We have an obligation to provide a harassment free environment for all employees. Additionally, it is important to us that our team members feel comfortable that our workplace is a safe and positive environment, and we will take strong action to insure that this feeling is maintained. Your behavior was inappropriate and further instances will not be tolerated.

To that end, this is a Final Warning. If you are involved in any further behaviors which disrupt the work environment, disrespect a coworker, or lead to the spread of negativity, further disciplinary action may be taken, up to and including the termination of your employment.

Jane, we hope that you are committed to moving past recent incidents and remaining a positive and productive member of our team.

_____   _____
Employee's Signature   Manager's Signature
Read and Acknowledged

_____
Witness's Signature

Sample: First and Final Warning—Behavior

Memorandum

[Date]

To: John Smith

From: [Your Name]

Subject: First and Final Warning—Behavior

On Thursday, [Date], Gregg Brown and I met with you to discuss the allegation that you allegedly approached a coworker in the men's restroom and solicited drugs, specifically, cocaine. You stated that you never had a conversation with anyone in which you solicited drugs and that you did not remember having a conversation with anyone in the men's restroom that day. At that time, you were placed on suspension while we conducted a complete investigation of this matter.

During the following two days, we interviewed several members of the staff. Ultimately, we were unable to find anyone to corroborate the allegation, or to confirm your assertions that it did not happen. As a result, we are reinstating you to active duty effective immediately, and we will pay you your salary for the days that you missed as a result of the suspension.

Due to the serious nature of this matter, I feel that it is important that I take this opportunity to reiterate the company policy regarding drug use or the possession of illegal substances while in our workplace. As stated in our company Employee Handbook, "Selling, purchasing, using, possessing or being under the influence of alcohol, any illegal drug, or any controlled substance not prescribed by the employee's own physician while at work or on the premises is strictly prohibited. Any employee found to have violated this policy may be subject to immediate termination." It is also a breach of our policy to retaliate in any way against individuals who have, or may have, participated in our investigation. To do so is also grounds for immediate termination of employment.

In the future, should information to substantiate this allegation come to our attention or we find that you have violated this policy, disciplinary action may be taken, up to and including the immediate termination of your employment.

If you have any questions regarding this issue or memo, please come see me.

_____

Employee's Signature
Read and Acknowledged

_____

Manager's Signature

_____

Witness's Signature

Sample: Performance Warning

Memorandum

To: John Smith

From: [Your Name]

Subject: Written Warning—Performance

On [Date], we met to discuss my concerns regarding your negative communication style, especially when interacting with coworkers. We received feedback from a number of your team members that you were observed speaking to a coworker, Sally Adams, in a disrespectful manner. Your tone of voice and word choice was perceived as rude and abrupt.

Upon further investigation, we learned that this is a pattern of communication which you've exhibited toward other team members on a number of occasions. Several coworkers provided us with feedback that they feel you speak to them in a disrespectful way and that they do not enjoy working with you. I shared with you a specific example of this negative communication style that was brought to me by another manager, Gregg Brown. He observed you speaking to a coworker in a very demeaning way in an area where clients could overhear you. You've indicated that you were not aware that you were offending anyone, but these types of interactions are inappropriate and undermine your success. You will need to immediately change the way in which you communicate so that you support the team morale and build positive relationships.

Also, since client relationships are critical to us, you must be positive, energetic, professional and friendly when interacting with or around clients. Any further instances of rude or disrespectful communication in front of clients will not be tolerated and could lead to further disciplinary action.

I hope you accept this feedback in a positive and productive manner as it is intended to assist you in improving your relationships and your performance. These issues are very serious and need to be addressed quickly. If not resolved immediately, these issues could become job-threatening for you.

John, I am here to assist you in your efforts to make the necessary changes to your performance and communication style, and I would be happy to discuss any questions or concerns you might have regarding this issue.

_____   _____

Employee's Signature   Manager's Signature
Read and Acknowledged

Sample: Performance Warning—Bridging the Gap

Memorandum

[Date]

To: John Smith
From: [Your Name]
Subject: Performance Warning

This memo summarizes our discussion on [Date], regarding your performance. Gregg Brown, HR Manager was also in attendance at this meeting.

I began our discussion by stating that this was the third time we had met in the last few weeks to discuss your performance. Our first conversation was on [Date], when we met to discuss negative comments you made to a fellow manager regarding the new accounting process being rolled out to track expenses.

On [Date], we met to discuss your performance as part of your annual Performance Review. You received feedback that you need to increase your skills as a team player, and your acceptance of the new accounting system was an example of where we felt you could be more supportive of the leadership team. We discussed how, as a member of the management team, your attitude and behavior can set the tone for your employees. I stated during that meeting that we needed you to set a more positive tone for the team. Gregg was again part of this feedback process.

Finally, earlier this week, I also shared with you my perceptions that over the last several weeks, your overall performance had slipped. On several occasions, I observed you displaying negativity towards your coworkers and I've also noticed a significant lack of enthusiasm in the performance of your job responsibilities. I asked you then if there was anything wrong and you indicated that everything was okay.

Your performance is falling below expectations and you will need to make immediate improvements. You are expected to demonstrate a positive attitude and set the example for your team. Negative behavior towards coworkers is unacceptable. If there continues to be additional instances of negative attitude and behavior, further disciplinary action may result, up to and including Performance Probation and the termination of your employment.

John, I sincerely hope you are able to turn this situation around and I encourage you to use whatever resources are available to support your efforts. If there is anything you would like to discuss further, please come see me.

_____   _____
Employee's Signature   Manager's Signature
Read and Acknowledged

Memorandum

[Date]

To: Jane Smith

From: [Your Name]

Subject: Performance Probation Recap

On [Date], we met to discuss your performance. Overall, your performance was rated as unsatisfactory. There were several areas that were specifically noted as needing immediate improvement. They included your attendance, guest service, productivity, and overall energy.

At that time you were placed on Performance Probation. You were informed that your probation was for a maximum period of 90 days, during which time you needed to demonstrate and maintain significant improvement in these areas. As discussed today, you have shown the needed improvement in your performance.

As a result of your improved performance, we are taking you off of Performance Probation. You must continue to maintain your performance at an acceptable level in all areas going forward. Should your performance again slip to an unacceptable level, we reserve the right to skip probation and escalate the process. At that time, further disciplinary action may be taken, up to and including the termination of your employment.

Jane, please feel free to use the HR Manager and I as resources in your efforts to maintain these improvements. If you have any questions or concerns regarding your performance or this document, please feel free to come see me.

_____   _____
Employee's Signature   Manager's Signature
Read and Acknowledged

Sample: Performance Probation with Action Plan

Memorandum

[Date]

To: Jane Smith

From: [Your Name]

Subject: Performance Probation

On several occasions in the last year we have discussed your performance and the need for you to make improvements, especially in your communication skills and your overall organizational effectiveness. In August, Gregg Brown and I met with you to discuss issues that were impacting your effectiveness and your relationships with other managers on the team. On [Date], Gregg and I discussed and documented an issue involving your making negative and unprofessional comments during a meeting.

Issues involving your analysis and decision making skills, attention to detail, action orientation, and technical skills were addressed in your last annual performance review and then periodically throughout this past year. While some improvement has been noted, your performance is still unacceptable in several key areas.

As a result, you are being placed on performance probation. Below is an action plan which outlines the areas where you need to demonstrate immediate and significant improvement in your performance.

Organizational Skills
- Demonstrate proficiency with all computer and software systems that are used to manage the department.
- Execute all daily operational tasks according to company guidelines.
- Respond timely to calls for assistance from our customers.
- Accurately perform daily and week end reporting functions.
- Perform all duties timely and accurately.

Communication Skills
- Demonstrate effective listening skills; listen to others without interrupting, confirm your understanding by paraphrasing what has been said, ask follow-up questions.
- Express ideas clearly and succinctly when speaking. Confirm that others have understood by asking them to repeat back what you have said.
- Allow others to question your ideas or direction. Receive feedback in a nondefensive way that encourages them to provide you with feedback again in the future.
- Keep all comments regarding coworkers positive and professional.
- If you have an issue with an employee or peer, address the issue in a professional manner and in private.

Self-Management
- Effectively manage multiple tasks. Respond to requests in a timely manner.

- Demonstrate flexibility. Work effectively when the direction is unclear or conditions are rapidly changing.
- Take things in stride and give the appropriate amount of attention to matters.
- Demonstrate an understanding of your own strengths and weaknesses. Seek out and take advantage of opportunities for development.
- Learn from your mistakes and strive to not make the same one twice.

This probation period is effective immediately and will remain in effect for a maximum of 60 days. We will meet on a weekly basis to review your progress. During that time you need to demonstrate significant and consistent improvement in your performance, especially in the areas identified above. Failure to do so may result in further disciplinary action, up to and including Final Probation or the termination of your employment. During this period you are also expected to maintain a satisfactory performance level in all other areas of your job.

Jane, I am always available to assist you in your efforts to improve your performance. If you would like to discuss this plan or any other issue that may concern you, please feel free to reach out to me. I encourage you to use whatever resources you believe will assist you in this process.

_____   _____
Employee's Signature   Manager's Signature
Read and Acknowledged

Memorandum

[Date]

To: John Smith

From: [Your Name]

Cc: Gregg Brown, HR Manager

Subject: Final Performance Probation

Over the past several months we have been discussing your performance and the need for you to make changes in your leadership style and your organizational effectiveness. On [Date], we placed you on Performance Probation and gave you an Action Plan that was designed to help you address some of the areas where you were under-performing. Last week, we conducted your annual performance review in which you received an unsatisfactory performance score.

Because of your continued unacceptable level of performance, effective immediately, you are being placed on Final Performance Probation. To assist you in your efforts to improve your performance, we are again providing you with an Action Plan outlining the areas where you need to demonstrate immediate and significant improvement.

Leadership
- Provide clear direction for your managers and staff on a daily basis so there is no misunderstanding or confusion surrounding the goals for the department.
- Maintain a positive attitude and encourage staff to have fun and enjoy themselves while at work.
- Set clear priorities on a daily basis for yourself, your managers, and your staff. Ensure that emphasis is placed on high priority items.
- Lead by example in all that you do. Model good leadership behaviors to your managers to assist them in developing their own skills.
- Reward and praise staff publicly and counsel and reprimand privately.
- Problem-solve without looking to assess blame.

Team Management and Development
- Provide your managers and staff with all the necessary information and resources to do their job.
- Build your relationships with team members and managers. Earn and maintain their trust.
- Establish clear expectations for your managers, including roles, responsibilities and deadlines.
- Delegate effectively based on team member skills and workloads. Follow up with staff to ensure that responsibilities are understood and completed.
- Provide timely feedback to staff that is direct, clear, and honest. Solicit feedback from the staff regarding your performance and make adjustments as necessary.

- Document performance issues appropriately and in a timely manner. Address under-performance effectively without allowing a problem to linger.
- Encourage collaboration within your team in order to accomplish goals.
- Immediately address behaviors or issues that detract from the team's performance. Do not allow differences or issues between managers to become obvious to the rest of the team.

Communication
- Demonstrate effective listening skills; listen to others without interrupting, confirm your understanding by paraphrasing what has been said, ask follow-up questions.
- Express ideas clearly and succinctly when speaking. Confirm that others have understood by asking them to repeat back what you have said.
- Allow others to question your ideas or direction. Receive feedback in a nondefensive way that encourages them to provide you with feedback again.
- Do not rely on others to communicate critical information for you without follow-up.
- Communicate your disapproval with staff in a way that is clear, direct, and maintains the person's self-esteem.
- Practice an open door policy with others. Do not reprimand or penalize staff for going "over your head."

This probation period will remain in effect for a maximum of 45 days. During that time you need to demonstrate significant and consistent improvement in the areas identified in the Action Plan, as well as maintaining a satisfactory performance level in all other areas of responsibility. Failure to demonstrate significant improvement may result in further disciplinary action, up to and including the termination of your employment.

John, Gregg, and I are here to support you in your efforts to improve your performance. We will meet on a weekly basis during to review your progress. I am available to discuss this plan or any other issues that may concern you anytime. I encourage you to use whatever resources you believe will assist you in this process.

Employee's Signature
Read and Acknowledged

Manager's Signature

Witness's Signature

Acknowledgements

This book could not have been published without the encouragement and support of so many individuals. I am grateful to them all.

Thank you to Sue Simon and Bev Kolz at River Lights Publishing Services for their expertise, advice, and hand-holding throughout the publishing process.

To my committed and diligent proof-readers, Jennifer Higgins and Connie Vandever, I will be forever grateful for the time you spent pouring over the manuscript, taking notes, and providing me with such valuable feedback and insight.

Thank you to my family and friends who supported me along the way with your constant, caring inquiries into my progress and for your obvious pride in my success. Thank you to Jaime Lesley, Nicole Cozzocrea, Charles Spellman, Jennifer Hinckle, Christine Clifton and Sharon Flynn for being so generous with your opinions and advice. I will always be grateful for your friendship, love, and support.

To everyone who reviewed my manuscript and offered their feedback and endorsement, thank you for your time and support. It is appreciated more than you can know.

I would be remiss to skip my constant companions during the writing process; Lucky and Daisy. While writing can be an isolating experience, I was never alone with my loyal Beagles by my side.

And finally, thank you to all the people who I worked with over the years whose lessons, intentional or otherwise, inspired the teachings in this book. Thank you!

About the Author

KATHY RYAN, SPHR, is owner and founder of Pinnacle Coaching Group, LLC. Over the last 25 years, Kathy has influenced thousands of people in the business and nonprofit sectors through on-site and remote coaching and training. She is able to deliver practical wisdom with a perfect balance of reality-based advice and lighthearted humor. Her expertise covers a wide range of subjects including leadership, communication, human resources management, motivation, team dynamics, performance management, and personal development.

Kathy has a degree in psychology and history from Dickinson College in Carlisle, Pennsylvania, and has earned a lifetime certification as a Senior Professional in Human Resources from the Society for Human Resources Management. She has been certified in the use of the Myer-Briggs Type Assessment (MBTI) since 1995, and uses it, as well as other assessments, as tools for self-discovery in her consulting and coaching practice.

Kathy is also co-author of the book *The Baby Boomers Handbook for Women.* She has written and published numerous articles on leadership and other personal development topics, as well as publishing the blog, *Inspired Leadership,* at *www.CoachKathyRyan.com.*

You can contact the author at:
Pinnacle Coaching Group LLC.
P.O. Box 772377
Orlando, Florida 32877
Email: *Kathy@PinnacleCoachingGroup.com*
Website: *www.PinnacleCoachingGroup.com*

You can follow her at:
www.Facebook.com/kathyryan.author
www.Linkedin.com/in/coachkathyryan
www.Twitter.com/coachkathyryan

Index